GREENING THE BUILT ENVIRONMENT

Maf Smith, John Whitelegg and Nick Williams

Earthscan Publications Ltd, London

The Earth deserves to be recognised as our common home.
As every culture knows, to destroy one's own home is folly indeed

Ernst Ulrich von Weizsäcker

First published in the UK in 1998
by Earthscan Publications Ltd

Copyright © Maf Smith, John Whitelegg and Nick Williams, 1998

Published in association with WWF-UK

A catalogue record for this book is available from the British Library

ISBN: 1 85383 403 3 paperback
       1 85383 404 1 hardback

Typesetting by JS Typesetting, Wellingborough, Northants
Printed and bound by Biddles Ltd, Guildford and King's Lynn
Cover design by Andrew Corbett

WWF-UK is a Registered Charity. No 201707. In the US and Canada, WWF
(World Wide Fund For Nature) is known as World Wildlife Fund.

For a full list of publications please contact:

Earthscan Publications Ltd
120 Pentonville Road
London, N1 9JN, UK
Tel: +44 (0)171 278 0433
Fax: +44 (0)171 278 1142
Email: earthinfo@earthscan.co.uk
WWW: http://www.earthscan.co.uk

Earthscan is an editorially independent subsidiary of Kogan Page Ltd and
publishes in association with WWF-UK and the International Institute for
Environment and Development.

CONTENTS

FIGURES, TABLES AND BOXES

FIGURES

Note: the authors would like to thank Martin Rowson and Anne King of The Building Service Research and Information Association (BSRIA) for permission to reproduce Figure 3.3 and Nick White of the Hockerton Housing Project for permission to reproduce Figure 3.5. They would also like to thank Emma Heathcote for illustrating Figure 4.1.

TABLES

BOXES

ACRONYMS AND ABBREVIATIONS

BNRR   Birmingham Northern Relief Road
BSE   bovine spongiform encephalopathy
CEC   Commission of the European Communities
CFC   chlorofluorocarbon
CHP   combined heat and power
CPRE   Council for the Protection of Rural England
dB(A)   A-weighted sound level in decibels
DIY   do-it-yourself
DoE   Department of the Environment (to 1997; now Department for
        Environment, Transport and the Regions (DETR)) (UK)
DSM   demand side management
EIA   Environmental Impact Assessment
EJ   exajoule (1 × 10^{18} joules)
EPA   Environmental Protection Agency
ETR   ecological tax reform
EU   European Union
GJ   gigajoule (1 × 10^9 joules)
ha   hectare
IPCC   Intergovernmental Panel on Climate Change
IRA   Irish Republican Army
ISEW   Index of Sustainable Economic Welfare (UK)
kWh   kilowatt hour
LCA   life cycle analysis
LETS   Local Exchange Trading Systems
LTO   landing and take-off
MAI   Multilateral Agreement on Investment
NAFTA   North American Free Trade Area
NASA   National Aeronautics and Space Administration (US)
NEC   National Exhibition Centre (Birmingham, UK)
OECD   Organisation for Economic Co-operation and Development
PM_{10} particulate matter (<10 microns)
PNR   private non-residential (parking)
RCEP   Royal Commission on Environmental Pollution
RMI   Rocky Mountain Institute
SEA   Strategic Environmental Appraisal
SMUD   Sacremento Municipal Utility District
T5   Terminal 5 (London Heathrow Airport)
TDM   traffic demand management
TERN   Trans European Road Network

UPVC	unplasticized polyvinyl chloride
VAT	value added tax (UK)
VOC	volatile organic compound
W	watt
WHO	World Health Organization
WRI	World Resources Institute
yr	year
ZEV	zero emission vehicle

I

WHAT ARE WE DOING HERE?

*'tree is leaf and leaf is tree – house is city and city is house – a tree is a tree
but is also a huge leaf – a leaf is a leaf but it is also a tiny tree – a city is not
a city unless it is also a huge house – a house is a house only if it is also a
tiny city'*

Aldo van Eyck

At Manchester University, England, the University authorities built a new block
of student residences known as Whitworth Park, which amongst resident students,
members of the University and local people, rapidly became known as 'The
Toblerones'. This nickname comes from their peculiar shape; they are triangular
in profile, and the roof extends from the apex almost to the ground. The windows
of the flats jut out from this roof as if the whole building were a planners'
nightmare of loft extensions. Yet the main reasons for this design were allegedly
not aesthetic but financial. According to University folklore, the design stems
from an agreement between the University and the City Council over funding
of the residences, for which the Council had agreed to pay roofing costs. The
result: buildings with little wall area, and large roofs. It makes an amusing story,
but also defies our intuitive grasp of logic and good design. Cost is undoubtedly
a factor, but whose cost; the University's, the Council's? And surely allowing
cost to literally shape all other factors shouldn't be encouraged. Yet 'The
Toblerones' are symptomatic of the way we treat our built environment.

The built environment, consisting of our homes, places of work and leisure,
is what makes up the fabric of our cities, towns and villages. The buildings which
surround us provide shelter and retreat, yet can also foster within us feelings of
well-being, of awe, of the special associations which come from place, and of
belonging. They can also fail to do these things, and indeed work against such
positive associations, fostering within us feelings of alienation, fear and
dissociation. They are also the backdrop for our communities, a term now back
in vogue, as we begin to wake up to what we have lost or given away.

Put simply, we have allowed concerns such as cost to take pride of place
over other things we value, to the extent that we are now noticing the decline

and disappearance of non-costed items such as peace and quiet, security and child independence. Cost means building homes and offices with minimal permissible insulation standards, it means using low space standards and it means creating a cut throat construction industry whose adversarial nature is hardly conducive to producing quality buildings. Yet perhaps it is not so much a concern with the cost of things, but the way we have allowed cost to be so narrowly defined. When the cost of a new building is considered, it is rare that energy-in-use costs are given much thought, let alone concerns of the resultant cost to the local and global environment. Such considerations have been viewed as externalities in the same way that owners of the dark satanic mills of the early Industrial Era regarded health and safety issues as something outside their responsibility. Instead such externalities should be viewed as integral to any design and construction process.

This is not the fault of the construction industry as such, but of the way our economy as a whole functions. This means that economists, governments and industry have tended to assume that there are no limits on the availability of resources, or on the ability of the planet to absorb waste and pollution generated by human activities. In response to this, Daly and Cobb note that:

> 'Sometimes the most obvious things are the ones we overlook. The ecosystem, of which the economy is a subsystem, does not grow. Obviously the world is not static. But equally obviously the diameter of the earth is not expanding . . . Consequently the economy becomes larger relative to the ecosystem and stresses the parent system to an ever greater degree'

Daly and Cobb, 1989, p 143

Think about all the nature films we have seen: we know that young birds and animals begin their lives totally dependent upon their mother. They can only eat as much as the mother can give them, and when they need more they must forage for themselves. As species, however, each group can only consume as much as is available; there are natural limits which cannot be overstepped, and we humans are as bound by that rule as any earwig, blackbird or cheetah. All the US dollars, mining technology, power stations and factories in the world cannot change what is a physical fact. This means that the economy (ie the activities of society) must have a proper scale relative to the ecosystem. Any activities, or change that takes place within our society, must therefore take place within these limits.

Change of some kind in our immediate environment is always inevitable and, ironically, often crucial to balance in society. In much of the change that has taken place, however, there has been too little consideration of wider issues such as the fostering of community and minimization of our impact on the environment. Such considerations have always been important to society, yet ironically, as our power over our environment has increased – mainly through technology, but also because of the role of industry, governments and planning – so our inclination to ignore such issues has grown. Furthermore, while there is now a heightened awareness in society over how certain activities – for example transport – impact upon the environment, awareness of the impacts of buildings, in their construction, use, refurbishment and disposal, is generally low. This is despite the fact that the construction sector has a pivotal place in the economy and has one of the largest impacts upon the environment.

Ravetz calls the built environment the 'container and context' of our lives, and goes on to note that:

'the system of the built environment has complex interlinkages . . . The questions cover both technical, economic and social issues, and there are few clear pathways or precise targets for sustainability. The challenge is to make the linkages between environmental limits..., other social and economic goals, and . . . needs and opportunities'

in Town and Country Planning Association and
Manchester Metropolitan University, 1996

This shows that in looking at the built environment, we are considering more than just collections of buildings. Instead, we can think of the built environment as the physical result of the impact of environmental, economic and social pressures, as illustrated in Figure 1.1. It is the impact of these three influences working together which produces our built environment around us. If the built environment is to be made sustainable, then we must therefore look to these interlinked causes.

Analysis can also look into the stocks, flows and patterns of the built environment (Expert Group on the Urban Environment, 1996), which are as follows:

- Stocks: buildings, land, open space, streets and other tangible features.
- Patterns: spatial and temporal patterns in urban and rural forms, neighbour-hood design, street layouts.
- Flows: the pressures of urbanization, pressures on rural communities, house-hold trends, demands for energy, transport, materials, waste, etc.

Viewing the built environment in these terms leads us to a general model which clearly shows the interrelated nature of many of the issues and problems of the built environment, as set out in Figure 1.2. This means that any specific action can affect other more distant parts of the system in ways that are not always obvious. One of the challenges of sustainability is therefore the framing of policies which reflect this apparently chaotic nature. The driving forces in the model are social and cultural pressures for space, mobility and consumption, as shown in the left hand column of Figure 1.2. The various *stocks* and *patterns* are thus the intermediaries between these demand trends and the resulting environmental impacts (Town and Country Planning Association and Manchester Metroplitan University, 1996). Analysis of the model can help us see just how large and widespread our impacts upon the environment really are.

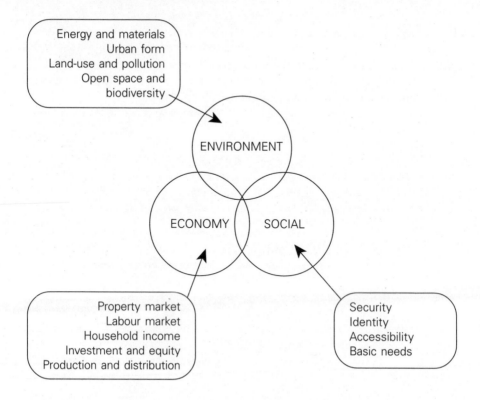

Figure 1.1 *Scope of the Built Environment*

The challenge to contemporary thinking on the built environment, is the adoption of more holistic models of development, management and planning which recognize this complex web of interrelationships. The criticism of planning, especially as it relates to urban development, is that it tends to simplify the relationships existent in our society, which manifest themselves in the built environment in general. Alexander, in his paper 'A City is Not a Tree', dismisses such thinking:

> '. . . *artificial cities . . . have the [branching, separate, compartmentalized] structure of a tree . . . When we think of trees we are trading the humanity and richness of the living city for the conceptual simplicity which benefits only designers, planners, administrators and developers . . .'*

> *'In any organized object, extreme compartmentalization and the dissociation of internal elements are the first signs of coming destruction. In a society, dissociation is anarchy. In a person, dissociation is the mark of schizophrenia and impending suicide'*

> Alexander, 1965, pp 130–131

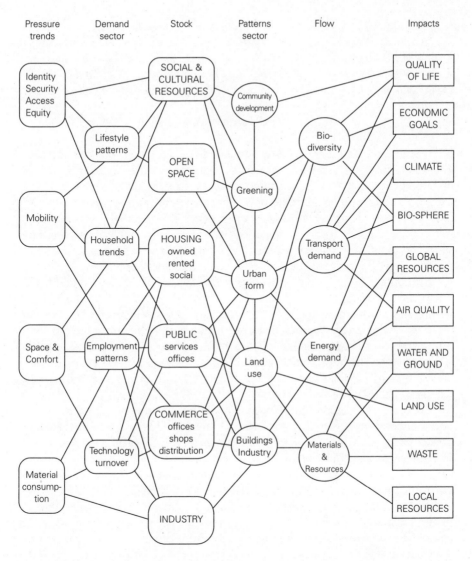

| Pressure trends | Demand sector | Stock | Patterns sector | Flow | Impacts |

Source: adapted from Town and Country Planning Association and Manchester Metropolitan University, 1996

Figure 1.2 *The Built Environment: A General Model*

Ignoring this complexity of influences leaves us ill prepared to tackle problems within our built environment. Instead modern building practices have appeared reckless to the extent of the damage they have caused to our immediate and global environment. Coming to a realization of how much environmental and social damage we have caused in so little time ought to humble us at least slightly. As Roodman and Lenssen point out:

'buildings fall short if they only provide comfort, security, and modern amenities. To the extent that modern structures have become destructive to the world around them, they can be seen as more primitive than traditional structures. Although they have improved in many ways since the industrial revolution, buildings will have to evolve much further if they are to answer all human needs'

Roodman and Lenssen, 1995, pp 14–15

It has been estimated that each year some three billion tonnes of raw materials – 40 per cent of the total flow into the global economy – are used in the manufacture of construction materials throughout the world (Roodman and Lenssen, 1995). These materials must be quarried (or perhaps harvested) and processed. Environmental impacts are produced at all of these stages. The process is also incredibly wasteful: in the US, for example, construction of an average house produces seven tonnes of waste (Brickner et al, 1994), much of which is landfilled.

In terms of energy use, the two dozen nations belonging to the Organisation for Economic Co-operation and Development (OECD) consume about half the world's commercial energy, and of this, nearly 40 per cent is used to run the heating, air conditioning and lights in homes and offices (Flood, 1993). Because the bulk of this energy comes from the burning of fossil fuels, buildings are responsible for a large proportion of carbon dioxide (CO_2) emissions and the resultant global warming. In the UK, for example, it has been estimated that energy use in buildings accounts for 48 per cent of the country's total CO_2 emissions (Pout, 1994).

We are buying more and more appliances for our homes, whilst industry is becoming ever more capital (and machine) intensive. This leads to a greater and greater energy demand, much of which comes from CO_2-producing fossil fuels. It is now recognized that our energy problem is increasingly not one of exhausted supplies, as was thought in the 1970s (Meadows et al, 1972), but one of global environmental damage because of rising levels of greenhouse gases in the atmosphere. To halt and reverse this process, it is therefore imperative that we reduce our *energy intensity*. This will not only involve using energy more efficiently, but ultimately will also involve learning to fulfil our needs with less energy (Weizsäcker, 1994; Weizsäcker et al, 1997).

In addition to the energy problem, we are still faced with the problem of increasing levels of material use. Rising consumption is leading to greater and greater levels of material usage, requiring more quarrying and extraction, energy for production, transport over longer distances, and in most cases, energy in use. To put a stop to this, both greater efficiency in material usage (for example through reuse and recycling) and, ultimately, learning to use fewer materials (for example by making buildings last longer and reducing our rates of consumption) are required. In short, reducing our *materials intensity*. It has to be recognized that nations in the North are using above and beyond their quota of energy and materials. Accepting that there are limits to the amount of energy and materials that can be used without polluting our environment and exhausting material reserves means that we all have to learn to live within our means. The Wuppertal Institute call this our *Environmental Space*:

> '*The quantity of energy, water, land, non-renewable raw materials and wood we can use in a sustainable fashion is called our **Environmental Space**. This criterion is input/use-oriented . . . [or] based on estimates of output/sink capacities. As modern economies not only use national resources, but are built on international commodities trade the calculation of Environmental Space a national economy uses has to be based on an estimate of the global supply for that respective national economy. The available environmental space gives a ceiling to the permitted level of use of natural resources, which can be used in very different ways to meet the demands of a society*'

Friends of the Earth Europe, 1995, p 11

Energy and material intensity will be used as key concepts within *Greening the Built Environment*, because they serve as useful indicators of our impact upon the present and future environment. An important point to make is that the two are usually linked, meaning that success will only be possible if both are reduced together: for example, the only household appliance American consumers bought less of in 1995 was the electric corn-popper (Morgan, 1996, p 139), suggesting that energy and material intensity in the US are still increasing. If we are truly to reduce our impact upon the environment and ensure a sustainable future, then we will need to do more than reduce our consumption of electrically popped popcorn. The concept of *environmental space* will help us come to terms with the scale of reductions in intensity necessary if we are to meet sustainable development criteria.

One of the purposes of this book, then, will be to raise issues surrounding consumption and demonstrate how we might begin to reduce what is, and will be shown to be, the sizeable negative impact buildings and their arrangement in settlements currently have on our environment and on our lives. Crucial to our thinking in this book is also the recognition that the stability of society is linked to the health of the environment, and furthermore, that problems which will be highlighted are themselves only symptoms of more fundamental problems in the way our economy and society are currently structured. Seen in this light, environmental degradation, whilst a problem, is also a symptom of a faltering economy. Therefore, to stop this degradation it will be necessary to tackle the problem at source. In suggesting this, we are following responsible industries which have recognized that end of pipe solutions are not the most effective means of addressing pollution. Better solutions lie in not producing the pollution in the first place. One person coming to such a realization is Dr Braden Allenby, Research Vice-President of American Telephones and Telecommunications (AT&T) Inc, who puts it like this:

'I began to focus more and more on the need to deal with problems rather than symptoms. For a lot of people that was pollution prevention. It was clear to me that was not where the real focus should be for industry. The focus had to be on the design process'

Charter, 1996, p 8

The challenge, then, goes deeper than simply reducing the environmental impact due to production, for example brick manufacture, or activities, for example energy use. It must also look at how our built environment has been designed, using the widest possible meaning of the word. At root, design means having control over how an object is shaped, and of its intended purpose. Design considerations involve not just what colour a house should be, but start out with questions of function, before addressing issues such as material use, land use and planning. Doing this will mean all those involved in this design process will adopt new perspectives and new ways of thinking. More fundamentally, more mundanely even, this also involves opening up this process to ordinary people and allowing them active involvement in, and a feeling of ownership of, the built environment around us all. It is these people who have to live and work in this built environment, yet at present have little, if any, say as to how it is shaped. Winston Churchill once said, 'We shape our dwellings and afterwards our dwellings shape our lives'. The same is true of the streets, estates, villages, towns and cities we live and work in. In short, our built environment. This is why much of our built environment is so unsatisfactory. High-rise flats were designed and built by those who do not have to live in them. An important element of sustainability, and any design which embraces sustainable development, is therefore acceptance of equity and social responsibility.

This book will raise crucial issues for the design process, including the impacts of building materials, energy use and energy efficiency. Wider questions will also be addressed, such as transport, equity, health and community. If this design process is to be successful it must be open and non-hierarchical. The process must also be one where local scales, local control and influence are paramount. This is what Sale (1980) terms 'human scale' in his epic work of the same name. Spreiregen (1965) explains it as follows:

'The proper size of a bedroom has not changed in thousands of years. Neither has the proper size of a door nor the proper size of a community . . .'

'Scale: by that we mean buildings and their components are related harmoniously to each other and human beings. In urban design we also mean that a city and its parts are interrelated to people and their ability to comprehend their surroundings'

Spreiregen, 1965, p 12

The concept of human scale came originally from architecture, so it is perhaps fitting that this book should use it as a key concept for issues affecting the built environment. In order to tackle problems present in the built environment, it is suggested that the scale must be *appropriate* for the task in hand. Scale must be appropriate because no proposals for a change towards sustainability are likely to work without a consideration of function, size and location, all of which can be seen as factors of scale. Furthermore, if people are to become involved in and gain a sense of ownership of their built environment, then the appropriate scale must be a human one, one they can relate to.

Another important recognition in the book is that many apparently disparate problems actually have a common beginning and are best tackled together. If this is not done, the result is an environmental equivalent of robbing Peter to pay Paul. Sale calls this the problem of the 'double bind' because:

> *'The crises of the present . . . have grown so large, so interlocked, so exponential that they pose a threat unlike that ever known. It has come to the point where we cannot solve one problem, or try to without creating some other problem or a score of problems, usually unanticipated. Then we are suddenly faced with the task of coming up with new solutions without enough time to figure out their consequences, and when we hastily put that solution into effect, it goes on and creates another set of problems'*
>
> Sale, 1980, pp 26–27

In terms of the built environment, this means, for example, not designing buildings which rely heavily on such technologies as air conditioning to keep them 'comfortable' or 'liveable', because doing so will only lead to a building using more energy and may even make the building unhealthy to work or live in. It also means not building more parking, roads or out of town development to solve traffic problems, because doing so is likely to fuel traffic growth. This makes the original problem worse, and at the same time introduces a whole host of other problems by fracturing communities, putting people's health at risk, and weakening local economies.

Thinking differently, holistically, however, is the way to extricate ourselves from the fine mess we have found ourselves in. Holistic thinking makes sense if we have rejected end of pipe solutions as not going far enough. The challenge, then, is to follow the mess of pipes back to the source, the common causes. This might seem to make the task in hand harder: rather than solve one problem we must now solve *how many*? In fact, it means that solutions will be easier to come by, and results simpler to achieve. Michael Corbett, the developer of Village Homes, an environmentally aware housing development in California, sums it up this way: 'You know you're on the right track when you notice that your solution for one problem accidentally solved several other problems' (Hamilton, 1995, p 43).

So far this introduction has delved into some of the key issues which will crop up throughout this book. Another one is that of *sustainability* which will be looked at in Chapter 2. There, we will examine the development of the concept, and especially how it applies to the built environment. While growing use of the term has led to a loss of clarity which needs to be addressed, what is important for us about sustainable development is its recognition of interconnections between a number of crucial areas. These are: environmental degradation; inequality; the future stability of society and the environment; and lastly, participation in and control of the decisions which affect these areas. Sustainable development then, is not just a concept, but also the design tool we have been waiting for, since it allows a holistic approach, recognizes how issues are bound together, and allows a large amount of participation and control in its use. In the DIY world, the guiding principle has always been 'if all else fails read the instructions'. In sustainable development, however, the principle must surely be: 'if all else fails, look for new instructions'. This is because sustainable development is a process to be engaged in, not a goal to be reached. Therefore what is required of us all is to become involved, and to do this, we need the information to help us make informed choices and a forum in which the different voices of the users of the built environment can be heard. This book will hopefully provide valuable insights into what issues must be tackled and how this might be done.

Chapter 3 will look at energy use in the built environment, and assess how its impact can be reduced. A sustainable energy strategy for our built environment will involve in the first instance increasing levels of energy efficiency and working much more closely with the natural environment in the design and construction of buildings. More fundamentally though, this chapter will put the case for the need to adopt demand management strategies and to move to much more locally based forms of power generation which are better suited to meeting the demands of sustainable development.

Chapter 4 will look at the environmental impact of the construction industry in terms of its materials use. Materials intensity in this industry is increasing at a time when the environmental consequences of this are becoming ever clearer. The construction sector also seems fixed on using a relatively small number of materials and construction types which block innovations needed for sustainability. New forms of working which maintain the best of the old while embracing the best of the new are important overall. There is therefore a need to reject unsustainable methods and look to the use of a wider range of materials and new practices to help reduce our materials intensity.

Chapter 5 will consider the impacts of transport and land use planning and how these relate to the built environment. Studies have shown that a significant proportion of the environmental impacts of construction stem from transport, and with the increasing globalization of the building materials sector, this impact looks set to increase. Sustainable development criteria would question such developments. While much has been written about the impacts of transport, it is worth going into detail about how transport specifically affects the built environment. Considering land use planning is important because it impacts upon transport intensity, energy use, community, economic development and sustainability. Through responsible planning that encourages development within communities, discourages road transport, promotes sensible energy and material usage, and adopts sustainable development criteria we can reduce this impact.

Chapter 6 will look at how the built environment can impact upon people's health. Despite the western world having reduced the incidence of many infectious diseases through public sanitation measures and improved nutrition, there is growing concern that modern building practices and materials are bringing with them health issues of their own to counteract past health gains. Sick building syndrome is one manifestation of this. Furthermore, the contemporary urban environment is not conducive to healthy lifestyles and for many people is highly stressful. New patterns of illness have emerged which can be traced to the urban milieux in the same way that cholera and smallpox could be traced to the filthy cities of the nineteenth century. Design and planning considerations can also foster feelings of positive health through provision of buildings and environments suitable to the needs of their users. Examples of this range from provision of natural light in offices, to the naturalistic styles of architecture associated with the Steiner movement.

Chapter 7 will look at issues of sustainability and social equity, and stress that both are dependent upon each other. Housing can be seen as a good example of how society has failed to deliver basic needs to a significant minority of people. However, simple provision of environment-friendly basic amenities to the population can produce large-scale gains through community support and economic stimulation while also reducing people's dependency on other agencies for their welfare and stability. The chapter will also show how provision of energy efficiency measures can produce very real and significant benefits in terms of increasing people's real incomes. Such moves are important if sustainable development is to have any chance of being realized.

Chapter 8 will look into the concept of sustainable communities. As noted earlier, the notion of a community has become much in vogue of late, yet there are concerns that the term, like that of sustainable development, has been used so often that it has lost some of its potency and meaning. Especially relevant here is the notion of scale. There are different kinds of communities which function at different levels, for example the village, town and city, though within each of these there may be other community groupings. For such geographical communities, however, the built environment is often integral to their vitality, because it is here that the community must live and work. This chapter will assess in more depth how these different communities can be strengthened and why this is important.

Chapter 9 will look into how the form of our built environment has been encouraged by an economy which sends out the wrong signals and encourages unsustainable practices. To make our built environment sustainable, there is therefore a need to change these signals through a 'greening' of the economy. Much has been written about environmental economics, but this chapter approaches the topic from the particular focus of the built environment and provides some insights into how a sustainable economy will work within the built environment.

Finally, Chapter 10 will summarize the issues raised and present, in policy terms, what is needed to realize the potential shown in the preceding chapters. We will return to key themes, and express potential gains in these terms.

11

In the same way that the book covers a number of related subject areas, so the book is also aimed at a number of different groups who might find what it has to say useful. Students of building, land use, environment, geography, planning, architecture, health and public policy should all find something of interest here. If the aim of the book is to bring a wide range of topics under one roof, then hopefully it will help users to make links between different topics in their own research. Practitioners working in fields as varied as construction, planning, environmental management, transport and health should also find something of interest here: not just in their own specialist area, but also for making links between different areas. It is worth saying again how the subject areas covered by the book are interlinked. *Greening the Built Environment* might be a useful way for practitioners to gain more insight into other areas which impact upon their work, and whom they in their turn affect.

This chapter began with a quote from Aldo van Eyck which highlights the importance of interaction in buildings and the built environment. Van Eyck is saying that for a house or a city to be judged a success it needs to fulfil many different demands and meet a wide variety of needs. This can only be done through inclusion of all the relevant concerns at the design stage. Similarly, if our built environment is to satisfy the needs of people, then we must not seek simple solutions but embrace the diversity inherent in society, and adopt a holistic approach towards problem solving. The topics set out in this book may be varied, but they are also closely interconnected. To help bring about sustainability, then, we must embrace this diversity and look for solutions within it. In *Human Scale* Sale discusses the idea of self sufficiency and the ability of a community to meet its own needs. He notes that such ideas are often criticized for being simplistic, and responds in the following way:

> '. . . *in fact I wish to complexify, not simplify. It is our modern economy that is simple . . . Diversity is the rule of human life, not simplicity . . . It is when a society complexifies and mixes, when it develops the multiplicity of ways of caring for itself, that it becomes textured and enriched*'

Sale, 1980, p 403

We would agree with Sale in looking amongst such diversity for solutions. *Greening the Built Environment* sets out where we might start looking.

2

THE BUILT ENVIRONMENT AND SUSTAINABLE DEVELOPMENT

'The future is purchased by the present'

Dr Johnson

The built environment provides us all with the most direct, frequent and unavoidable images and experiences of everyday life. The presence or absence of buildings, the geometry of spaces, the human scale of architecture and relationships between spaces and buildings and deeply felt feelings of security, fulfilment, gregariousness and community all take their cue from the shape, form and quality of the built environment. In this chapter we will argue that the built environment is a product and an amalgam of physical structures, the absence of such structures, the availability of open spaces and the relationships between spaces and between buildings and spaces. The quality of the built environment in its widest possible meaning is determined by the quality of the spaces between buildings and the opportunities for creative interaction with others in the spaces that separate buildings and give cities their distinctive qualities. The built environment can also be used to describe rural areas particularly in the sense that rural areas increasingly function as part of what geographers used to call the 'non-place urban realm'. The non-place urban realm concept describes a lifestyle where the emphasis is on high levels of mobility, long distance interactions by physical and electronic means and a relative lack of involvement in the detail of daily life in the village, hamlet or settlement where 'home' is temporarily located. These lifestyle factors blur rural–urban distinctions just as shopping patterns and working arrangements blur them.

The built environment as a term with some meaning beyond the mere descriptive has to be flexible enough to include the patterning of space-time structures through lifestyle arrangements that connect the rural and the urban, the developed world and the developing world and the social and the physical. These patternings determine the shape and form of cities, the level of investment in transport infrastructure, the provision of land for new housing, the shape of retailing and leisure activities and the nature of tourism. They also continuously redefine community. In this chapter we shall explore the definition of the built environment in its widest possible meaning and use sustainable development as a metric that will permit a better understanding of current failures and possible futures.

SUSTAINABLE DEVELOPMENT

The built environment is a result of a number of social and economic processes that are central to, and determine the rate at which we proceed in the direction of, sustainable development. More importantly the built environment exhibits very strong positive feedback mechanisms so that tendencies towards non-sustainability are very quickly reinforced by other developments triggered by a prior set of changes. An example of this positive feedback process is the conversion of agricultural land to land for new housing. This land is likely to be on the edge of an existing settlement or even for a new settlement. It will be developed with generous car parking provision and new highway infrastructure in areas not well served by public transport and will then contribute to increased levels of traffic, pollution and road danger that will in their turn add to the pressure for more roads, bypasses and parking in the centre of the nearest town or city. The built environment is a major agent of change (in this instance) in generating non-sustainable lifestyles.

Global changes in the rate of consumption of raw materials and energy, the conversion of agricultural land to developed land, the loss of rain forest both tropical and temperate and the associated waste, pollution and loss of biodiversity have been documented in great detail. At the global level successive reports from the World Resources Institute and United Nations Environment Programme (the latest in WRI, 1996) have documented the increasing severity of environmental problems and the threat to sustainability from over-consumption, water shortages, pollution and global warming. These environmental problems are inextricably bound up with social and health problems which are exacerbated by rapid population growth in developing world cities and excessive resource consumption in cities of the developed world:

> '*In the wealthiest cities of the developed world, environmental problems are related not so much to rapid growth as to profligate resource consumption. An urban dweller in New York consumes approximately three times more water and generates eight times more garbage than does a resident of Bombay. The massive energy demand of wealthy cities contributes a major share of greenhouse gas emissions*'

WRI, 1996, p 2

It is clear that the much quoted but totally unsubstantiated claim that economic growth will improve environmental quality is false. The Dobřiš assessment of the quality of the European environment could not be more direct about the end state of a long period of economic growth and increases in standard of living: 'The report confirms the poor quality of the European environment . . . (and) . . . identifies serious threats and stresses on the environment, natural resources and human health which have to be tackled more efficiently.' (Commission of the European Communities, 1995, p xi).

The deterioration of Europe's environmental quality against a background of significant increase in incomes and standard of living over the last 30 years should sound clear warning signals both to policy makers in Europe who have overseen this decline and to their colleagues in developing world countries who have signalled that a similar path will be followed in their countries.

The Dobříš assessment highlighted 12 prominent European environmental problems (see Box 2.1). All are generated, sustained or rendered more intractable by the scale of our commitment to a built environment and life style founded on the principle of consumption without responsibility.

Box 2.1
TWELVE PROMINENT EUROPEAN ENVIRONMENTAL PROBLEMS

- Climate change
- Stratospheric ozone depletion
- Loss of biodiversity
- Major accidents
- Acidification
- Tropospheric ozone and other photochemical oxidants
- Freshwater management
- Forest degradation
- Coastal zone threats and management
- Waste reduction and management
- Urban stress
- Chemical risks

Source: Commission of the European Communities, 1995, p 599

The built environment in developed countries is maintained and developed on the availability of fossil fuel energy sources which are priced at levels significantly below those at which prices would be if full account had to be made for all the environmental, land use and human health consequences of such a level of dependency (see Chapter 9 for a fuller discussion of pricing). This fossil fuel dependency determines the shape and size of, and distances travelled in, our urban and regional systems. We are an energy intensive and distance intensive society. This contributes to our preferences for buildings with a high energy content in their materials and the transport of those materials and it determines the degree to which we must convert land from non-developed states to developed states to meet this demand for energy and materials. Our preference for buildings with an embodied energy content far higher than is needed for that building to function well and deliver what is required of it, is matched by our preference for long distances over which we commute and by modes of transport that consume large amounts of fossil fuel energy. The energy demands of the building (in materials and in use) are as non-sustainable as the travel demands made by the occupants.

These high levels of demand for fossil fuel energy arise because energy prices do not reflect their environmental costs. They are underpriced. A different pricing regime and one which thoroughly internalized the external costs of all the environmental 'bads' would produce a different built environment. The built environment we now have is an artefact of underpricing and should be recognized as such. Its principal characteristics are shaped by a rising demand for more road space, car parking, housing, low density business parks, aggregates, out of town shopping centres, space greedy university campuses, fast food drive-in restaurants and the sterile spaces that often surround the paraphernalia of a fossil fuel society based on cars and lorries.

This patterning of the built environment consumes materials and energy on a scale that causes severe problems with so-called greenhouse gas emissions and with the production of chemical compounds. These compounds are implicated in local pollution and in global problems such as ozone layer depletion. They also cause the acidification of precipitation, lakes and streams and tree dieback. The food production systems on which we depend with their high levels of (fossil fuel based) chemical dependency cause water and waste pollution problems. The demand for land and the partitioning of land into ever smaller plots by new roads and linear developments lead to loss of biodiversity and species extinction. The growth in tourism partly as a response to the need to escape from seriously degraded urban environments causes devastation in coastal areas and the loss of coastal habitats. High levels of consumption produce high levels of waste particularly in a society that is inclined towards disposal rather than conservation. Waste consumes scarce land, pollutes ground water through landfill leachate and pollutes the atmosphere through incinerator emissions. The totality of this high level dependency on wasteful industrial, agricultural and transportation systems produces health problems, stress problems, heightened accident problems and an increased incidence of major technological and managerial failures, for example BSE, climate change, auto-immune disease, road traffic accidents, chemical spills and nuclear accidents.

The built environment in this nexus of problems, issues and societal malfunction is both a cause and an effect. It is ideal, therefore, as a starting point for understanding more clearly where and why things are going wrong and what, if anything, can restore a better balance of benefits and disbenefits to all the world's population whether North or South, urban or rural, rich or poor. The built environment is pivotal and can be managed, manipulated and shaped to restore health, equity, satisfying lifestyles and non-exploitative relationships between people and people, people and places and people and nature.

IS OUR BUILT ENVIRONMENT SUSTAINABLE?

The answer to this question depends on the definition of sustainable development. There is a measure of agreement about the principles of sustainable development though less coherence on the practical definitions and implementation of the concept. The principles include some or all of the following:

- Development that meets the needs of the present without compromising the ability of future generations to meet their own needs (the Brundtland definition).
- Development and consumption that ensure we live within our 'environmental means' sometimes expressed as living on 'interest' from the environment rather than 'capital'.
- Development that is based on a strong sense of equity and social justice. Large differentials in income and wealth globally and within the developed world are not compatible with the principle of living within environmental capacity limits.
- A requirement that we should not 'trip' critical environmental thresholds such as levels of greenhouse gas emissions that trigger irreversible climate change or levels of pollution that damage the respiratory health of children.
- A preference for the involvement and participation of individuals, communities and organizations at every level in taking 'ownership' of the problems and developing strategies for solving problems as 'stakeholders' rather than bystanders. These ideas are developed under the general banner of Local Agenda 21 strategies (see Chapter 10).

The United Kingdom is fairly typical in its response to the rigours, preferences and injunctions of sustainable development. It has a sustainable development strategy (Department of the Environment, 1994a) in which these principles are developed and applied to a number of economic and governmental sectors. It has a strong commitment to economic development that in practice takes precedence over other (particularly environmental and health) considerations and ensures the dilution of sustainable development principles (see the discussion below of Heathrow Terminal 5 and Manchester Airport's second runway). This dilution tendency which manifests itself in the spread of urbanization and the loss of agricultural and 'green' land is strongly entrenched in all countries and in the activities of the European Commission. Even in its most narrow sense the 'built environment' is increasing in its size and variety of expression as the rising demand for travel and transport, shopping and leisure expeditions ensures the spread of tarmac and concrete and the loss of green land and biodiversity.

IMPLEMENTING SUSTAINABLE DEVELOPMENT

In spite of the conceptual confusion and lack of coherence in implementing sustainable development there has been some progress in laying down ground rules. The European Commission's publication on sustainable cities has shown exactly what sustainability means in practice and has advanced the definition of a sustainable built environment in a way that 'provides strategies for sustainability incorporating ecological aspects into the development of the built environment' (Expert Group on the Urban Environment, 1996, p 40). Sustainable development has a number of practical features that can be implemented directly in policies aimed at the built environment:

- environmental limits;
- demand management;
- environmental efficiency;
- welfare efficiency;
- equity.

Environmental limits

The environment imposes thresholds for certain human activities in terms of resources, absorption of waste and maintenance of life support services such as temperature and protection against radiation. These resources are intrinsically of value to humanity and should not be 'traded' against the benefits of a particular development (eg Manchester Airport's (UK) second runway) or a particular activity as a whole (eg air travel). If we do not have clean air and clean water, an atmosphere that shields us from harmful radiation and soils and climate that enable food to be produced, we are unlikely to be in position to enjoy the benefits that were identified when an original trade-off was made. There is already evidence that we are breaking or risking breaking some important environmental capacity constraints. As defining these capacity constraints is difficult it will be necessary to invoke the precautionary principle where the avoidance of potential critical risks to the physical ecosystem must be given a substantial weighting in the decision making process. The precautionary principle is explicitly endorsed in the Maastricht Treaty and by extension formally part of the policy of all 15 Member States in the European Union. The fact that in practice it is not implemented highlights a recurrent problem in sustainable development.

Demand management

This is a critical concept and policy that follows an acceptance of environmental capacity limits. In the UK it has been government policy for some years to forecast the increased demand for road transport and then build the roads thereby ensuring that the forecast demand was indeed achieved. This 'predict and provide' approach is the opposite of demand management and has been rejected by the United Kingdom Royal Commission on Environmental Pollution in its Eighteenth Report (1994). It is still the basis of airport planning in Europe and in North America. Demand management involves more subtle and responsive planning to meet basic objectives rather than some derived demand. Hence it is possible to reduce energy consumption by a variety of conservation and efficiency measures as an alternative to building new power stations. It is possible to reduce waste and transport by improving (respectively) recycling and reuse and better accessibility to goods and services.

Environmental efficiency

There is now a considerable body of evidence that much business and governmental activity not informed by environmental concerns and strategies is inefficient (Welford and Starkey, 1996 and Berman, 1996). According to the Commission of the European Communities (Expert Group on the Urban Environment, 1996) the principle of environmental efficiency means 'the achievement of the maximum benefit for each unit of resources and waste produced' (p 41). Environmental efficiency can be increased in several ways (op cit, p 41):

- Increasing durability so that environmental costs are spread over a longer useful life.
- Increasing the technical efficiency of resource conversion, for example through greater energy efficiency or recovery of waste heat.
- Avoiding the consumption of renewable natural resources, water and energy faster than the natural system can replenish them.
- Closing resource loops for example by increasing reuse, recycling and salvage.
- Simplifying and avoiding the need for resource use (non-renewable).

These points will be returned to later in this chapter under the heading of 'Factor 4'.

Welfare efficiency

Environmental issues cannot be separated from social issues. The principle of welfare efficiency expresses the direct equivalent of environmental efficiency and describes the objective of gaining the greatest human benefit from each unit of economic activity. Welfare efficiency requires a much more diverse social and economic system with many more possibilities for satisfying lifestyle requirements than at present. It also requires a much more diversified and 'opportunity rich' built environment so that geographical space does not become rigidly compartmentalized and specialized and capable of utilization only through the expenditure of vast amounts of fossil fuel energy. It requires a built environment that in all its manifestations protects and enhances health (see Chapter 6).

Equity

The poor are worst affected by environmental problems and least able to solve them. Environmental policies have the potential to deliver significant improvements in the quality of life, health and job prospects of the marginalized, dispossessed and socially excluded in both developed and developing societies. There are not many rich people in developed societies who live on streets with 60,000 cars per day or on a housing estate next door to a chemical factory. There may, however, be some poor people and some people with very little choice about residential location and much else. The residential preferences of the rich have always been a good indicator of a high quality environment. Wealth itself is, however, an environmental problem and is not sustainable if it is deployed to support ever-increasing amounts of energy and material use and to support environmentally damaging and severely compressed space-time experiences in sensitive habitats and ecologies (an activity pattern sometimes known as tourism). Equity for people now living must accompany sustainability's concern for equity for future generations: 'Even the narrow notion of physical sustainability implies a concern for social equity between generations, a concern that must logically be extended to equity within each generation' (World Commission on Environment and Development, 1987, p 43). Equity is discussed in more detail in Chapter 7.

ECOLOGICAL FOOTPRINTS

One measure of our non-sustainability is the extent to which the maintenance of ordinary everyday life in cities has become dependent on vast tracts of land throughout the world and increasingly concentrated in the developing world. William Rees has defined the 'ecological footprint of cities' as the land required to feed them, to supply them with timber products and to reabsorb their carbon dioxide emissions by areas covered with growing vegetation. Defined in this way London's ecological footprint extends to 50 million acres, 125 times greater than its actual surface area of 400,000 acres or nearly equivalent to the entire productive land area of Great Britain (Sustainable London Trust, 1996). This is almost certainly an underestimate. The total mass of concrete, cement, steel and aggregates pouring into London to maintain and expand its property inventory would almost certainly require the addition of many more acres that have been involved in global mining, quarrying, manufacturing, transport and associated waste disposal. London's resource consumption is quantified in Table 2.1.

Giradet (1996) has carried out similar calculations for Hong Kong which has the highest concentration of people on the planet. The key point made by these calculations or mass balance audits is not that cities represent huge sinks in the global movement of materials and energy (which is part of the definition of a city) but that cities make little or no effort to convert their large one way flows into circular flows or closed loop systems. Even more significant is the

Table 2.1   *The Metabolism of Greater London*

Resource	Annual Input (million tonnes)
fuel (oil equivalent)	20.0
oxygen	40.0
water	1002
food	2.4
timber	1.2
paper	2.2
plastics	2.1
glass	0.36
cement	1.94
bricks, blocks, sand and tarmac	6.0
metal	1.2
	Annual Output (Waste) (million tonnes)
industrial and demolition waste	11.4
household, civic and commercial waste	3.9
wet, digested sewage sludge	7.5
carbon dioxide	60.0
sulphur dioxide	0.4
nitrogen oxides	0.28

Source: Sustainable London Trust, 1996, p 10

extent to which developing world cities like Calcutta are converting their circular, quasi-closed loop systems into linear systems (Box 2.2).

The input–output statistics for Hong Kong or London show a dramatic failure in basic housekeeping and indicate the extent to which we expect to live off 'capital' and not 'interest'. On a more positive note they also show the potential that remains untapped for reducing energy demand and fuel consumption, recycling urban waste as nutrients for food production, extending the acreages for urban food production, substituting local supplies where appropriate for those that have travelled long distances and creating a built environment with the opportunities for replacing the linear 'one-way' system with a closed loop system.

The concept of an ecological footprint is simple and profound. The average Canadian uses 4.3 hectares of land to support his or her lifestyle (Wackernagel and Rees, 1996). This total is made up of a large number of components (eg food, energy and transport) and is further categorized as land areas consumed by energy demand (including embodied energy in products), degraded land (or land allocated to the built environment) and demands made on gardens, crops, forestry and pasture. Energy and degraded land account for 60 per cent of the total land taken up in meeting the demands of the citizens of Canada. Housing

---

Box 2.2
RECYCLING IN CALCUTTA

Calcutta is a city of 14 million inhabitants in West Bengal (India). The eastern fringes of this city are marked by an area of wetland 78 km² in area. Over the past 100 years this area of wetland has developed as part of a very sophisticated waste and nutrient capturing and recycling system. The wetlands take all the sewage and waste water from Calcutta through drainage channels and canals where it is used for fish cultivation and irrigation of vegetable growing plots having been cleansed by the natural action of a large mass of plant matter and sunlight in ponds of no more than 3 m in depth. The wetlands also take the solid waste from all the households in Calcutta which is thoroughly scavenged for materials reclamation and reprocessing. The residues after scavenging are spread on the land and support three crops each year of vegetables (gourds, radish, cauliflowers etc) which like the fish are returned to Calcutta to provide abundant, cheap food. The whole recycling and recovery system provides employment for over 20,000 people and has a zero fossil fuel energy require-ment. It is currently under threat from the expansion of the urban area of Calcutta and the development of the planned township of Salt Lake City. The elimination of a free, non-polluting and high employing waste disposal system that also feeds 14 million people is likely to create significant problems of extra cost, pollution and urban poverty. These problems are not being addressed as Salt Lake City expands.

Source: Ghosh, 1996

---

alone accounts for 21 per cent of the total size of the Canadian citizen's ecological footprint which is considerably larger than that of an Indian citizen (see Table 2.2).

The high levels of consumption in North America represent a sequestration of global resources never before seen in history. The consumption levels support

Table 2.2 *Comparison of Consumption Levels*

Consumption per person	Canada	USA	India	World
CO_2 (tonnes/yr)	15.2	19.5	0.81	4.2
Vehicles per 100 persons	46	57	0.2	10
Paper consumption (kg/yr)	247	317	2	44
Fossil energy use (GJ/yr)	250	287	5	56
Fresh water withdrawal (m³/yr)	1668	1868	612	644
Ecological footprint (ha/person)	4.3	5.1	0.4	1.8

Source: Wackernagel and Rees, 1996, p 85

a lifestyle and a design of built environment that is non-sustainable. It is non-sustainable because it is not available to the total population of the world. The world quite simply runs out of land if North American consumption levels are extrapolated to the population of India and China. The consumption levels are non-sustainable because they depend on inequalities. Inequalities in global consumption are essential if existing ecological footprints are to be maintained. Wackernagel and Rees (1996) put this more bluntly: 'if everybody lived like today's North Americans, it would take at least two additional planet Earths to produce resources, absorb the wastes, or otherwise maintain life-support' (p 15).

The high levels of consumption are associated with large amounts of waste and pollution (World Resources Institute, 1996). These are causing health problems and global warming/climate change problems that affect North American just as much as they affect Indian citizens. They may be triggering irreversible climate change and exceeding known environmental capacity limits. The reality of ecological footprints is that the excess consumption of the developed world can only be maintained at the expense of the under-consumption of the developing world.

Changing this situation is a central objective of sustainable development policies. Lifestyles, consumption and the built environment can be transformed to be more conserving, less wasteful and more nurturing of health and community. There is already abundant evidence that such a change represents a win–win situation. The achievement of sustainable development objectives does not involve a lowest common denominator policy or the adoption of 'policies of impoverishment'. Sustainable development involves a transformation of material and energy flows that makes full use of all available resources and at the same time enhances community and health objectives. One example of an advanced project working in this area is the Manchester 2020 project 'Sustainable development in the city region' (Town and Country Planning Association and Manchester Metropolitan University, 1996).

MANCHESTER 2020

The Manchester 2020 project presents a plan for the development of a radically different built environment for Manchester. It is a built environment that converts global and aggregate objectives about greenhouse gas emissions, waste and pollution into specifics about Manchester and in a way that could be implemented over a 25 year period. It is a blueprint for an ecologically sound built environment. At its heart are a number of targets, all of which would reduce the size of its ecological footprint, increase diversity of land use, create jobs, stimulate community enterprise and make full use of Manchester's resources in meeting Manchester's needs. The project demonstrates the extent to which the built environment is the key agenda for delivering sustainable development objectives. The plan is based on a vision (see Box 2.3) and a number of targets for the year 2020.

Box 2.3

MAIN TARGETS FOR MANCHESTER 2020

If there is one element essential for change, it is vision. A transformation within our lifetimes can see a Manchester which is green and beautiful, on a par with the great European capitals. Vibrant neighbourhoods filled with shops, studios and all kinds of housing. Exciting designs for buildings old and new, collecting their power from the sun. Tree-lined streets and squares, and parks and green corridors where one can walk or cycle for miles as if in the country.

Flowers and fruit trees flourish, along with the birds they support; and allotments and gardens are full of produce. The city's rivers and canals live again, supporting fish, insects and water-fowl.

Getting around the city will be simple – one card will access buses, trains, trams and taxis, with integrated door-to-door services, day and night. Most people will live within a short walk of shops and schools – pedestrian routes will be green and pleasant, while cyclists use a city-wide network of dedicated routes. Cars will still be needed by some, but pedestrians will have priority in all residential neighbourhoods and local centres. Air quality will improve so that a walk in the city will be pleasant and healthy.

Around the edge of the city, the fringe landscapes will no longer be the left-overs of motorways and power lines. Fields and hedges will provide rich wildlife habitats, and a patchwork of forests, gardens and meadows will be linked by leisure trails. Organic farms in the country and the city will meet a good proportion of the city's food.

The city's demands and impacts will move towards long-term sustainable levels. Demands on external resources will be minimized, most waste will be re-used and recycled. Industry and services will be creative and diverse, capitalizing on Manchester's lead role as a green economy of the 21st century. New patterns for the social economy and community enterprise ensures all human needs are met at the neighbourhood level.

Manchester's historical strengths of science and technology, education, sports and arts will no longer be compromised by dirt and decay. The city will offer variety and opportunity, and cease to fear the future it is creating. Sustainable development will harness the tradition of down-to-earth social cooperation and innovation in which Manchester has led the world in the past.

Source: Town and Country Planning Association and Manchester Metropolitan University (1996)

The key targets are:

- to reduce CO_2 emissions directly attributable to Greater Manchester by over 35 per cent;
- land use: clustering of urban form around local centres; up to half of all new housing in high density mixed uses;
- energy demand of buildings reduced by 30–40 per cent;
- road traffic reduced by 25 per cent in urban areas;
- public transport services tripled;

- open land: biodiversity doubled, chemical inputs halved, forest cover of 30 per cent;
- air quality: main pollutants reduced by 50 per cent;
- energy: stabilize growth in demand, 10 per cent from renewables;
- combined heat and power to one-third of all buildings in the city;
- employment: 50,000 jobs created in environmental and related industries.

The creation of a sustainable city region depends on minimizing resource and energy consumption (eg demand for concrete in new buildings), reusing waste matter in food production and recycling and retaining compact urban forms and land use patterns that can encourage walking, cycling and public transport and discourage use of cars.

Transport and land use must be considered together and are critical in achieving these objectives (see Chapter 5). An urban form that discriminates against walking and cycling to a rich concentration of facilities and activities available in a small geographical area is fundamentally non-sustainable and cannot be rendered sustainable by the application of technology, public transport or taxation. An urban form that can eliminate car dependency and encourage the use of non-motorized modes of transport is intrinsically sustainable. Wackernagel and Rees (1996) have calculated how much land must be allocated to a commuting trip of 5 kilometres in the USA. The land calculation takes into account how much green land is needed to absorb the carbon dioxide from fossil fuel mobility and how much road space is needed:

'. . . it turns out that a person living five kilometres from work requires an extra 122 square metres of ecologically productive land for bicycling, 300 square metres for busing, or 1530 square metres for driving alone by car. The land for the cyclist is needed to grow food while most of the bus passenger's and car driver's land is taken up by CO_2 sequestration'

Wackernagel and Rees, 1996, pp 106-107

This is almost certainly an underestimate. Land for car parking adds considerable amounts to an inventory based on road space alone (see UK calculations below) and land allocated to the plethora of car-oriented developments including salerooms, exhaust and tyre centres, drive-in restaurants, garages and service centres, adds more. As distances over which we travel lengthen in response to land use changes (eg in retailing) so the size of the ecological footprint goes up.

Land use is the key to other sustainable development objectives in Manchester. The report identifies 5000 hectares of vacant land which offer scope for local food production: 'together with under-utilised land along transport corridors and in institutional grounds and allotments food could be grown for 20,000 households' (Town and Country Planning Association and Manchester Metropolitan University, op cit, p 19). This local potential can be enhanced by recycling nutrients (sewage) locally and can reduce the ecological footprint by substituting short distance transport of food for long distance. Manchester's energy requirements would be significantly reduced through a multiple substitution of:

- short distance for long distance;
- recycled nutrients for chemicals;
- low processed foods for heavily processed foods;
- vegetable products for animal products.

This list also describes what Calcutta has actually achieved through a process of evolution and necessity.

Food issues go to the heart of the debate about sustainable development and land use and illustrate the irreducibles of life on a finite planet. If the planet's population consumes a diet of mainly meat products then we will have already surpassed the capacity of the planet to grow enough vegetable protein to support the cattle to feed the people. This is put into sharp focus in the work of Steinhart and Steinhart (1974) who have estimated that industrialized food systems require 5–10 calories of energy to obtain one food calorie, while 'primitive' cultures have obtained 5–50 calories of food for a single calorie of human energy expended. If we could achieve this level of environmental efficiency we will have achieved sustainable development.

NON-SUSTAINABILITY AND THE BUILT ENVIRONMENT

The focus on Manchester in the 2020 report is much needed. Manchester has experienced some fundamental changes to its built environment in recent years that make the shift towards sustainability very difficult indeed and present a number of methodological problems for the understanding of regional or sub-regional sustainability. Manchester is now ringed by a dense motorway network (M62, M602, M63, A57(M), A614(M)) and more is planned or under construction as in the case of the new motorway link through Daisy Nook, formerly a popular and habitat-rich green area accessible to several hundred thousand residents of Greater Manchester. With the support and encouragement of Manchester City Council, Manchester Airport has expanded rapidly in the last 10 years to become a major international airport in its own right and is now to build a second runway with a considerable negative impact on the rural environment of Cheshire.

These developments have transformed Manchester into a car dependent city. Businesses and retailing have shifted to motorway and edge of city locations. The land use system now requires higher levels of car use than it did 20 years ago. The presence of a major international airport has added to traffic levels and pollution and the combination of all these factors makes Manchester more difficult to deal with if a shift towards sustainable city status is the preferred policy option. The fuel consumed in Greater Manchester is dominated by car and lorry traffic to the airport and aviation fuel demands. As we have seen in the work of Wackernagel and Rees (1996) this will generate an ecological footprint considerably larger than if Manchester was not the location for a major international airport. Should this ecological footprint be attributed to the citizens of Manchester or to the citizens of whatever localities are supplying the passengers for the airlines? Does the fuel demand at the airport for air freighting green beans, lettuces or flowers from Africa to consumers in the north-west of England appear as a debit item on Manchester's ecological footprint/resource consumption inventory or on the household/local authority in Wilmslow or Southport consuming green beans from Africa? These questions are not ones of minor arithmetical significance. They go to the heart of responsibility for taking action to prevent global climate change and they go to the heart of achieving sustainable development objectives for regions and cities and for local populations whose health might be damaged by the noise and emissions from major international airports.

Manchester Airport was given permission in early 1997 to construct a second runway. The runway will destroy over 1000 acres of farmland in the Cheshire countryside, 43 ponds, mature woodland and will lead to a doubling of the traffic on the local motorway network (airport traffic will increase from 52,000 to 124,000 vehicles per day) which will have to deal with the additional demand. The inspector at the public inquiry into the runway proposal accepted that the runway would damage the health and environment of the local population and that it would lead an increase in greenhouse gas emissions at a time when international agreements were very clear that these emissions should be reduced. The large weight of evidence on local, regional and global impacts was deemed to be less important than the economic impact of the airport expansion on the region. The inspector at the inquiry recommended approval because of the economic development benefits for Manchester and for the whole of the north-west of England.

The airport inquiry and final approval of the project by government is very important indeed in terms of the light it sheds on the UK planning system and the probability that it can deliver sustainable development objectives. The commitment to these objectives is a lower order commitment when set against (presumed) economic gains. The job creation arguments presented at the runway inquiry were given far more significance than the environmental arguments notwithstanding the fact that these arguments can be challenged in detail (as they have been at the London Heathrow Terminal 5 inquiry) and notwithstanding that alternative investments and economic strategies can achieve higher levels of job creation through environmentally aware sustainable development strategies.

The reality of sustainable development in the UK when tested at road inquiries or airport expansion inquiries is far weaker than the rhetoric. Aviation represents a fundamental threat to the global environment (Whitelegg, 1997b) through its impact on global warming and a fundamental threat to residents in the vicinity of airports through noise and air pollution (National Resources Defence Council, 1996). Approvals to airport expansion plans fail the test of sustainability on at least these two counts. At Manchester the expansion plan fails on a third count which is the damage to habitat and ecology in the Bollin Valley, the loss of geomorphologically significant sites and the loss of biodiversity in a green belt area close to the homes of one million people.

In a study of one US airport (Chicago Midway) with one-fifth of the activity level of Manchester International Airport the authors concluded:

> '... that Midway's arriving and departing planes constitute a considerable source of particulate air pollution as well as toxic compounds such as benzene, 1.3 butadiene and formaldehyde, releasing far more of these pollutants than other industrial pollution sources within the 16 square mile study area. In fact, few of Chicago's industrial sources release as much benzene or formaldehyde as the planes flying into and out of Midway Airport. Nevertheless airports are exempt from the federal law that requires other toxic sources to report their toxic emissions totals'

National Resources Defense Council, 1996, p 8

The implications for the residents of Wilmslow, Stockport and Handforth of the Midway findings are severe. Their built environment will now include a major source of health damaging pollution, extra traffic, and higher levels of development of new industrial, commercial and residential activities that destroy green land. The principles and objectives of sustainable development have been rejected by the planning process that was supposed to put sustainable development at its centre (Department of the Environment, 1994a).

Aviation and the growth of aviation is a key lifestyle element in the developed world. Aviation has a huge impact on the built environment and on human health and yet continues to grow in its market share of total distance travelled and become deeply embedded in lifestyle choices and behaviour. Most people have flown to a holiday destination and expect to be able to continue to do so. Those who have not yet flown expect to do so in the very near future. Aviation has many positive images in the popular imagination and is also seen as an engine of economic growth. Its status in the debate about sustainable development is far more significant than its proportionate contribution to greenhouse gases or its impact on local air quality around Manchester or Midway. Aviation is a powerful metaphor for the contradictions and inconsistencies surrounding behaviour and policy in the area of sustainable development.

Aviation throws down a challenge to decision makers and politicians. There are only two choices. One is to add to the capacity of global aviation until everyone in the world takes as many flights as a US citizen now does and the other is to acknowledge the finite nature of environmental capacity and to plan for capping or reductions in the number of flights. The choices are currently being made throughout the world in favour of adding new capacity and this is a far more eloquent declaration of lack of commitment to sustainable development than any speech, treaty or convention. Aviation symbolizes the global rush towards non-sustainability cloaked in a rhetoric of green concerns.

The debate about aviation and its unconstrained growth has been focused for some time on Heathrow Airport. This location and this debate is of global significance and merits a more detailed case study approach in this chapter. The outcome of the debate about Heathrow's expansion will be the litmus test of the ability of sustainability arguments to influence the shape of the built environment across every sector of human behaviour. The largest expansion plan for airport development in Europe is the proposal for a new terminal (Terminal 5 or T5) at London Heathrow Airport. This is currently (summer 1997) at the planning inquiry stage and a decision on the planning application will not be made before the end of 1998. T5 will add 30 million to a 1996 total for Heathrow of 54 million passengers per annum. By 2015 the likelihood is that Heathrow will be handling 100 million passengers per annum. The impact of Heathrow on greenhouse gas emissions, NO_x emissions and the toxic releases identified at Chicago Midway will be severe. The severity in terms of public health will be compounded by the close proximity of large concentrations of population. The London Boroughs of Hounslow and Hillingdon are in close proximity to Heathrow as is the Borough of Windsor and Maidenhead.

T5, like Manchester's expansion can be expected to generate a large amount of new and relocated development either on the airport site or within a few kilometres and adjacent to the motorway network. This in its turn will generate extra vehicular activity with yet more noise and pollution. Even without the vehicular activity generated by new developments after T5 becomes operational the movement of passengers and aircraft alone will add a substantial burden of NO_x (which is health damaging) and carbon dioxide (which is the largest source of greenhouse gases contributing to global warming). Heathrow's impact with T5 is shown in Tables 2.3 to 2.5.

T5 would result in an increase in CO_2 emissions of 10 per cent when the with and without T5 situations are compared in the year 2016. This increase is clearly at variance with international obligations to reduce CO_2 emissions and with UK policy to reduce CO_2 emissions by 15 per cent from their 1990 level by the year 2010. On this simple criterion T5 is not a sustainable development and will frustrate national sustainable development objectives.

Table 2.3 *CO_2 Emissions from Passenger Car Traffic at Heathrow Airport*

	1992	2016 without T5	2016 with T5
Air passengers (mppa)	45	60	100
Car journeys (million) per annum	17.07	22.75	37.93
Vehicle kilometres (million)	85.35	113.75	189.65
Pollution (tonnes CO_2)	53,770	71,662	119,480

Note: A detailed explanation of the calculations in this table can be found in Whitelegg (1996)

Table 2.4 *Heathrow Airport's CO_2 Inventory (tonnes/annum)*

	1992	*2016 without T5*	*2016 with T5*
CO_2 from car traffic	53,770	71,662	119,480
Aircraft emissions from LTO cycle	562,600	696,000	725,000
Totals	616,370	767,662	844,480

Notes: A detailed explanation of the calculations in this table can be found in Whitelegg (1996).
LTO = landing and take-off.

Table 2.5 estimates the contribution of T5 to the oxides of nitrogen (NO_x) emissions in the vicinity of Heathrow airport. NO_x levels in 2016 with T5 are 35 per cent higher when compared with 2016 without T5. This is a serious deterioration in local air quality at a time when there are international agreements in place to reduce NO_x emissions.

Table 2.5 *NO_x Emissions at Heathrow Airport 'present' and 2016 (kg/day)*

Source/Species	*1992*	*2016 without T5*	*2016 with T5*
Aircraft	13,826	16,903	23,493
Road traffic	2106	2175	2276
Heating plant	608	752	978
Fugitive releases	0	0	0
Total	16,540	19,830	26,747

Source: Whitelegg (1996)

In addition to international agreements it is UK government policy expressed in 'The Health of the Nation' to reduce NO_x emissions in urban air from a 1990 baseline by 50 per cent by the year 2000 (Department of Health, 1991, p 102). The impact of T5 calculated by the proposers of the development itself is to deny over half a million urban residents in the west of London this elementary level of public health protection.

The built environment is intrinsically noisy. The Dobříš assessment of Europe's environment (Commission of the European Communities, 1995) identifies noise as a significant environmental impact and one that affects more than 50 per cent of the population in highly industrialized countries. Berglund (1993) estimates that 17 per cent of Europe's population is exposed to noise levels that have serious health impacts. These impacts occur at noise levels above 65 dB(A) and are associated with sleep disturbance, noise induced hearing loss, interference with speech communication, psychological problems, learning difficulties, high blood pressure and a decline in performance and productivity. The deprivation of use of gardens and balconies in fine weather and the inability to have windows open during summer when sleeping add another layer of psychological stress and loss of quality of life. Berglund (op cit) discusses in more detail the damaging effects of noise at levels lower than an average street (< 55 dB(A)) on learning in schools particularly where some of the children are learning through a language which is not their first language.

In assessing the impact of noise from the T5 development on residents living near to Heathrow Berglund concludes:

> 'The World Health Organisation evidence shows that in order to protect the majority of persons from being seriously or moderately annoyed during the daytime the sound pressure level outdoors should not exceed 55 dB(A) or 50 LAeq . . . the present situation at Heathrow warrants that the Terminal 5 project should be cancelled'

Berglund, 1995, p 23

The Dobřiš assessment (Commission of the European Communities, 1995, p 359) states that noise levels in the range 55–65 dB(A) have significantly increased through the 1980s and 1990s. Our commitment at national and European levels to higher levels of motorization and higher levels of air travel have produced a degraded urban environment that now fails over 100 million European citizens in basic health protection and guarantees of quality of life. On current evidence at public inquiries and in the outputs of the planning and development process this deterioration will continue producing the most unsatisfactory built environment (from the point of view of the individual who must endure the results) since people first began to live in cities and organize life around the principles of an urban civilization.

LOCAL AGENDA 21

Local Agenda 21 initiatives offer a route to a re-engineered built environment that meets in full the objectives of sustainable development. Agenda 21 is an action plan for the twenty-first century agreed at the Rio Conference in 1992. Its key principle and approach is its assertion of the importance of local action and local initiatives and the importance of local authorities and municipalities in achieving sustainable development. In Europe several thousand municipalities are developing local versions of Agenda 21. The Swedish Society for Nature Conservation has reviewed 300 of these projects and presented 49 of the best examples of local good practice (Bovin and Magnusson, 1997). The projects cover the whole range of transport, energy, housing and waste policy areas that figure so centrally in reducing fossil fuel dependency, reducing pollution and conserving the Earth's finite resources. The example of Orebro in Sweden is particularly instructive in its progress with a wide range of policy initiatives that are moving this city towards a sustainable condition. Orebro's policies have included:

- a bicycle plan to increase the use of non-motorized transport;
- a waste sorting plan to increase recovery and recycling;
- ecologically high performing apartment blocks;
- a transport–land use strategy to achieve a better balance between housing areas and workplace locations;
- housing to be constructed near to schools, shops, childcare facilities;
- heat and energy to be supplied from renewable sources;
- new construction will use demolition materials and local materials;
- rainwater from roofs to be collected and used in toilets and for gardening;
- cars to be eliminated from journey to work;
- car parks to be converted into green recreational areas.

The experience of Orebro shows that progress can be made in the direction of a sustainable built environment and in a way that benefits all sections of the community.

FACTOR 4

There is ample evidence that the developed world can reduce the size of its ecological footprint and practise environmental efficiency in a way that meets sustainable development objectives whilst increasing opportunities and human health. Walking and cycling in a well planned and high quality urban environment with ample shops, businesses, workplaces and schools within a 5 km range of a residential address can reduce energy use and CO_2 emissions by a factor of ten. Buildings can be constructed and materials sourced locally with a reduction of total environmental impact by a factor of at least 3.5 (Smith et al, 1995, 1997). Offices and homes can function perfectly well at levels of energy consumption 90 per cent lower than current buildings can provide for and organic farming can produce large crop yields with far less input of mechanical and chemical energy. We can reduce energy and materials in the manufacturing process, for example using fibre optic cable as an alternative to copper cable, and we can design products that have a very long life and can then be disassembled so that a high proportion of components can be reused or remanufactured.

The built environment has a key role to play in this re-engineering of our production and consumption patterns. Its role will be defined by the extent to which we can reduce the physical demand for fossil fuel mobility through careful land use planning (see Chapter 5), by a fully integrated approach to managing material resources throughout their life cycle, to extend the life of buildings, reduce the energy demand of buildings and fully utilize all waste products, however created, as valuable inputs to another process or activity. This re-engineering is a reconceptualization of human activity into closed loop (or nearly closed loop) systems where nothing is wasted, everything is reused or recycled, local resources and local skills are used to their maximum extent and land and water are conserved.

The idea of cranking up the efficiency of our production systems has been given practical expression under the term 'Factor 4'. It is possible to have a fourfold increase in productivity from the same resources, to have a built environment that delivers everything we need of it with a four fold reduction in per capita fossil fuel use and it is possible to double wealth and half resource use at the same time (Weizsäcker et al, 1997):

'we can accomplish everything we do today as well as now, or better, with only one quarter of the energy and materials we presently use. This would make it possible, for example, to double the global standard of living while cutting resource use in half'

Weizsacker et al, pp xxi–xxii

One of our objectives in the remainder of this book is to pursue the 'factor 4' philosophy. We do this on a much broader canvas than the originators of this expression. The built environment is a primary agent of change in moving towards much reduced materials and energy intensity and in this movement it must also deliver significant reductions in inequality and increments in welfare and employment. How can we get a significant increase in environmental performance of land use and buildings at lower energy consumption levels and better performance in health and equity? How can we multiply the beneficial effects of community coherence and citizen participation? How can we harness economic and environmental efficiency to reduce inequalities in wealth and income and how can we shift from an exploitative model of consumption to a conserving model? In the language of sustainability how do we learn to live off the interest and not the capital? We can factor up our performance and in some cases do much better than a factor of four. More importantly we can leave enough space (measured in land, clean air, clean water and material resources) for present and future generations to enjoy an improved quality of life whether they are citizens of Bangladesh or California. We must also have the modesty and the wisdom to learn from examples of best practice in cities like Calcutta and to demonstrate that the sophistication of an advanced industrial economy is a help and not a hindrance to the achievement of sustainable development.

3

ENERGY INTENSITY IN THE BUILT ENVIRONMENT

'It is depressing to have to admit that . . . fully air-conditioned glass-clad towers are still being erected from Australia to the Gulf and the Arctic to Singapore. It may not seem very important or relevant to our daily lives that for instance the Antarctic ice cap is melting at an increasing rate and that flowering plants are creeping ever northwards in Spitzbergen, but these and many other phenomena confirm the reality of global warming which will have a quite radical effect on the life of the whole planet if it continues to accelerate in such fashion. Before the end of the working life of some of the glass towers now being built, their feet could be washed by the waves of the seas that their excessive use of energy has helped to raise.'

Architectural Review, 1179, May 1995, p 4

In his book *The Green Imperative*, Victor Papanek notes that this century has seen two major changes which have never occurred before. One is that we have attained the power to change the natural order of the earth and throw it into disharmony. The other is that,

'we have nearly all – at least in the northern part of the globe – moved indoors . . . and most of us spend much of our time in homes, cars, workplaces, cinemas or public buildings whenever we are not shopping in malls, supermarkets or arcades.'

Papanek, 1995, p 10

This latter change might at first seem trivial in comparison to the first, but the two are linked. Whereas before, a life lived outdoors or in close contact with the outdoors could perhaps allow us to understand natural processes and the ability of and limits to the natural environment's capacity to deal with human activities, containment indoors has separated us from this understanding. Instead, we have increasingly sought to make buildings our own environment apart from nature. Modern buildings have, almost without fail, artificial heating or cooling systems and sometimes both. Between different buildings there exist large differences in terms of energy use and environmental impact.

Vast sums are wasted in heating and cooling buildings, and huge amounts of energy and materials squandered in making large, impressive glass-clad skyscrapers which tell us little except that we have the power to do these things. We have, after all, the power to go to the moon, yet few of us have actually been. Financial cost prevents us making the trip, and environmental cost ought to make us question the worth of many current building practices. As this chapter's opening comment from the *Architectural Review* noted, we are still designing and constructing buildings which will only put us in hotter and deeper water some 50 or 100 years into the future. These buildings will still be here when the architects, builders and current users are long gone, but it is likely that they will have become symbols of the destructive and short-term thinking characterized by the choices we are making now.

Our 'move indoors' has led to a position in which we no longer rely on our immediate environment for our food, fuel and building materials but are instead dependent upon distant players in the global market place for all these requirements. Our energy needs used to come from our immediate surroundings. Today, however, our wants are met in abundance by distant power stations burning fossil fuel. Cheap and abundant energy has been one of the main facilitators of our economic growth. Nordhaus (1994) estimates that the price of light per lumen hour has fallen by 800 per cent since the nineteenth century. Technological progress and so-called economies of scale have dramatically reduced the price we pay for energy, so that issues such as energy efficiency receive scant regard from many clients, builders and architects. The looming spectre of global warming, however, is providing evidence that there is an associated cost to our high levels of energy use for which we will all pay a price.

For many designers, 'green building' seems to mean little more than the use of more energy efficient light bulbs, or an extra 50 mm of insulation in the loft. Though such measures will undoubtedly help, they do not, unfortunately go far enough. More importantly, we must address the way in which we produce and use energy in our buildings and the built environment.

CURRENT ENERGY USE PATTERNS

The energy used in society depends largely upon power generated from fossil fuels. As well as being non-renewable, fossil fuels also release carbon dioxide as a by-product of generation, and this is the major contributor to global warming. It is already too late to stop global warming, and we are beginning to see the environment's delayed reaction to the damage already caused. Indeed, for many, rising annual temperatures, and falling rainfall levels are already a reality (Papanek, 1995, p 18). All that can be said, however, is that it is not too late to stop the situation becoming even worse.

Through sample drilling in rock, Arctic ice and soil, it has been established that during the last 12 million years the carbon dioxide content in the air never rose above 250 parts per million (ppm) until power generation using fossil fuels began. By 1958 it had risen to 315 ppm; to 340 ppm by 1988, and to 360 in 1995 (Papanek op cit; Brown et al, 1996). This increase in carbon dioxide content, along with increasing levels of other greenhouse gases such as methane, has led to a rise in global average temperatures as shown by Figure 3.1. According to the Goddard Institute of Space Studies, 1995 was the hottest year since records began in 1866 (Baird, 1996).

One of the chief concerns over global warming is not the rise in temperatures (which could in itself have dramatic consequences) but the disruption in weather patterns likely to result. According to the Intergovernmental Panel on Climate Change's 1996 report on global warming the incidence of floods, droughts, fires and heat outbreaks is expected to increase in some regions (IPCC, 1996). There are also concerns about falling levels of rain in Europe as evidenced by recent water shortages. In 1996, for example, Belgium went on drought alert when water reserves fell after what its Royal Meteorological Institute described as 'the most significant rainfall shortage since 1833' (*The Guardian*, 1996).

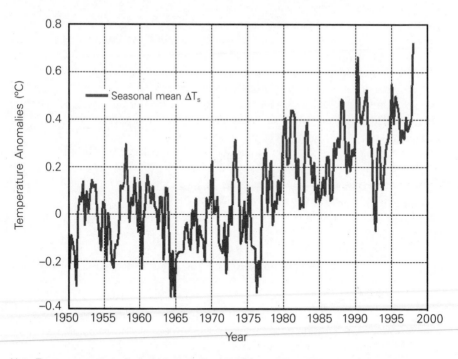

Note: Temperature anomalies are the variations in °C from 1951–1980 mean global temperature. To approximate mean global temperature add 14°C.

Source: NASA web page (http://www.giss.nasa.gov/data/gistemp/seas.GLB.gif)

Figure 3.1 *Global Average Surface Air Temperature, 1950–1997*

Paradoxically, alongside droughts, there has also been increased storm activity. In 1996, 44 floods worldwide claimed 6580 lives and cost insurance companies £140 million. In January 1995, the insurance industry was hit by severe flooding on the Moselle, the Rhine and the Maas, floods which were considered 'once in a century' events. Unfortunately, they were the second 'once in a century' events within 13 months, Germany having been flooded in late 1994. In the summer of 1997, severe flooding again hit Germany, as well as Poland, the Czech Republic and Romania. More than 120 people died, while at the flood's height, more than 7000 square kilometres of Poland were covered. In Frankfurt, the Oder rose more than 6 metres above its normal level. Munich Re, the German reinsurance firm, estimated the cost of the damage of this third 'once in a century event' at more than DM 10 billion (£3.5 billion) (Radford, 1997). Much of this cost, some of which will be uninsured, will be in lost agriculture and lost productivity, but a significant cost is likely to stem from damage to the built environment.

As well as an increase in instances of flooding, there are concerns about the growing severity and frequency of storms, notably hurricanes. The south-eastern United States has been hit by a number of serious hurricanes in recent years. Although loss of life has been reduced due to effective warning systems, economic damage has been unprecedented. On 24 August 1992, Hurricane Andrew virtually flattened 235 square kilometres of Dade County in Florida, destroying 85,000 homes and leaving 300,000 people homeless. Total losses were put at $30 billion (Brown et al, 1996). However, Robert Sheets, then director of the National Hurricane Centre, estimated that if Andrew had moved only 30 kilometres north, it would have covered New Orleans in 6 metres of water and caused damage of $100 billion (Rapaport and Sheets, 1995).

Damage from flooding and storms, when coupled with rising sea levels, is likely to lead to increased problems in our built environment, much of which is sited on the coast or on river plains. According to Gerhard Berz of Munich Re:

'The increased intensity of all convective processes in the atmosphere will force up all the frequency and severity of tropical cyclones, tornadoes, hailstorms, floods and storm surges in many parts of the world, with serious consequences for all types of property insurance.'

Berz, 1996, p 20

Between 1990 and 1996, the worldwide insurance industry has paid out US$48 billion on weather-related losses, compared with losses of US$14 billion for the previous decade. As a first step, many insurance companies are reducing cover in areas of high perceived risk (Brown et al, op cit). According to Dr Andrew Dlugolecki of insurers General Accident, weather-related events have almost doubled the cost of household buildings insurance over the last 10 years, and insurers have begun charging differential rates for areas prone to subsidence, flooding and storm damage (Baird, 1996). As the effects of global warming become more apparent, it is likely that certain areas will suffer, and insurance costs increase. Excessive increases would make certain areas virtually uninsurable, an effect which would create major problems within the built environment. All the above should remind us that society in general and the built environment in particular is still dependent upon and prey to the processes of the natural environment. It should also hit home just how relevant the problem of global warming is to much of our built environment.

The events described above may not be connected to global warming, and may merely be unprecedented meteorological distortions. However, they may be early indications of man-made changes to our climate and merely the first signs of what is to come. If this is the case, then some of our towns and cities are already beginning to feel the consequences of the unsustainable behaviour which has been encouraged by society. Any rational response would be to begin tackling the causes of global warming immediately. It could be that the predictions on global warming are alarmist, though the bulk of scientific evidence says not. However, the cost of action in the future will be so great that action now must be seen as prudent and cost effective. After all, prevention is always the best cure.

Energy use is associated with economic activity, therefore the greater the level of activity, the greater the amount of energy use. However, the energy use ratio in much of the developed world has been falling, as industry and housing have become more efficient in the way they use energy. In the UK, the energy ratio has been falling since the 1950s. Our CO_2 emissions per unit of delivered energy have been falling, a fact due mainly to the move from coal towards gas. However, despite this fall in CO_2 emissions per unit of energy used, total emission levels have actually risen slightly, because of increased levels of consumption (Pout, 1994). The World Energy Council, in its report 'Energy for Tomorrow's World' estimated that in 25 years, energy use will have increased by 88 per cent over the 1990 level representing a growth rate of 3 per cent per year. Most of this energy will come from fossil fuels. With an estimated world population of 8 billion by 2020, the report predicted a 44 per cent increase in greenhouse gases by this date driven largely by the increased use of fossil fuels by developing countries. Even in the developed world however, growth in energy use is predicted (Smith, 1996). In the UK future projections show increased levels of energy use of between 11 per cent and 20 per cent per decade (Department of Trade and Industry, 1995). The main causes are as follows:

- a projected growth in the number of households and in available industrial and commercial space;
- rising levels of disposable income and resultant consumption;
- rising standards of internal comfort;
- rising levels of household and commercial equipment.

However, the IPCC has calculated that a 60 per cent reduction in CO_2 emission levels is necessary to avert the worst consequences of global warming (Jacobs, 1996). The world consumption of commercially traded energy[1] (ie excluding

---

1 1988 figures

sources like fuel wood) amounted to 337 EJ, 80 per cent of which was produced using fossil fuels. In the European Union (EU), the total energy demand was 45.1 EJ in 1988, 46.7 EJ in 1990 and 50.8 EJ in 1991.[2] The proportion generated using fossil fuels was approximately 85 per cent, with the remainder being predominantly nuclear. This means that the EU is responsible for over 14 per cent of world energy demand, yet its population makes up only 6.4 per cent of the world total. Energy consumption is therefore inequitably distributed (Friends of the Earth Europe, 1995).

In its study 'Towards Sustainable Europe' the Wuppertal Institute in Germany uses the concept of *environmental space* to set out a recommended level of energy use for the European Union (Friends of the Earth Europe, 1995). This concept recognizes that the world can only generate a fixed amount of fossil fuel energy over a set time period, because the natural environment is limited in its ability to assimilate the pollutants produced. This limit is called the Earth's carrying capacity. It is important not to exceed this capacity, and it is also important that the ability to produce pollutants within this capacity is shared out equitably, so that one nation or block of nations does not overuse resources and force other nations to use less or to suffer the environmental consequences of something they have no or little responsibility for. Using more than this equitable figure means that a country or region is using up more than the recommended level of environmental space. If others do likewise, then the result will be increased environmental degradation.

In using more than its recommended environmental space, the EU is using more than its equitable share, resulting in environmental impacts which are above and beyond the natural environment's ability to assimilate. Environmental space targets can be compared with actual consumption levels; the difference between them is the unsustainability gap. Figure 3.2 sets out the 'Sustainable Europe' assumptions, and the key findings are as follows:

- global emissions of CO_2 are now about 4 tonnes per capita per year;
- to stay within our environmental space, the EU must reduce its CO_2 emissions to 1.7 tonnes per capita per year by 2050;
- the current European CO_2 emission level is 7.3 tonnes per capita per year, ie 4.3 times higher than environmental space calculations allow. Such high usage will make it virtually impossible to meet the IPCC target, meaning that intermediate targets will be needed.

Various international conventions have all recognized the need for action to reduce greenhouse emissions, yet it is becoming increasingly clear that commitments by the industrial world to reduce CO_2 emissions fall far short of changes

---

2 EJ equals exajoules. One exajoule is 1,000,000 gigajoules, or 1,000,000,000,000,000,000 joules. 50.8 EJ is equivalent to leaving 16,200,000,000 100W bulbs permanently on for one year. The Wuppertal Institute put per capita energy use in Europe at 123 GJ/year, which is equivalent to leaving 39,224 100W bulbs permanently on for one year.

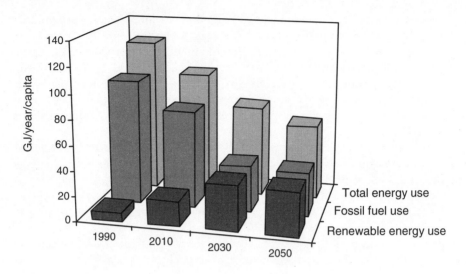

Source: adapted from Friends of the Earth Europe (1995)

Figure 3.2   *Sustainable Europe Energy Assumptions*

actually needed. Action is needed in all areas, with a key sector being buildings. Estimates of global energy usage in buildings give a figure of at least 40 per cent (Roodman and Lenssen, 1995). It is more instructive however, to break these figures down and see which sectors of building activity are most damaging. UK annual energy consumption broken down by sector shows that 56 per cent of energy is consumed in the use of buildings and 10 per cent used in the production of building materials. Two-thirds of UK energy use stems from or is associated with building construction and use (Connaughton, 1993). The significance of buildings in addressing CO_2 emission reduction targets is therefore obvious.

Addressing energy use at a regional and local level is also necessary. Estimates for Greater Manchester show that the city is responsible for 0.14 per cent of the world's greenhouse gas with buildings in Greater Manchester themselves accounting for 0.08 per cent of emissions (Town and Country Planning Association and Manchester Metropolitan University, 1996). Manchester is a city with a number of social problems, but in its bid to regenerate, it will need to do so whilst also cutting energy use, a task which requires a different approach to how we build and use our buildings.

This chapter will concentrate on energy used in buildings and look at how we can: (a) reduce the energy demands of our buildings while (b) changing the types and method of energy supply to meet sustainable development criteria. However, it is also important to remember that transport is a major user of energy in the built environment. There is therefore little use in us 'solving' the problem of profligate energy use in buildings if nothing is done to reduce the energy expended by vehicles driving between all these different buildings. US research has shown that energy use due to transport is often as great as that due to building use. The research modelled the energy use of two contrasting households, one living in a typical suburban house constructed to high energy efficiency standards, the other living in an 88 year old 'energy hog' house located in a traditional urban neighbourhood. Despite using more energy for heating, the latter household used 10 per cent less energy overall because its use of an automobile was significantly lower, given easy access to services within the neighbourhood and the provision of good levels of public transport (Browning et al, 1998).

This modelling is confirmed by Goodacre (1998) whose work on energy use in Lancaster, England has shown large-scale differences in energy use between households. Surveys have revealed that while the more wealthy members of the community tend to have the more energy efficient homes, they also drive significantly more. This increased car use is often enough to eradicate any energy savings made in the household. This is a subject addressed in greater detail in Chapter 5. Here though, we need to be aware of the interrelationships between these two forms of energy use.

REDUCING OUR ENERGY USE

Building with not enough thought on how to protect users effectively and efficiently from the environment, or indeed, to harness the environment to the good of building design must be seen as a wasted opportunity. Too often buildings are designed with little thought for working in tandem with nature, through the use of technologies such as passive solar heating or cooling. A quick look at most new developments around us will show that buildings tend to go up with little thought over orientation to incident solar radiation.

Even worse, architects often seek to design out the influence of climate. The windows of modern offices and factories often face north so as to minimize changes in brightness inside the work area. Instead of relying on natural lighting and heating, designers prefer the security of expensive, energy guzzling lighting, heating and cooling technologies. In doing this architects 'eliminate the element of life which can breathe vitality into otherwise sterile places and breathe joy into the human heart.' (Day, 1990, p 178). Saying this reminds us that the provision of natural light not only saves energy, but can also help to promote good health.

In northern countries buildings should, if possible, be sited so that living and working spaces face towards the south and make the most of solar gain. Too often, however, lack of good sunlighting is not seen as a problem, because design shortfalls can be overcome through overspecification in a building's heating system. This is an expensive and wasteful way of satisfying user comfort. The same goes for buildings which underspecify insulation, instead relying on artificial heating, or for buildings seemingly designed to overheat in the summer. Again, a large expensive cooling system is seen as the solution, even though it will only tackle the symptom of the problem, not the actual problem itself. Treatment of the symptoms rather than the causes does not remove the problem and often creates new problems of its own. It is also a very expensive remedy. Sustainable development however, is all about dealing with the root causes of such problems; causes which often have wide impacts, thereby necessitating the adoption of a holistic approach to problem solving.

Le Corbusier once proclaimed, 'I propose one single building for all nations and climates' (Brolin, 1976). The advent of huge heating and air conditioning systems in offices, factories, homes and hotels around the world shows perhaps that this is increasingly the case. Rather than learn about an area's climate, and seek to work with it, it is easier and quicker simply to overspecify the building services. Golton refers to these technologies as 'inappropriate', and makes the point that just because they rely on modern technology it does not necessarily make them more sophisticated. On the contrary, they allow architects and building service engineers to abdicate their responsibility for issues such as climate control. The responsibility has been passed to machines which can fulfil this brief, but only with a huge cost in terms of energy used and the health impacts on building users (Golton and Golton, 1995). In our use of such inappropriate technology we are ignoring the fact that we are surrounded by a perfectly acceptable climate, and are instead seeking to install a new one, as illustrated in Figure 3.3. In those cases where we are not surrounded by an acceptable climate architectural design can still produce the desired result as in the case of traditional architecture in India, Mexico and West Africa, and modern examples, notably in the US and Scandinavia.

Some architects in the West are rediscovering the use of natural ventilation and solar heating as a way of harnessing the power of the sun. Figure 3.4 shows plan diagrams for the new library at the Anglia Polytechnic University, designed by ECD and Ove Arup. The building is designed to utilize the heat of winter sunshine, using materials of heavy thermal mass to collect and store heat for gradual release overnight, thus reducing morning heating needs. In the summer, shades prevent direct sunlight entering and heating up the building. Natural ventilation minimizes heating of the building, and at night, removes any excess heat stored in the thermal mass (Evans, 1993). The overall result is a large reduction in heating, cooling and lighting costs, as well as the provision of a healthier building. The building is a good example of climate sensitive design and the use of appropriate technologies such as thermal mass and natural passive ventilation.

In California, the Davis Group and the Pacific Gas and Electricity Company built the Davis House (an experimental domestic house) which avoids the use of air conditioning in a region where summer temperatures of 40°C are not uncommon. Designers saved money on equipment and reduced energy needs by insulating the house well, positioning the windows to capture sunlight effectively and efficiently at certain times of the day and year, specified a light coloured roof to reflect rather than absorb sunlight and used materials of heavy thermal mass to absorb heat in the day and release it slowly at night.

Source: Martin Rowson, reproduced with the kind permission of The Building Service Research and Information Association (BSRIA)

Figure 3.3   Building an Environment Apart from the Natural Order

43

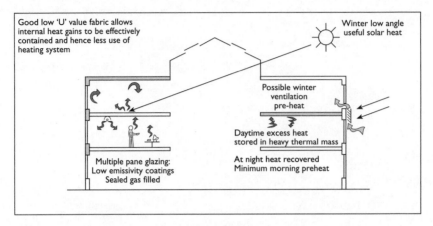

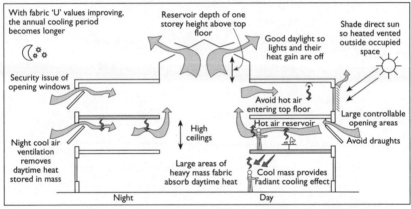

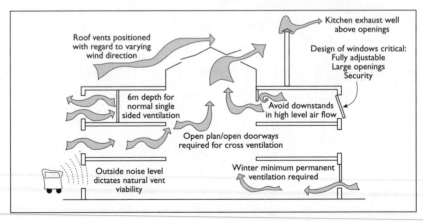

Note: The U value is a measurement of energy loss in W/m²K. The lower the value, the higher the level of insulation.

Source: Adapted from *Architects Journal* (1993) 2 June, p 47

Figure 3.4 *Anglia Polytechnic University Library*

Measurements show that the house should reduce energy use by 60 per cent, as compared with standard houses of its size (Roodman and Lenssen, 1995; Weizsäcker et al, 1997).

In Frankfurt, recent developments have shown that commercial buildings can be ecologically responsible. In the late 1980s the German Commerzbank was looking to acquire a key site for its new head office, though the proposed site was occupied by a number of small businesses and community groups. In return for the site, the organizations specified that a new office building be built for them on an alternative site. The result was the Ökohaus, a cultural and business centre built to ecological specifications, which opened in 1992. According to its architects Elbe and Sambeth, the 7000 m² development is an 'alternative example to Frankfurt's usual business premises' while 'respecting ecological principles in its entirety and in its details, at costs not excessively above the usual.' To reduce energy needs, the Ökohaus utilizes passive solar gain by building conservatories and has waste heat recovery from a resident print works (Göldner, 1994a, b). Subsequently the Commerzbank began to work on its new headquarters, which, now nearing completion, is apparently 'widely regarded as the greenest of green buildings' (O'Neill, 1996). The building, Europe's tallest at 850 feet (260 m) and with 56 storeys, cost £250 million, and utilizes natural light and natural ventilation. The building's three sides take it in turns every four storeys to support a garden 35 metres across and with enough space above for a tree or two rising four storeys.

Working with the climate is a positive design feature, and will hopefully reduce the energy use of the building as compared with other 850 ft high skyscrapers. Comparing the result with the Ökohaus, however, the results are surely less spectacular. The Ökohaus was designed to accommodate no more than 30 small and medium sized organisations, a criterion 'appropriate for its neighbourhood, compatible with the use of traditional load bearing materials, and consistent with the idea of communication and interaction.' (Göldner, 1994a). The Commerzbank, however, while having substantially reduced heating, cooling and lighting – all worthy goals – has been built using high-performance construction methods and materials which require large amounts of embodied energy. Furthermore, while natural lighting and ventilation are likely to improve substantially the working environment of bank employees, one should ask what effect the bank has on the surrounding area in terms of providing an open, welcoming environment. On this, it is worth noting the words of Christopher Day (1990, p 13): 'We rarely experience larger buildings as architectural objects, but where we do, it is usually because they are forceful and dominating. Such buildings impose their presence on us and – most particularly – are imposed upon their surroundings'.

Such comments serve to demonstrate that to be truly sustainable, a building needs to address a wide range of concerns, and not simply reduce energy use. It is through balancing such concerns and approaching them holistically that architects and designers can produce truly 'green' and sustainable buildings.

ENERGY EFFICIENCY

Designing with climate in mind involves letting the best of the climate in, but sometimes of course climate needs to be kept out. Given the fact that most buildings have been with us for quite some time, and will be around for a fair while longer, issues such as orientation and design for climate may have only limited application. Energy efficiency, however, is something which can be successfully applied to all buildings. Energy efficiency measures range from simple provision of draught proofing to the installation of double and triple glazed windows and use of thick layers of insulation in walls, ceilings and floors.

Perhaps one of the foremost examples of energy efficient construction is the Rocky Mountain Institute in Colorado. Though located high in the Rocky Mountains at a height of 2165 metres, where the winter temperature can fall as low as $-40°C$, the building's heating comes almost solely from its occupants and the sun. Two wood stoves are also used occasionally, though they contribute less than 1 per cent of the building's heating needs. The reason for this independence from energy generation is super-insulation[3]. The walls, floor and roof are insulated to very high standards, and the (predominantly south facing) windows are fitted with double glazing with an argon filled cavity. The argon reduces heat transmission through the glazing, while the glazing itself is coated with a low-emissivity (low E) film which further enhances the insulation properties of the double glazing. Aiding the insulation is a huge volume of thermal mass which stores heat for days of little sun. As well as use of the walls and floor for thermal mass, the building has been partially buried, leading to further heat storage and energy efficiency. Appliances used in the building such as the fridge, freezer, computers and photocopiers have been chosen with energy use in mind, and a heat exchanger ensures that any waste heat is reused as part of building ventilation. It has been estimated that the building uses about one-tenth of the energy that would otherwise have been expected, and the extra cost of construction has been offset by savings of more than 99 per cent of space and water heating costs and 90 per cent of the household electricity costs (Vale and Vale 1991, Weizsäcker et al, 1997).

Research and experience have shown that the installation of high levels of insulation can give dramatic reductions in the running costs of buildings, and justify any extra expenditure needed, as shown below. Reducing heating and lighting costs is particularly important for those on low incomes who suffer from fuel poverty. Unfortunately, low income households also tend to have the lowest levels of insulation, meaning that heating costs make up a disproportionate part of their income. This fact has serious impacts on the health and equity criteria of sustainable development and will be explored in subsequent chapters.

---

3 The walls have a U value of $0.14 W/m^2K$, and the roof a value of $0.09 W/m^2K$. Current UK Building Regulations specify using a minimum of $0.45 W/m^2K$ for the walls, $0.25 W/m^2K$ for the roof and $0.40 W/m^2K$ for the floor. The lower the value, the better the level of insulation.

Research comparing alternative housing specifications has shown that environmental impact and financial costs can be reduced significantly for a minimal extra construction cost. One piece of research compared two social housing developments of identical size and function but with different specifications. One, the Control, was built to current UK Building Regulation standards and used standard central heating technology. The second, Eco-Type 1, was a desk specification with high levels of insulation and a shared gas condensing boiler to provide heating. Both have the same south-west orientation. Computer modelling revealed that over an assumed 60 year lifetime, Eco-Type 1 would cost £6500 less to run than the Control, yet environmental design features resulted in only a marginal increase in construction costs (of 1.1 per cent). Savings stemmed from the fact that:

- major repairs for Eco-Type 1 would be around 13–14 per cent lower than for the Control;
- the tenant running costs (mainly space heating) of Eco-Type 1 would be about 35 per cent lower;
- management and maintenance costs for Eco-Type 1 would be 30 per cent lower.

While the specification of Eco-Type 1 involved the use of low embodied energy materials, that of the Control involved no consideration of environmental impact in specification choice. Life cycle analysis (LCA) of the two buildings found that 90 per cent of the reduced environmental impact stemmed from specification of 'super-insulation' (ie levels of insulation significantly higher than current UK standards) and the provision of a gas condensing boiler which was shared between the households. These specification choices meant that the environmental impact of heating for Eco-Type 1 was 75 per cent lower than that of the Control, as is shown in Figure 4.4 of Chapter 4. Consideration of appliance use and lighting was excluded from the calculations, but careful appliance choice and the use of low-energy light fittings could have further reduced the impact of Eco-Type 1 (Smith et al, 1995).

A FRESH VIEW ON ENERGY

Our modern lives tend to take energy as a given, something which we have a right to; yet this is a right which has only been available and claimed relatively recently. Recent liberalization of energy provision has changed the perceptions of energy providers, with energy once again being seen as a commodity to be bought and sold. This has brought with it concerns about energy availability, inequality and dependency – concerns which must be addressed. It also, however, provides us with an opportunity to rethink how we use energy and look towards more sustainable solutions which are more appropriate to our future.

This section has so far concentrated on energy efficiency and energy sensitive design, looking into the ways in which buildings can reduce energy demand. This focus is for a very good reason: namely that the best way to save energy is to avoid producing it in the first place. Environmental space targets (see above) show that our profligate use of energy is unsustainable, and technological advances mean that we can conduct many of our activities much more efficiently. Hunter and Amory Lovins have pioneered the concept of 'negawatts' in an attempt to promote new models of energy generation and usage. At the heart of their argument is the conviction that it is cheaper to save energy than to produce it in the first place. The research on energy efficiency in housing set out above supports this view, demonstrating that if householders or building managers wish to save money, then the best way to do so is by investing in energy efficiency measures. Yet this is also true on a larger scale. In the US, the Pacific Electric Company distributed thousands of low-wattage light bulbs at no cost to its domestic customers, and also has a programme of insulating customers' houses for free. At first glance it might seem pretty idiotic that a company which makes money from generating electricity should wish to help its customers use less. Closer analysis shows that it is actually a hard-headed business decision based on long-term planning and recognition of the concept of demand side management. By helping its customers it is avoiding the need to build a new power station that would cost $185 million (Ingersoll, 1992), a move that would be a huge drain on the resources of any company, even one as large as Pacific Electric.

An even more radical approach has been taken by the Sacramento Municipal Utility District (SMUD), a publicly owned utility serving a population of less than one million customers in California. The company relied primarily on a 20 year old 900 megawatt nuclear reactor, which on paper was its greatest asset but in practice was a noose around the company's neck. After prolonged plant shutdowns, SMUD's customers voted to close the plant permanently, and the company began the search for alternatives. SMUD turned to S. David Freeman, one of America's true energy revolutionaries, who while at the Tennessee Valley Authority in the 1970s had cancelled 8 of the 12 nuclear reactors under construction. At SMUD, he turned to demand side management, investing 8 per cent of its gross revenues on reducing customers' energy use through provision of efficiency measures, such as low energy lighting, the installation of solar water heaters on customers' rooftops, solar panels and the planting of shade trees. The company also heavily subsidized the installation of solar water heaters, offering a rebate of $863 on systems costing less than $3000. Customers paid the balance as part of electricity bills over a ten year period. By early 1994, over 1800 systems had been installed.

Investments are also being made in wind farms and cogeneration plants and the company is considering new measures such as subsidizing the purchase of electric vehicles. The company also plans installing 1 megawatt of distributed photovoltaic systems each year until the turn of the century. The work of SMUD and other such utilities has shown how cost effective demand side management can be, with electricity prices for SMUD customers significantly lower than those for customers of neighbouring utilities still shackled to nuclear plants and supply side thinking (Flavin and Lenssen, 1995).

It has been calculated that a megawatt of capacity is actually eight times more expensive to produce than one 'negawatt of uncapacity', because a negawatt has low capital costs and no running costs, while a megawatt of capacity involves high capital costs and high running costs. Furthermore, to provide extra capacity involves the construction of generating plants which are expensive and take a long time to construct. This is time when the capital investment has been spent but is not producing any return. Any money spent 'producing' negawatts produces savings quickly and cheaply. As Vale and Vale note: 'People often object to the building of power stations, but it would be hard to object to the receipt of free light bulbs.' (Vale and Vale, 1991, p 47).

But why, if saving energy is so much cheaper and more profitable than generating it, do more power companies not go down this route? The answer lies partly in the way we have been trained to think and partly in the scale at which we are attempting to tackle our problems. Power companies are comfortable with generating and providing power, not doing precisely the opposite, so the idea that you can make more money by promoting energy efficiency has been slow to be accepted. Also, because companies are used to generating power, it is easier to go on doing this than to embrace new methods (Weizsäcker et al, 1997). Furthermore, power companies are often too large to respond to such problems. Power generation and demand-use forecasting and planning often take place nationally, yet the closer the power company is to users, then the easier it is to forecast user demands, and to begin working with users to cut that demand. At a national level such communication becomes ineffective, reduced to adverts in newspapers and on television urging people to install draught proofing or to lag their hot water tank.

LOCAL PROVISION OF ENERGY

Energy used to be a local issue. Communities were often formed out of the need to group buildings together as protection from the climate, and when electricity generation began, it was usually local authorities or local businesses who built power stations and connected local homes, offices and factories. Yet these systems were slowly conglomerated into huge companies who now provide power from a small number of big power stations. These economies of scale make economic sense for the companies, yet provision of energy from smaller, more locally based plants is surely the way forward if we are to meet our future energy needs in a more sustainable manner.

The use of technologies such as combined heat and power (CHP) and district heating can provide heat to large buildings, factories and neighbourhoods much more efficiently than large power stations. Renewable energy generation can also take place on very small scales. Even large developments tend to work better when undertaken by communities and regions. The important realization is that scale is all-important in moving towards sustainable methods of generating the power we need.

It is only at the local level that we can begin to take responsibility for reducing our energy needs, and again at the local level that we can best begin to adopt new methods of power generation. Economies of scale have given us cheap power at immeasurable cost to the environment and an unhealthy concentration on a few sources of fuel. Through choosing to exploit sources of fossil fuel in such a rapacious manner, we have produced the problem of global warming. However, in turning away from fossil fuel many exponents of alternatives preach the gospel of nuclear power. In the UK, for example, the National Fossil Fuel Obligation requires that 5 per cent of national electricity consumption should come from renewable energy sources by the year 2000. To achieve this, a 10 per cent levy was applied on all electricity bills and used to subsidize electricity supplies generated without fossil fuel (Hewett, 1995). However, the bulk of this levy was used to support nuclear power generation, yet it is hard to see how nuclear power could be regarded as sustainable, given even a scant reading of the precautionary principle. Furthermore, as power generation has led to reliance on a small number of fuels, so it has also seen us become dependent on a small number of providers, and we have lost the will or the means to control our system or to change it for the better. As Vale and Vale note: 'People constructed their buildings together because of the mutual benefit to be obtained. A policy of cheap energy removed this generator of traditional community as surely as did the automobile'. (Vale and Vale, 1991, p 70)

Douthwaite (1996) compares our use of fossil fuels to an addict's use of hard drugs. We are so dependent upon these fuels, we will do almost anything to get our regular fix of them. Of most concern is the damage this addiction inflicts on the environment. At the local level communities are wrecked through activities such as open-cast coal mining or put at risk through the siting of nuclear power stations, and at a global level we are all put at risk by global warming. Our reliance upon fossil fuels has been the end result of a process of rationalization and efficiency gains which has seen power generation concentrated in fewer and larger power stations. Economies of scale produce this, yet there is evidence that such energy policies are counter productive and actually bad for the economy because of their in-built inefficiencies.

The concept of negawatts shows that it is often more cost efficient for energy utilities to spend money on energy efficiency and conservation, than to invest capital in new power stations. In a similar way, it can be shown that it would be better for the economy to make do with less power and to look to more local and appropriate means of generation. However, such thinking bucks the trend in current energy policy, and for this reason is described as uneconomic. Across Europe, countries are linking up their electricity grids in a bid to share the problems of top-heavy generating systems. The UK and France, for example, are linked together, and the two countries rely on this link to meet peaks in demand in their countries. When this link went down, however, in 1996, the UK grid came very close to shutting down. The reasons seem farcical, but stem from the fact that the interconnector between the UK and France shut down at the same time as viewers put on their kettles at the end of 'Call Red', a TV drama about helicopter-borne medics. The National Grid also admitted that the number of these 'major events' is increasing for the first time in 15 years (Barrie, 1996).

The power industry's answer is bigger and better links between different countries and provision of greater spare capacity through the construction of new power stations. Liberalization of energy markets is also seen as a better way for supply companies to meet the needs of their customers by allowing them to shop around for electricity, whether this electricity is produced locally, or from across the continent. Sending electricity from one end of Europe to another is a very wasteful process, and necessitates the use of larger pylons and power cables. Despite this, the establishment of an internal market for energy in the European Union is seen as a priority. Interconnecting national energy supply networks is high on the agenda of energy policy, and guidelines are currently being drawn up for a Trans-European Energy Network in order to 'create the technical, administrative, legal and financial conditions favourable to energy exchange across national boundaries.' (Hewett, 1995, p 54). While such energy liberalization will provide consumers with the option of purchasing power from cleaner and renewable sources (Kåberger, 1996; Tickell, 1997) its main impact will be to increase our dependence upon larger power sources sited increasing distances from where we live and work.

Yet it should not be this way. If power were generated and used locally, consumers would have greater control over how it was generated. The energy used would be more appropriate to the surroundings, for example it could be wind power in exposed, upland areas or biomass in lowland ones. Energy generation and use at a local level would also be a better employment generator than generation in large power plants (that is, it would be less capital intensive and more labour intensive) and it would help to support local economies by providing employment and keeping money in the community. For example, an audit of the neighbouring towns of Newport and Nevern, in West Wales, found that they were losing £250,000 a year in payments for 'imported' energy (Conaty, 1995). Douthwaite (1996) uses this figure to calculate that a community uses over one-quarter of its income to buy energy (including for transport and the amount used in producing items bought by members of the community) from outside the local area. The Rocky Mountain Institute calculates that the amount a typical town spends on energy purchased from outside is equivalent to the payroll of 10 per cent of its population. In Osage, Iowa (population 3800) the equivalent of 60 new jobs were created by implementing a variety of energy efficiency measures, and $1.2 million that had leaked out of the community to pay energy bills now stays in people's pockets and recirculates in the local economy (RMI, 1995). Such movement of money out of the community can weaken the local economy by removing money which could otherwise support local industries and local shops – a problem discussed in Chapter 9 – yet it is within the capabilities of most communities to generate all their own energy needs from local sources (Douthwaite, 1996; ETSU, 1996a).

Energy generation which is locally based works best with renewable resources such as small-scale solar power, wind farms or the use of biomass. By utilizing a variety of sources communities can safeguard their energy supplies from outside influences such as rapid rises in oil prices. In Sweden, biomass provides 15 per cent of the country's primary energy consumption, much of this generated locally through combined heat and power (CHP) schemes burning wood, municipal waste or both. In Austria, almost 100 district heating schemes are in place, fuelled mainly by materials from the country's plentiful conifer forests. This represents 10 per cent of the country's total energy consumption (Hewett, 1995).

Even regarding the use of fossil fuels, it is much more efficient and cost effective to generate power locally on a small scale than in large, isolated power stations. A prime example of this is the use of CHP for community heating. The economic benefits of CHP stem not from energy suppliers taking advantage of economies of scale but from the efficiency of the technology. CHP and district heating schemes are highly efficient at converting primary fuels into usable forms of energy. Whereas conventional steam thermal power stations convert about 40 per cent of energy input into electricity and dissipate the remainder as waste heat, CHP schemes attain efficiencies of over 80 per cent by using this heat for homes or industry. Because of this, these schemes can significantly reduce CO_2 and other pollutant emissions in comparison to individual sources of production. For example, the introduction of 13 CHP schemes in Leeds and Birmingham was estimated to have reduced CO_2 emissions per unit of delivered energy by 38 per cent. Furthermore, CHP often works best at a smaller scale. A recent survey in the UK found that 83 per cent of CHP installations were of less than 1 megawatt (Department of Energy, 1994). A recent report has suggested that 10,000 new jobs could be created through the generation of 6 gigawatts of CHP in the UK (New Economics Foundation, 1996). Furthermore, many of these jobs would be at the local level and therefore widely spread through the country.

An example of how communities can help to foster local forms of generation can be found in Denmark. Four per cent of Denmark's energy comes from wind generation, and there is a commitment to increase this significantly. Of that currently generated two-thirds comes from collectively owned machines operated by wind power guilds. Wind power guilds bring local people together to invest in wind turbines for their area, and people are happy to invest because energy from these turbines has a guaranteed premium price. Importantly, all members of a guild have to live in the same electricity supply area and within 3 kilometres of its turbine. According to Flemming Tranæs of Danske Vindkraftværker (DV) with reference to the wind power association:

'The idea was that if anyone in the area around a turbine suffered any inconvenience from it, it should be those who enjoyed its advantages. Well-to-do people from the cities were not to be allowed to invest in turbines and gain the advantage of cheaper electricity without being affected by any noise or *visual disturbance at the turbine sites. This approach fits in well with the co-operative idea: that you establish your enterprise in the area where you live and among the people with whom you share your life, for good or bad.'*

Tranæs, 1996, p 204

This approach perhaps partly explains the high levels of acceptance of wind farm developments in Denmark. Concerns about large wind farms being imposed on communities are irrelevant if it is that community clubbing together to generate renewable power locally. At the end of 1995, DV's members owned 2090 turbines, and 52,500 people were members of its associated turbine guilds, although many guilds have not joined DV (Douthwaite, 1996). There is no reason why such an approach could not be used for other forms of power generation and used to help make communities in our built environment self-sufficient in energy generation.

A UK study of the market town of Hatherleigh, Devon, found that all of the town's electricity needs could be met by utilizing a combination of renewable resources (ETSU, 1996a). Interestingly, solar and wind power do not count among the recommended fuels, because of concerns that the solar panels might detract from the traditional appearance of the town, and because wind speeds were comparatively low. Instead, the researchers found that the greatest potential lay in the planting of energy crops and the production of biogas from slurry to fuel a CHP plant. The only drawback lay in the fact that these forms of generation were more costly than current energy supplies. Given, however, that the cost of fossil fuel generation is subsidized by the economy and the environment (see Chapter 9 for a fuller discussion of this point), increasing use of renewables should be recommended. The Hatherleigh study is important, however, for showing that a fossil-fuel-free future is not something to fear, as there is vast untapped potential for using new fuels.

The Danish Government, as part of its Action Plan for Energy, are promoting a gradual shift from fossil fuels to renewables, as well as putting in place demand side management to ensure that each unit of generated power is used as efficiently as possible. As part of this change, the Government is planning a 'renewable energy island' as a demonstration that local communities can be self-sufficient. The plan is to designate a local area – for instance an island – which over a period of a few years will change until all its energy needs (including for the transport sector) are met through the use of renewable energy (Miljø and Energi Ministeriet, 1996). Similarly, Newark and Sherwood District Council in England are building a 2 megawatt biomass community power station as part of Broughton Energy Village 2001, which will make the parishes of Broughton and Ollerton self-sufficient in energy needs (NSDC, 1995a).

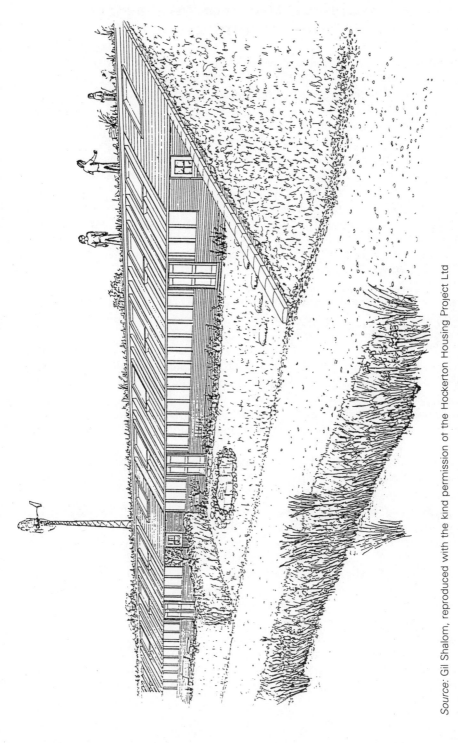

Figure 3.5 *Hockerton Housing Project*

IN CONCLUSION: AWAY FROM DEPENDENCY, TOWARDS AUTONOMY

Autonomous housing is housing which is independent of services such as electricity, water and gas which we normally see as necessities to all new developments. This might mean that the housing is not connected to the National Grid, or which generates at least as much power as it consumes and feeds back into the grid. A prime example of this concept is the previous home of architects Brenda and Robert Vale, designed in line with the principles outlined in their first book *The Autonomous House* (Vale and Vale, 1975). Sited in a conservation area in Southwell, Nottinghamshire, the house is of a traditional appearance, at least on the outside. The building relies upon a highly insulated solid thermal mass to provide long-term heat storage; this assists both heating and cooling. A two storey conservatory provides heating needs through passive solar heating, while a solar array mounted on a garden pagoda provides over half of the remaining power needs. In 1995, the solar electric system generated 1762 kWh, of which 40 per cent was used in the house and 60 per cent exported to the local utility. Planned improvements in the heating system should mean that the solar array can provide for all the house's needs. As well as providing for most of its energy needs, water is collected from the roof and filtered for drinking and sewage is collected on site and composted (Currivan, 1996; Greenpeace, 1996).

The Vales are also architects for a project close by at Hockerton, near Newark, where construction is underway of a terrace of autonomous earth-sheltered housing. The idea came from Nick Martin who is the developer and main builder. When completed the residents will be responsible for the supply of their own power and water and will deal with their own waste. Electricity use will be minimized through high insulation levels, and passive solar heating. Electricity will also be generated using an on-site wind generator. Water will be collected and stored for use, and used water (including sewage) dealt with and cleaned using a reed bed system. Sketches of the houses are shown in Figure 3.5 on pages 54–55 (Martin, unpublished).

Newark and Sherwood District Council has also been a significant player in the project, and has supported the development, even though on paper it contravenes all relevant planning guidelines. Their commitment is also such that they are considering developing autonomous housing themselves for new council tenants. The Council's Housing and Investment Programme for 1995/96 sets a target of the provision of 100 autonomous homes by the year 2000 (NSDC, 1995b), and its Broughton Energy Village 2001 project aims to provide new employment opportunities, increase energy efficiency and promote environmental improvement by reducing CO_2 emissions by 60 per cent (ETSU, 1996b).

In looking at autonomous housing, we do not propose that all houses be made independent and self-sufficient. Rather than do this, we have used autonomous housing as an example of what can be achieved. Autonomous housing is entirely realizable, economic, and sustainable. Furthermore, it is about as far away from current building practices as it is possible to get. The situation today is one of dependency: upon superquarries for our aggregates, tropical rain forests for our timber, large power companies and national grid systems for our power, and large water companies to provide our water for drinking, washing and gardening and to take away our sewage. We are reliant upon others for our housing, when not so long ago it was within the ability of most to construct themselves a simple dwelling. This reliance is part of the change that has occurred in society, and is in part an inevitable consequence of the specialization of our lives. Today, none of us are jacks of all trades. Few are masters of more than one. This dependence increasingly means that we have little control over our situation or our surroundings. We are taken for granted when decisions are made, because there is little need to ask us. Instead we have become dependent upon others making our decisions for us.

Sustainability, however, demands that we regain some of this control, and in return we reduce our dependence upon others. It can seem easier to rely upon other people and places for what we need, but as these others have become people we do not know, or the places ones which we have no concern for, so we have degraded our environment and put our own lives and stability at risk. Providing energy in a sustainable manner will help reverse global environmental damage, while a more local focus on generation and use will concentrate people's minds on the need for demand side management and the availability of local fuel sources. It will help promote a sustainable built environment through encouraging demand side management at a town and city as well as a regional and national level, resulting in moves to increase levels of energy efficiency, utilize passive solar heating and cooling and seek to meet more of our needs from local renewable fuel sources. All these policies, if followed, will assist the strengthening of our local economies and communities, and contribute to the solving of related problems in planning, health and equity. These are all issues which will be returned to in subsequent chapters.

4

MATERIALS INTENSITY IN THE BUILT ENVIRONMENT

'Our economy is such that we "cannot afford" to take care of things: Labour is expensive, time is expensive, money is expensive, but materials – the stuff of creation – are so cheap that we cannot afford to take care of them.'

Wendell Berry

The pursuit of sustainable development with its emphasis on reducing materials intensity necessarily puts buildings at the centre of any sustainability debate. Building construction, use and disposal are responsible for a significant part of environmental destruction, and there are, moreover, many simple ways to reduce building impacts. Through simple choices made in design, construction, DIY and refurbishment we can do much to reduce the scale of this impact.

In environmental building design, many of the changes needed are of a technical nature and may involve no more than making different choices over issues such as materials specification, insulation thickness, and so on. Following such design changes, more difficult, cultural changes – affecting how we use our buildings and how our resulting lifestyles affect the environment – will be needed. This is a recognition that to make our buildings environmentally benign, we cannot just replace one material with another. Rather, what is needed is a different approach to the construction and use of buildings and of the built environment, to ensure that the wide variety of concerns – which are embraced by the concept of sustainability – are taken into account. For example, we cannot just replace brick with wood: we must also change the way in which we use these materials and the buildings we make from them.

We must begin to see our buildings in a much wider perspective, that is not only as short-term design and construction projects considering how they look, work with their surroundings, and meet the needs of users. We also need to look forward to the future – buildings are after all creatures of long life – and examine the effects of the decisions we are making now. Sustainability demands that we take this long-term view: what will the future be like for our children, our grandchildren, the future occupants of our buildings? As Margaret Thatcher famously said in one of her few speeches on the environment, 'We do not have a freehold on the earth, only a full repairing lease' (Thatcher, 1988). Architects and building users ought to be able to understand this concept. If we are to be sure we can put a stop to or make good any damage caused before our tenancy expires, then we need to be aware of our buildings' impacts right across their life cycles.

LIFE CYCLE AWARENESS

When we think of life cycles, it is not usually buildings which come to mind. An important element of ecology and ecological thinking is the recognition that natural processes work in cycles. The idea of waste is not a natural concept, because nature makes use of all, yet waste and wastefulness are seemingly unavoidable within modern society. Growing concern over the environment is leading to the recognition that our society and our economy cannot separate themselves from the natural world, a realization which leads to the conclusion that we must work more closely with these natural cycles in our day-to-day activities. This is a statement which applies to buildings as much as to any other part of our society.

When we think of the natural world and envisage the dwellings and burrows of other animals, we tend to view these as wholly different from our more advanced buildings, and indeed they are, for what all these others have in common, and what our modern buildings lack, is harmony with the environment. While we continue to view our buildings as mere shapes and forms which have little impact upon, or interaction with the natural environment, we will continue to degrade that environment. If, however, we saw them as being a part of that environment, then we would be better placed to realize their impact, and hence go on to reduce it. Above, we referred to buildings as 'creatures', a description which might seem misplaced. We should recognize though that buildings change the area in which they are built and themselves change over time. Furthermore, through their use they impact on the environment as surely as any living thing can do. They are also the creations of creatures which need to live their lives in harmony with, rather than apart from, natural processes and cycles. This is a key element behind the concept of ecological building design which seeks to ensure that our built environment works in harmony with ecological processes.

It is because of this that we need to look at a building in terms of its life cycle, that is from its conception through to its destruction. In terms of the impacts of this life cycle, we also need to look beyond this physical life, at the processes involved in material extraction and the fate of the materials upon demolition. Knowing this, we can then seek to reduce these impacts by reducing the energy and materials intensity. The life cycle of a building consists of:

- quarrying and refining;
- production of raw materials;
- manufacturing of building products;
- on-site construction;
- building use;
- afterlife: ie demolition, reuse and disposal.

All of the above phases consume materials, energy and water and result in emissions to air, water and soil.

Life cycle analysis (LCA) is one increasingly used method of quantifying environmental impacts of materials and products. It involves the systematic collection of data at different stages in the life cycle of a product to gauge its impact in terms of pollutants generated. The drawback with LCA, however, is that it is a complex and slow process, requiring a mountain of data for each product. This means that it can be an unwieldy design tool, and out of the reach of most buildings professionals. However, LCA methodologies can provide useful information about a large number of building components, and this information, together with common sense reasoning, can guide choices about building materials and building designs.

Figure 4.1 shows a schema of an LCA of a door. The figure shows that a complex series of stages are required to bring the door from tree to frame.

Sustainability demands that choices about buildings do not just consider issues of cost and suitability, but also environmental impacts. As the LCA of the door shows, these impacts are widely spread. To ensure their reduction, awareness of impacts across the life cycle is required: this means minimizing waste and energy use, lengthening the lifespan of buildings and their components and promoting the reuse and recycling of building components after the demolition of the building. This limits the depletion of raw materials and reduces the impact due to manufacture and usage. Most raw materials used in construction are freed up again at the end of their or the building's life. High grade reuse or recycling of these materials can help to lessen the demand for new materials (Anink et al, 1996).

The ultimate aim is to integrate the life cycle as much as possible, that is to work towards a looped system in which products and waste re-enter the system as an input rather than exit as unwanted waste. This cycling mirrors natural processes like the carbon cycle to ensure that our demands for new material and energy inputs are lessened. The basic checkpoints for reducing our materials intensity are as follows:

- Maximize use of renewable and recycled sources.
- Minimize use of non-renewables, and use efficiently when unavoidable.
- Use materials with least environmental impact.

On a sustainable level, awareness of a building's life cycle means looking into the future and gauging what effects it will have on forthcoming generations. We

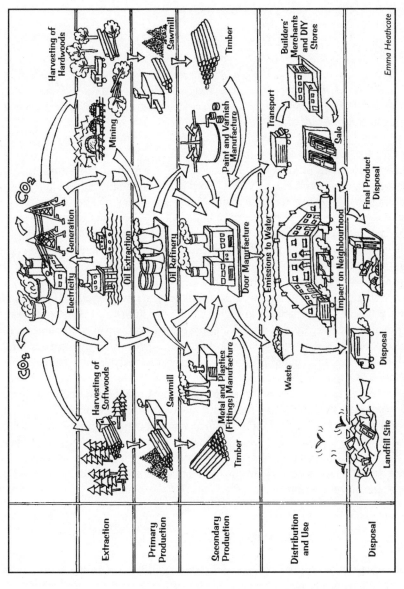

Figure 4.1 *Life Cycle Analysis of a Door*

also need to be looking around us now, and seeing what effect our buildings have on current users: how they are impacting on people's health, on local communities, on people's own sense of belonging.

Christopher Day (1990) has described the experience of visiting hospitals in good health, yet feeling half alive when he left:

> *'after sitting for hours in rectangular grid-patterned, vinyl seating, fluorescently-lit, overheated corridors. The brutal vandalism of buildings unfailingly imposed on the landscape can have the same effect. Architecture can be life-suppressing or even crushing, not only to our finer sensitivities but to our feeling of freedom. In some places one feels a trapped statistic, not a valued member of society'*

Day, 1990, p 9

This feeling is one shared by many people. The situation as we find it is one of damage to the environment and to society. Individually and collectively, our buildings work against us by damaging our environment. They waste resources and energy and encourage patterns of living which themselves add to this damage. The design of these individual buildings, and of the built environment they collectively share, is also failing to support both our society and the sense of community we seem to be searching for. Indeed, its current shape may well contribute to feelings of isolation and a lack of community.

Building design and the overall condition of the built environment can affect people's feeling of well-being and ultimately have long-term consequences upon our health, an issue dealt with in Chapter 6. It is also worth remembering that it is the poor in society who will tend to bear a disproportionate share of the cost of bad building and planning ideas. For example, poor construction standards in social housing lead to damp and fuel poverty. Poor planning decisions can promote traffic growth while moving shops, hospitals and schools further away from people's houses. These are all impacts which disproportionally affect the poor, not least because the better off in society have the means by which they can escape or defend themselves against negative trends in society. This is an equity issue which will be addressed in Chapter 7. Here, it is worth noting that a more holistic approach to design and construction can help us avoid such problems in the first place.

THE BUILDING INDUSTRY IN OUR SOCIETY

The construction industry is one of the pivotal industries of the world and has a dynamic position in our economy. The construction industry as a whole needs a strong economy if it is to survive and prosper, yet the wider economy itself is also heavily reliant upon a vibrant construction sector for its own well-being. In Europe and the United States, the recessions of the 1980s and early 1990s were felt first by the building industry, with job losses and empty order books a common story. Because of all this, the industry has also been seen as the way in which we can 'build ourselves out of recession', with increased activity in the construction sector being hailed as a stimulant for renewed economic activity.

As will be shown in Chapter 9, however, there are serious concerns about how economic growth damages the environment, with the market sending out the wrong signals and encouraging the wrong types of behaviour. This is particularly true of the building industry, owing to its size and resource intensive nature. It is estimated that the building sector is responsible for 50 per cent of the material resources taken from nature, 40 per cent of the energy consumption (including energy in use) and over 50 per cent of the waste generated by society (Anink et al, 1996). If we are to reduce our energy and materials intensity then we must reduce the overall amounts used in the construction sector, and from this begin to use the buildings industry to promote change in the wider economy. Furthermore, Chapter 9 will highlight concerns about the overall health of the economy and show how changes in behaviour within the construction sector can aid the economy and society as a whole.

THINKING OF MATERIALS

Traditionally, the materials we used for building tended to come from what lay around us and what we could use. This is why Aberdeen was built of granite, much of it quarried within the city. It also explains why the original American settlers built their houses from wood, mud or even straw. Stone may have lain beneath their feet but most did not have the time or tools, skills or money to extract, cut, face and stack it into any shape or form which resembled a building.

Historically, dependence of society upon local resources has been the primary factor in shaping our buildings, and over the years, decades and centuries, such factors have shaped what we see as our vernacular architecture. The Oxford Dictionary defines vernacular architecture as 'concerned with ordinary buildings, not cathedrals', yet perhaps we should use a wider definition than this. Vernacular architecture was shaped by necessity and by dependence on the immediate environment for resources (with resources also meaning money, skills and labour). Perhaps, then, we need to define our vernacular as a common sense approach built out of necessity. Traditionally we built according to our limits. Today, however, there are no apparent limits. Building form is defined by our technology, by global markets and by consumer taste. Traditionally, resources had to be used wisely, because their scarcity and the effort needed to manufacture them were automatically understood. We now use more and more of them, and bring them from further and further away.

Research by Golton (1994) has shown how the way we build has changed over time. By looking at two Cypriot houses from opposing ends of the twentieth century, he clearly demonstrates that modern buildings do not rely upon their locality for building materials, but source them from around the globe. For the traditional house, most materials came from no more than 15 km away. The stone was quarried in the hills around the village; timber joists, floor boards and partitions came from a neighbouring village; roof stones came from a village about 16 km away and mud used in roof construction and between the wall stones came from the excavations for the building. Only reeds for a reed lattice above the roof joists and gypsum for plastering came from further afield, but this distance was only about 50 km.

In contrast, materials for the modern house were international in origin. While the brick clay, bricks, sand, gravel, cement and facing stone were all sourced on the island (though at distances usually over 50 km), some timber came from the USA, steel reinforcements came from Belgium, aluminium for doors, window frames and other fittings came from Greece and Italy (though the aluminium was processed on the island), glass came from the UK and Belgium, carpets came from Italy and ceramic tiles from Italy and Spain. Materials also came from Russia, Greece and Japan and it is worth noting that the raw materials for most of these imported products probably came from still more different countries.

The difference in construction methods between these two buildings has contributed to a higher level of comfort for the occupants of the modern house, yet the material usage and the energy needed for material manufacture and transport have increased dramatically. Furthermore, the modern building was found to be less effective than the traditional building at modifying the climate, suggesting that the building was less rather than more efficient.

The Cypriot research shows that while modern buildings have improved our lives, increasing levels of resource consumption have imposed a large environmental cost. This increase stems from a flaw in our economic system which assumes that natural resources are infinite. Assuming this leads to wasteful practices with little regard for the environment. There are, however, very definite limits in terms of the total amount of resources, the rate at which these can be extracted, the energy we need to extract and process materials, the rate at which the natural environment can absorb the pollutants we generate and the number of holes we can dig in our countryside.

These arguments will be explored in greater detail in Chapter 9. For now, it is sufficient to restate that we are wholly dependent upon our natural resources, and that the growing scale of our activities has increased rather than decreased that dependence. The challenge for us now is to reduce the impact of our activities without threatening our quality of life.

The concept of *environmental space* (see Chapter 3) is a useful indicator in showing how far we need to reduce levels of resource use. Using this indicator, the Wuppertal Institute has calculated that world usage of wood needs to be reduced by between 40 and 60 per cent if the timber industry is to become sustainable. In line with principles of equity, this means that Europe needs to reduce the use of raw materials by between 80 and 90 per cent (Friends of the Earth Europe, 1995). Figure 4.2 shows production of cement – which serves as a prime example of the overuse of non-renewable materials – in various countries, and shows that there are wide disparities in levels of use.

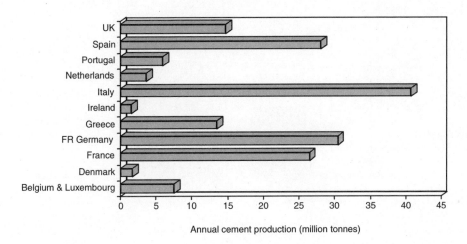

Source: Adapted from Friends of the Earth Europe (1995)

Figure 4.2 *Production of Cement Within the EU*

Cement is one of the most important bulk materials, and represents nearly one-third of the global production of non-energetic materials (ie excluding those for energy generation). Production of cement produces various pollutants, and overproduction means that pollutants are generated beyond the environmental carrying capacity: faster than they can be assimilated by the environment, thus causing environmental degradation. Furthermore, resource estimates show that in the long term, cement production will suffer from exhaustion of the non-renewable resources used in its production. This eventual exhaustion creates an obligation to use supplies wisely. However, growing levels of construction throughout the world mean increasing levels of cement use and pollution, hastening the moment when raw material reserves are exhausted. The West is a large-scale user of cement in construction, yet the environmental problems associated with its production necessitate sharing out that amount of production which can be carried out within the earth's carrying capacity. This equitable approach brings us to *environmental space* calculations for countries and regions. The EU currently uses 175 million tonnes of cement each year, which equates to 15.2 per cent of world production, yet its population makes up only 6.4 per cent of the world total. Calculations for the EU show that we need to reduce our annual consumption from the current level of 536 kg per person per year to between 64 and 96 kg per person per year. This represents a reduction in use of between 82 and 88 per cent (FoE Europe, 1995). Globally, cement production needs to fall by between 58 and 71 per cent. These environmental space requirements are shown in Figure 4.3.

In reading these reduction targets, some readers may respond that there are well-proven stocks of most non-renewable materials, meaning that there is no

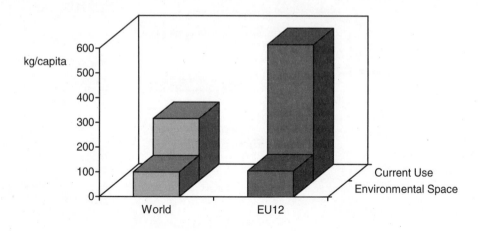

Note: EU12 excludes states joining since 1990

Source: Adapted from Friends of the Earth Europe (1995)

Figure 4.3   *Environmental Space Targets Globally and Within EU*

pressing need to reduce material usage. The flaw in this view, however, is that it is not primarily the scarcity of materials which is the problem, but the associated impact of their extraction, production and use. For example, iron and aluminium (as bauxite), exist in the Earth's crust in abundant quantities. From the source end, this means that these metals can be considered essentially unlimited. However, the impacts of extraction and processing severely limit the rate at which we can safely use these stocks, meaning that the sink capacity is limited.

The extraction of non-renewable resources often involves a number of processes from extraction through to refining and because most materials exist in low concentrations, the finished product is usually only a small percentage of what came out of the ground. This leads to 'overburden', that is the soil and rock moved to get access to the wanted material but not further used for processing. In open cast mining, the overburden and spoil left over generally exceeds the area of the mine by a factor of 3–5 times, and are often sources of contaminants such as dust, silt and nitrates (Meadows et al, 1992). Extraction and processing also require large inputs of energy which, as we have seen, need to be reduced, as well as leading to pollution of the environment. The Wuppertal Institute calls this unwanted part the 'ecological rucksack', a term which helps convey the unseen impacts that accompany production of all materials. Our major problem right now lies in the need to reduce the load of this ecological rucksack. The obvious, indeed the only, solution is to reduce resource use.

In the longer term, whether this happens or not, resource availability will become a problem because of the fundamental non-sustainability of the whole global population trading up to consumption patterns and material requirements of the average Californian. Particularly relevant to the construction industry is the fact that after fossil fuels, stocks of sand and gravel are likely to be the first to become exhausted in our economy (FoE Europe, 1995).

Most non-renewable resources do exist in fairly substantial quantities in the earth's crust, but the majority of deposits exist in concentrations too low to make extraction cost-effective. This means that as resources are used up the concentration of usable materials will decrease, resulting in larger and larger ecological rucksacks. Even with reductions in resource use, as resources become depleted the impacts of mining them will increase. Figure 4.4 shows the consequence of this depletion for metal extraction. It can be seen that as the amount of usable metal in the ore falls below 1 per cent, the amount of rock that must be mined, ground up and treated per ton rises rapidly (Meadows et al, 1992), thus increasing the eventual overburden and size of the accompanying ecological rucksack. As the average grade of copper ore mined in Butte, Montana, fell from 30 per cent to 0.5 per cent, the overburden per tonne of copper rose from 3 to 200 tonnes. This rising curve of waste is closely paralleled by a rising curve of energy use required to produce each tonne of the end product (Meadows et al, 1992).

Tons of waste per ton of metal

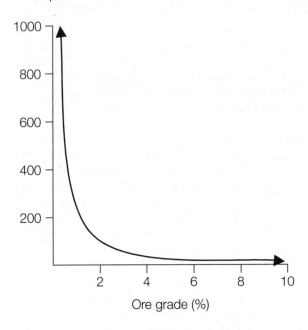

Source: Meadows, Meadows and Randers (1992) *Beyond the Limits*, Earthscan, London

Figure 4.4   *Tons of Waste Per Ton of Metal*

Increasing rates of extraction of aggregates for both building and road construction are also a source of concern. Because of the high cost of transporting bulky aggregates, transport distances have tended to be relatively low (though the environmental impacts of these distances make up a significant proportion of the transport element of construction) but market forces are leading to more quarries, including a number of superquarries. The UK uses some 300 million tonnes of aggregate per year, which is roughly equivalent to a small skip load of aggregate for every household in the UK (Atkinson et al, 1994). Traditionally aggregates came from local sources, yet with reduced transport costs and better transport links, the trend is for materials to be supplied from further and further away. Particularly worrying is the trend towards reliance upon rural coastal areas for aggregates. Redlands Aggregates has plans for a superquarry on Mount Roineabhal on the Isle of Harris in western Scotland. It is reckoned the proposed quarry would be either the world's largest or second largest, and would supply 10 million tonnes of aggregate per year over a 60 year lifetime. At the end of its lifetime the quarry would leave a crater 370 metres above sea level and 180 metres below it, 1 km broad and 2 km long. The market for the quarry would primarily be south-east England, but would also have an international element (Link Quarry Group, 1996). In adopting such an aggregates strategy, we are choosing to blight one area simply because another is overusing available resources.

The rise of these superquarries is being fuelled by the continued growth in demand for aggregates, despite calls for the use of more recycled material. UK planning decisions made about new quarries have to take account of government forecasts, with each area expected to provide a set amount of aggregate. However, these forecasts have been criticized because they are in effect demand-led and put together by local authorities, representatives of government and the aggregates industry. No governmental environmental body is involved in the process, and the methodology used remains a secret (Adams, 1991). In effect, the decision-making process hides 'a cartel of prices for the industry so that real prices are less than they were 20 years ago' (O'Riordan, 1993, p.42). This leads to a situation in which the materials intensity of aggregates is increasing, and hinders reuse and recycling because of the free availability of low cost aggregate. For example, the Royal Commission on Environmental Protection has noted that 'in order to move towards sustainable development and protect the environment, there needs to be a general policy objective; to reduce substantially the demands which transport infrastructure and the vehicle industry place on non-renewable resources' (Royal Commission on Environmental Pollution, 1994, p 8).

Over-reliance upon non-renewable materials might suggest that we should instead begin seeking to use renewable materials such as wood much more widely. This might be true, but does not mean that we simply adapt current practices to make greater use of renewables, because current practices also give cause for concern about future supplies of renewables. We can only guarantee future supplies of renewable materials if we allow regeneration and protect stocks of these materials. Within Western Europe, each of us uses 0.66 cubic metres worth of wood every year (m^3 per capita per year). Wuppertal calculations show that the environmental space for timber in Europe is 0.56 m³ per capita per year, which necessitates a reduction of 15 per cent of current levels of use (FoE Europe, 1995). Fifteen per cent is a realizable target, but one that will be made difficult by increasing reliance upon renewable materials. The solution must be to use materials much more efficiently, as well as to be creative with materials we can use in our buildings and remove materials from the waste stream so that they can be reused.

As we have seen, our society is overusing materials, when it is becoming clear that large-scale reductions in use are needed. Meeting any targets for reductions will also be made more difficult by increasing levels of building activity. This activity is driven mainly by signals from the economy, but also by the needs of society for more and new types of building. This itself is a response to shortfalls in existing building provision and changing needs and preferences. Any work towards reducing our materials usage must therefore be able to deal with these growing demands, or tackle the root causes of such change.

It will also become increasingly important to reduce the impact of construction through careful design and materials choices. Research by Smith et al (1995, 1997) has shown that ecological design changes in building specification could produce a reduction in the environmental impact of construction, refurbishment and demolition (ie not including energy in use) of 70 per cent. The research was an LCA project comparing a standard housing design and a design taking account of ecological criteria. One, the Control, was of standard block construction, the other, Eco-Type 1, was of timber frame construction. Furthermore, while materials in the Control tended to be those of standard use, specification for Eco-Type 1 involved taking ecological criteria into account and choosing materials that were seen to be environmentally responsible. A key element of the research was that any ecological materials specified had to be commonly available, 'practical' and utilize proven, standard technology or processes. For example, this meant excluding the use of such techniques as straw bale construction in Eco-Type 1. Through use of greener design principles, it is believed that reductions in impact of an even greater amount could be achieved. The LCA results comparing the impact of the two buildings are shown in Table 4.1 and Figure 4.5.

Looking at such studies does not mean that all buildings must be built to some new 'eco-spec'; green design does not work like that. If then, this book is not going to provide a new blueprint, how can we move towards sustainability? The answer lies in using new design and use criteria which will lead us towards buildings of a lower environmental impact. Furthermore, by looking at the use of buildings and of the built environment, we also believe that people can begin to reduce the impact that their lives have upon the environment. Again, these criteria themselves are not a blueprint but a list of issues which must be considered and assessed if buildings are to become sustainable. We must all become aware of the importance of such issues, indeed, changes in our environment will force us to become aware of them. These criteria are as follows:

Table 4.1   *Relative Impact of Eco-Type 1 and Control*

Item	Control (Eco-points)	Eco-Type 1 (Eco-points)	Reduction in impact of Eco-Type 1	
			Eco-points	Percentage
Construction and major repairs	12.80	3.82	8.98	70
Transport of materials	1.10	0.51	0.59	54
Energy for space heating	109.00	27.30	81.70	75
Disposal of materials following demolition/disassembly	0.49	0.00	0.49	100
Whole life totals (60 years) excluding space heating	14.39	4.33	10.06	70
Whole life totals (60 years)	123.39	31.63	91.76	74

Source: Smith et al (1995)

- reducing the environmental impact of materials used;
- reducing obsolescence and increasing longevity;
- increasing reuse and recycling;
- doing more with less;
- adopting new ways of working;
- using local materials and skills.

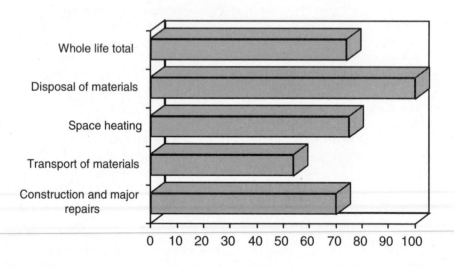

Source: Smith et al (1995)

Figure 4.5   *Impact of Eco-Type 1 as a Percentage of Control*

REDUCING ENVIRONMENTAL IMPACT

There are a number of ways of assessing the environmental impact of building materials, from the use of highly specialized LCA through to the application of common sense. Most research has tended to confirm what has long been the view of those adopting a common sense approach, namely that the lower the level of processing needed in the production of materials, the lower the environmental impact. This will mean that energy use in production will be lower, which is itself an important aim. This energy is called the *embodied energy*, and is a term well understood in green building and design.

Connaughton (1993) has shown that embodied energy of construction materials accounts for 10 per cent of UK energy use while other research puts the proportion even higher. Tucker and Treloar (1994) estimate that embodied energy figures represent 19.5 per cent of total energy consumption in Australia. Embodied energy studies can provide data about energy values per tonne or per cubic metre of material, but presenting these figures is problematic because of the differences in use and density of materials. Instead, it is helpful to look at case studies of buildings and the contribution of each material to overall energy use.

Figure 4.6 shows the relative contribution of different materials to the overall energy requirements of the UK construction sector. From this, it can be seen that five key materials account for over 50 per cent of the total embodied energy in new buildings.

An important point is the realization that materials of lower embodied energy not only consume less energy in their production, but also that this lower figure is a good indicator that less steps were needed in manufacture. Thus the more complex a material, the greater the amount of processing needed. As this increases, so does the need for other raw ingredients for production, and the resultant

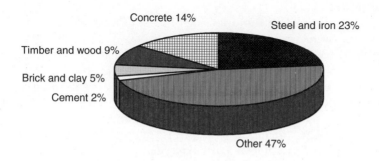

Source: Connaughton (1993)

Figure 4.6 *Contribution of Various Materials to the Energy Requirements of the UK Construction Sector*

pollution. Put another way, the higher the embodied energy of a product or a building, the higher the material intensity.

A good example of this is plastic. In the manufacture of various plastics there are about 15 stages of synthesis. At each of these stages energy is required and pollutants generated. Furthermore, each of these stages is about 50 per cent efficient, meaning that the final product is composed of only about 0.002 per cent of the original raw material used for its manufacture (König, 1989). This means that plastic is a material with a high embodied energy, though this high value is only an indication rather than the true value of the environmental damage caused by its production. These figures are given weight by the results of a Swedish embodied energy study, which showed that although plastics made up only 2 per cent of a building's mass, they were responsible for 12 per cent of its embodied energy (Adalberth, 1994).

REDUCING OBSOLESCENCE

If we look around our towns and cities, and even our villages, we can all see redevelopment going on. Old buildings are continually being demolished to make way for the new. These old buildings, from the mundane to the distinctive, are deemed inappropriate and thus removed from the landscape so that we might build something bigger and better. At the extreme end of this we have redevelopment like that in the City of London, where the Old Baltic Exchange, severely damaged by the IRA bomb blast of 1992, is to be demolished to make way for a new tower designed by Sir Norman Foster. If built, the tower will have 92 storeys and be 1200 feet high, making it Europe's tallest. The proposal has been met with criticism from many quarters, however, and looks set to face a public inquiry even if it is given the go-ahead by the Corporation of London. The Baltic Exchange's previous owners are also annoyed because the Exchange was sold off after the bomb blast on the understanding that it was to be refurbished, not redeveloped (Meikle, 1996).

Demolishing one building and disposing of most of the materials, only to build another one (whatever its environmental credentials or lack of them) must be seen as a step back from taking environmental responsibility seriously. These buildings are not usually demolished because they are literally worn out, but for other, more mundane reasons, most notably to make money profits. After all, if the Baltic Exchange could have been saved after a bombing, then why not most other buildings?

The key factor determining obsolescence is utility (Golton and Golton, 1995), which the Collins English Dictionary defines as: 'the ability of a commodity to satisfy human wants'. If a building is not felt to be fulfilling its utility, then it must be obsolete and it can fail this test for the following reasons:

- structural obsolescence;
- economic perspectives;

- use perspectives;
- social perspectives.

(Golton, 1991)

The problem for our society is that it is the last three considerations that usually form our views on whether buildings are past their sell by date. In urban development, the primary driving force is that of profit, and market behaviour encourages the regular demolition and replacement of buildings. In Hong Kong, for example, the city centre is almost devoid of old buildings. The Old Bank of China building, built in the 1950s and now being refurbished after the Bank moved into its newer prestigious IM Pei designed skyscraper, is something of a rarity because of its age. Most buildings in the centre of Hong Kong are less than 20 years old, and buildings over 40 years old seem to be considered relics. This continual replacement and refurbishment of buildings is a trend affecting many commercial buildings today, though in Hong Kong businesses tend to take such market economics to the logical extreme. For shops, offices and property developers, there is an ongoing race to keep buildings and their interiors interesting, which ultimately means keeping them new. This behaviour means that commercial buildings can have embodied energy values greater than the operating energy (Connaughton, 1993; Lawson, 1994). These processes are seen at their most extreme in Hong Kong and Las Vegas (see Chapter 10), but are widespread throughout the capitalist world.

The capitalist imperative, which ignores real economic costs (Daly and Cobb, 1989), produces an environment in which it is preferable to demolish perfectly sound buildings and replace them with new ones. Similarly, social considerations and changing user perspectives also lead us to demolish buildings well before the end of their expected life. As we demolished terraces and so-called slums because they were unsuitable in the 1950s and 1960s, so we are now demolishing the tower blocks which replaced them to rebuild more traditional terrace-like developments. While there may be problems with tower blocks, and most are reluctant to build such social housing today, it still seems absurd and costly simply to wipe the slate clean before other options have been tried out.

Sustainability must therefore mean challenging user perspectives which seek to reduce a building's life unnecessarily. More obviously, however, we must build buildings capable of standing the test of time. Investment costings usually assume a lifetime of 60 years and sometimes of only 25 years. These assumptions are based, in part, on inappropriate economic models, though also on a lack of faith that buildings might last longer.

Social housing is particularly susceptible to the problem of inferior construction, having been built more to fulfil the needs of statistics than as dwellings in their own right (Day, 1990). The system-built tower blocks we see in so many towns and cities in the UK are notorious for the poor quality of construction, as are the timber frame houses of the 1970s. The result, of course, is that they wear out sooner. They are also so riven with defects and problems that the buildings acquire such a negative image that owners see little option but replacement instead of refurbishment. British council housing suffered from a negative image because of this approach, which meant that the ending of council house building in the early 1980s met with little resistance. Housing associations took over responsibility for the provision of social housing, though ongoing government cuts mean standards within these associations are falling as they struggle to provide decent accommodation within laid down cost restrictions (Rudlin and Falk, 1995).

This said, it is possible to build decent housing which fulfils environmental criteria, will have a long life and which is of low cost. Brenda and Robert Vale designed a pair of houses in Cresswell Road, Sheffield for the North Sheffield Housing Association. The house designs took account of energy conservation water conservation, and used healthy building materials, yet were constructed for less than the Housing Corporation permitted cost. On top of this, room sizes were 13 per cent above Parker Morris space standards (Vale and Vale, 1993; Rudlin and Falk, op. cit).

The houses cost £6500 less than the Housing Corporation's permitted cost for conventional housing, yet include a wealth of environmental design features. Costs were kept down through using the lowest grade materials fit for the purpose and through careful design. Materials chosen had low embodied energy and were not likely to be detrimental to indoor air quality. Where possible, materials were obtained from local sources so as to provide local employment and minimize transport distance. The basic construction is in locally manufactured brick, concrete and untreated softwood from sustainable sources. The insulation contains no CFCs and recycled newspaper has been used in the roof. Timber rainwater gutters were used. Linoleum has been used instead of vinyl flooring throughout the ground floor and in the bathroom. This avoids the possibility of outgassing of vinyl chloride monomer from sheet vinyl. Cupboards and wardrobes were made from softwood to avoid formaldehyde vapour which can be given off by chipboard furniture. Interior painting used water-based non-vinyl emulsion paints to cut out solvent emissions. High levels of insulation were installed, and water use cut by including low flush toilets and water butts with the houses. The houses are built to a good specification because if social housing is to have a long life, it must perform well; otherwise, residents and landlords will have a low opinion of it and it will be replaced with an alternative. Department of the Environment research also suggests that energy efficient housing will last longer through reducing problems of damp and because of better treatment by occupants (Energy Efficiency Office, 1994).

Through the construction of high quality buildings, we can go a long way to reducing our turnover of buildings and the materials which go into them. Furthermore, if environmental design considerations are applied to the built environment in general, then it is less likely that buildings will cease to fit into their surroundings. Holistic concerns applied to planning and architecture, along with the application of environmental considerations to economics, should mean we value what we have around us and do not need to replace it all with this year's latest model. What we have will be good enough. Short building lifetimes are unacceptable because they necessitate the extraction and use of new materials. If, however, demolition led to large scale reutilization of materials, then it might be acceptable to reduce building lifespan (Lawson, 1994). Ideally the two approaches ought to go hand in hand.

INCREASING REUSE AND RECYCLING

Once a building has reached the end of its natural life, there is still much that can be done to reduce its overall impact. In discussing impact, the focus is often on energy use and material manufacture, yet disposal is one area where significant impacts can and do occur. The UK produces an estimated 70 million tonnes of masonry and concrete waste each year of which only 4 per cent undergoes high level processing to produce secondary aggregate. A further 29 per cent goes to low level uses on or near the site of origin (Golton et al, 1995) meaning that two-thirds of building rubble still goes to landfill. In other countries, however, government targets are encouraging more reuse and recycling. In Germany, a target of 60 per cent has been set from 1995 onwards.

Historically, materials were seen as expensive and reused as a matter of course. In modern building practice, however, changes have meant that it has become increasingly difficult to reuse or recycle materials. Economic forces often play a part in the low level of reutilization, but so also do professional attitudes that issues such as recycling are outside the remit of the construction industry. Research, however, shows that even under current economic conditions, much greater reuse and recycling is possible. A Franco–German research project showed that with careful planning it was economically viable to reutilize 94 per cent of a timber frame house, meaning that only 6 per cent needed to be sent to landfill (Ruch et al, 1994). Other estimates suggest that it should be possible to recycle about 75 per cent of building materials (Lawson op. cit).

Short-term considerations also mean that current practices discourage future reuse and recycling. Bricklayers formerly used lime-based mortars, which meant that bricks could be easily knocked apart at the end of their useful life. The move to cement-based mortars, however, has meant that the bricks are bonded so firmly together that they can only be separated with a wrecking ball or sledgehammer. This in turn means that at best they can only be ground up for hardcore, though in truth most are simply landfilled. Old bricks, bought by those seeking a more traditional look may have been used a number of times previously, but using cement mortars ensures they have no future place in other buildings.

In the electronic and automotive industries designers and manufacturers are looking seriously at the concept of design for demanufacture. This is because of concerns about the spreading of producer responsibility legislation, which will give manufacturers responsibility for the ultimate disposal of their products. Such legislation has already been passed in Germany and Scandinavia. Legislators are finding that doing this leads to companies designing products which are either suitable for reuse or can be easily taken apart and recycled. This is a long way from the modern house or office which is usually dismantled using brute force. If construction firms are to face up to their environmental responsibility, then it is vital their designers look seriously at the problem of future dismantling. There are a few examples in current practice which may help practitioners. In Australia, cost effective methods of joining structural timbers are being developed, which will allow easy disassembly. Also in Australia, a method of using building blocks without bonding won the 1992 Australian Design Award (Lawson, 1994), while in France, architect Renzo Piano used mortarless brickwork in his 1989 extension of the IRCAM building in Paris. The system used aluminium frames to hold the clay brick components forming a permeable skin protecting the masonry behind (Piano, 1992).

Technology is now available that can grind up used concrete, and the resulting powder can be mixed with additional cement to make new concrete, thus reducing the need for new resources. Used wood can also be ground up and the resulting fibres used. One Californian company makes a material called 'grindcore' from old newspapers, cardboard boxes and timber. This grindcore is moulded to maximize its strength yet minimize weight. The company feels that it will soon be possible to build entire homes with these new beams, studs and panels (Roodman and Lenssen, 1995).

Another way to reduce impact is to use recycled materials from other processes to make building materials. Insulation materials are now available which are manufactured from recycled newspaper. The resulting fluff is sprayed with boron to give it fire retarding properties and can be used in roofs, floors and timber frame walls. In a study for the EU Insulation Eco-label, the consultancy dk-TEKNIK found that this recycled paper insulation had the lowest environmental impact of all the types of insulation tested (dk-TEKNIK, 1995). It also has a better thermal performance than many other insulation materials and is comparable in cost.

DOING MORE WITH LESS

A primary aim, whatever the material, must be that of efficient usage. As has been seen above, environmental space requirements show that our overall consumption is too high, and this applies to nearly all consumer goods and materials, not just a critical few. Furthermore, because of energy use in manufacture, efficiency of material use is yet another good way to reduce our energy needs. A new approach to buildings is needed which involves both prudence and creativity, linked to higher standards, flexibility and consumer satisfaction.

In the developed world, however, modern day practices work against such an approach. Materials are usually seen as cheap to the extent that building materials wasted during construction account for about 20 per cent of the total. This is caused through inaccuracies when ordering and specifying, spoilage during transport or storage, or because of damage or off-cutting at the installation stage (Harland, 1993). Some damage is of course unavoidable, but there are limits which we have already overstepped considerably. Typical construction in North America generates 20–35 kilograms of solid waste per square metre of floor space, much of it reusable, yet in constructing the Green Home in Waterloo, Ontario, the builders generated only 5 kilograms of waste, with most of what would normally have been landfilled reused or recycled instead (Roodman and Lenssen, 1995).

In seeking creative solutions, however, help is at hand. While some answers undoubtedly lie in looking at more traditional approaches to construction, we can add to this perspective the use of new technology and new building methods to help us use materials more efficiently. Historically, builders used what lay around them, and this changing creativity slowly led us to our current views of vernacular architecture. Similarly, in slum dwellings in the developing world people build with what they can, waste nothing and produce surprisingly sophisticated houses from minimal resources. Such dwellings are hardly luxurious, but their major problem lies in the lack of any sanitation, not poured concrete. In terms of ecological impact, such houses surely rate nil, since all the materials are effectively scavenged. This is of course reuse and recycling as it was traditionally practised.

The central challenge is one of design where the objective is to minimize material use and maximize comfort and economy. This kind of thinking has influenced the design and construction of a series of houses at Hornby Island, near Vancouver. Built by Lloyd House, a former carpenter, the houses used driftwood washed up on the island's beach. House seeks to use the warps and splits in the wood to add to the design of the house, and sees these visual qualities as signs of the history of the timber. Also, the houses are not drawn but allowed to evolve in construction, with spaces evolving out of the available material (Helliwell and McNamara, 1978). An important consideration in the building of these houses is the general awareness of environmental issues, with residents actively involved in recycling and composting (the absence of any building legislation on the island has removed many barriers to construction). As Vale and Vale (1991, p 121) note:

'If the interest in recycling now being manifested in Western societies brings with it anything like the respect for materials that is found among the builders and designers of Hornby Island, a very different architecture may be the result, with materials again forming the starting point for architectural design.'

In calling for ecological housing, we must therefore be sure that we use materials sensibly, and balance legitimate concerns. An example of this is the use of concrete as thermal mass. While the use of high thermal mass will reduce energy consumption through aiding passive heating and heat storage, this cannot simply rely on large-scale use of concrete. Environmental space criteria demand that we seek to use our non-renewable resources more prudently. For example, reclaimed aggregate can be added to concrete to reduce the use of new resources. Hollow concrete blocks or elements can be used for ground or party floors. Alternatives can be found to avoid the use of certain materials altogether. For the ground covering beneath a suspended ground floor, for example, shells may be used instead of concrete, sand, clay granules or the more common polyethylene or polyvinyl chloride membranes. Shells, if gathered sustainably, are a renewable resource and also need minimal processing (Anink et al, 1996).

Materials such as timber can also be used more efficiently. In timber frame construction, builders are increasingly turning to 'glu-lam' beams. These beams, made from glued laminated sheets or scraps of wood, greatly increase the strength of the wood, and use up to 75 per cent less wood than normal beams. Such beams need adhesive bonding, however, so any considerations about their use need to be balanced with concern about the glues used, though products which avoid or limit the use of solvents like formaldehyde are coming on to the market.

Materials like glu-lam show what is possible if new approaches to waste are used. By taking what was a waste product, and turning it into a useful material, manufacturers are helping to divert material away from landfill, and to reduce our need for new material. We can also look for new sources of materials. In the UK, Stramit Industries use straw to produce their Stramit Board 'Easiwall', which is a wall partitioning system. The manufacture of the board involves compressing straw using heat and pressure (and no adhesives) to make an entirely natural board in a variety of thicknesses. The board conforms to building regulations and is perfectly suited to its purpose, meaning that there is no loss of performance in specifying the product, yet the advantage is in using a healthy, environmentally sound material manufactured from what modern day farmers often see as a waste product.

Straw can also be used to construct whole buildings by using the straw bale method of construction. Again, this is an example of using our materials prudently, by seeking to widen the number and type we use. Straw bale building is a traditional building form from Nebraska, which has attracted renewed interest because it is inexpensive, easy to use, fire resistant and environmentally responsible. According to Ross Burkhardt (1994), it could 'revolutionise home construction methods'. Straw bale houses dating back to the turn of the century are still in use and in good condition in the Sandhills area of Nebraska. Residents built these houses because the area had no trees and the sandy soil prevented sod construction used by many other settlers from that era. Because of this, they turned to the native rangeland grasses for their building material, and used mud to plaster the buildings. The method of construction was used for houses, barns and churches until the 1940s when the increasing availability of more conventional materials supplanted this vernacular method (Myhrman, 1993).

For the modern builder, straw represents an alternative to the large-scale use of timber, stone, block or brick: all of which are in short supply. Straw is completely renewable, and unlike timber, is fast growing, meaning that millions of tonnes of this material are produced annually. In the USA alone, farmers burn enough each year to build an estimated 5 million houses (Roodman and Lenssen, 1995), yet the sale of straw bales represents a new source of income for what farmers see as a waste product. Selling the bales on to builders therefore results in a 'win–win' situation for farmers, builders and the environment (Steen et al, 1995; Burkhardt, op cit). Straw bale construction is also becoming increasingly popular in Europe, notably Norway, France and the UK.

Straw is only one of a number of traditional building forms being redis-covered and updated. A traditional UK building type is the cob building. These were cottages made from rammed earth and straw (Ellis, 1947) and examples still survive today. Recently, builders have been re-appraising this method, and it is becoming increasingly popular in the USA, Australia, France and Germany. Earth building uses a material which might in theory be classed as a non-renewable resource, but which is available in abundance, is cheap and needs minimal processing or transport. Earth building is done through rammed earth construction or through use of machines which manufacture earthen blocks on site available for use. Embodied energy estimates vary because of the different methods of block manufacture, but studies indicate that earthen blocks have a value 100 times lower than an equivalent amount of concrete (Houben, 1994) and 500 times lower than that of bricks (Roodman and Lenssen, op cit).

An approach towards building which seeks to use that which is commonly available will also seek out alternative products. At the beginning of this section, we showed that environmental space calculations indicate that Europe must reduce its use of timber by 15 per cent and cement by about 85 per cent. Figures for the USA, Canada and Australasia are likely to be similar, if not higher. If we are to meet these targets, then industry must begin not only to use these materials more efficiently, but also to look around for new ones. Traditional building methods, together with the application of modern, but appropriate technology can provide the answer.

Traditionally, variety in building types, forms and materials was regional. Today, however, variety seems to come more from the extent of materials processing or from small marketing differences. What is most confusing though, is how with such an unlimited canvas of modern materials, our building types tend to look the same and to contain the same mistakes. We can surely learn from adopting not just different styles of kitchen fittings, but also different building types and technologies. Doing this would be prudent and it would also ensure that raw material resources are available to future generations.

USING LOCAL MATERIALS AND SKILLS

The use of local materials is an important element in the movement towards a more sustainable construction sector, because by doing this it will also be possible to fulfil other objectives. The phrase 'Think globally, act locally' has become something of a mantra in the environmental movement, almost to the point of cliché, yet its use continues, and is apt here, because of an increasing realization that the best way to solve our global problems is through local action. As was discussed in Chapter 3, an increasing number of people are of the view that through strengthening local economies and communities, we can produce a society whose impact on the environment is automatically, rather than purposefully small. Using local materials and skills for construction could be a major contribution to strengthening these communities.

Fairlie (1996) gives three reasons why the use of local materials should be encouraged: they are easily accessible, easily accountable and easily assimilable. Firstly, because of their accessibility, builders can avoid bringing materials great distances, which will reduce pressure on our roads and cut carbon dioxide emissions. Secondly, local materials are accountable. In the modern building world, we use bricks from the other side of the country, or even from across Europe, aggregates from superquarries in remote rural areas, and wood from half a world away. Our plastic fittings come from oil which may have been extracted in Saudi Arabia, refined in another country and then manufactured in yet another. Our copper for pipes and wiring may have been mined and processed in South America. We buy products from around the world simply because they are all that is available at the builder's merchants or at our local out-of-town DIY shed, and not (usually) because of our taste for the exotic. In buying such products, however, we have no knowledge about how materials are extracted and processed or how employees are treated. In short, materials are likely to be grossly unsustainable. Furthermore, because materials come from half a world away, our awareness of their scarcity is practically nil, because we do not see the effects of their production, or know that mines in different areas are becoming exhausted.

If, however, we were reliant upon local resources for our materials, this would ensure more responsible use. Firstly, it would encourage people to use a wider range of materials such as straw, recycled paper insulation or earth. Secondly, it would lead to more responsible use. The organization Common Ground, which campaigns for local distinctiveness and responsibility, is keen to see local quarries in use which serve local people. This is because:

> 'it is important that people experience/appreciate the impact of their own expansions. It is more likely then that things are kept in proportion, that materials are regarded as precious, and appropriate use is made of them, rather than, for example, the grinding down of good building freestone for road ballast.'
>
> Clifford, quoted in Fairlie, 1996, p 59

If people were therefore more reliant upon, and more responsible for their local resources, then it is likely they would see how rare they really are. This would not necessarily mean that there would be no regional, national or even international trade, but that it would not be the norm. Before people sell outside their area, they should perhaps satisfy local needs first. This was of course the traditional approach. People were reliant upon what lay around them. They did not have access to large lorries and motorways to move vast amounts of brick, block and aggregate around the country. However, having this transport infrastructure has brought supposed advantages and freedoms. One such freedom is that a builder in Scotland may choose to use bricks from South Wales, while a builder in South Wales may choose to use stone from Scotland. There is really little advantage in that.

The third reason for using local materials is that they are easily assimilable: that is they fit into the landscape and the vernacular. Before we had such a cornucopia of materials able to be delivered to everyone's doorstep and building site, almost everything was built from the same local materials. This is why we have vernaculars. If, however, residents of Bath had been able to use limestone from Cumbria or granite from Scotland, perhaps their city would be a bit different today. Perhaps it would look like every other city?

However, action is being taken to address this dependence on outside sources for materials, and one of the more interesting projects is a study by the Ecological Design Group at Robert Gordon University, Aberdeen into what environmentally benign materials are available in the bioregion of Aberdeenshire. A bioregion is a (bio)geographic zone which can be identified by the cultural, ecological, environmental and economic parameters, which when combined are particular to it alone. This differs from a region, which is commonly delineated by political and administrative boundaries. The aim of the project is to find what materials are available and to test methodology for applying the approach across Scotland. The pilot project found that many building materials could be sourced from within a single bioregion and identified materials not currently being produced but which could be encouraged and markets found. The report concludes that a wide range of economic, social and environmental aims could be achieved through encouraging local sourcing of construction materials (Ecological Design Group, 1996).

IN SEARCH OF A NEW VERNACULAR

There are many openings through which we can and must make current practices sustainable. A key term which has cropped up throughout this chapter has been that of vernacular, and it is here that some solutions might lie. Vernacular is often used to describe the look of our traditional, common buildings, but the term also denotes the way in which we traditionally built. This means that:

'Traditional building styles developed by finding inspired solutions to problems that arose through access to only a limited range of materials. Modern architects, with literally thousands of building materials and products at their fingertips, instead paste . . . detail over a non-existent problem. If we are to rediscover an architecture that is dynamic yet remains authentically

traditional, then we can only do so by giving builders free rein to solve fundamental problems with a similarly limited, but updated, range of basic local materials.'

Fairlie, 1996, pp 60–61

Vernacular architecture has also become something cherished by planners as they attempt to make modern buildings 'fit in'. The problem in doing this, however, is that traditional construction had no concept of planning consent and, looking back, our traditional buildings seem to sit well together. Modern ones, built to fit in, seem out of place. As Fairlie notes:

'For over 20 years, the planning profession . . . has tried to recreate artificially, usually with ghastly results, the architectural integrity that was natural in pre-industrial buildings. Nowadays even supermarkets try to don the vernacular, for example the discount shopping centre just off the M40 marketed as a "development which would blend with and enhance the local environment . . . The distinctive personality of the scheme is that of an English village street with its mixture of cottage style shops and premises modelled on traditional rural industries, such as the traditional blacksmith's shop".'

Fairlie op cit, p 59

This leads to 'superficial neo-traditionalism' which 'has gone a long way towards destroying and devaluing precisely the traditional qualities that professionals and the lay public alike believe that they are safeguarding' (Darley, 1993). What we are seeking to safeguard, is what is common around us. However, as Andrew Wyeth (1987) has declared: 'The commonplace is the thing, but it's hard to find'.

These common, traditional qualities stem from the vernacular of place, which Jackson defines as follows:

'Mobility and change are the key to the vernacular landscape, but of an involuntary, reluctant sort; not the expression of restlessness and search for improvement but an enduring patient adjustment to circumstances . . . natural conditions play their part and so do ignorance and a blind loyalty to local ways, and so does the absence of long-range objectives: the absence of what we would call a sense of future history.'

Jackson, 1984, p 140

This vernacular approach also had lower environmental impact than our modern day activities. The challenge then, must be to return to this low impact, without needing to return to Victorian, Edwardian or even medieval styles or to an 'ignorant' or 'blind' approach.

Within green building, there is an important debate about the concept of a new vernacular. Amongst practitioners there are those seeking to use technology and advances in building construction to reduce a building's impact, for example through promoting energy efficiency or 'intelligent' buildings. On the other hand, there are those seeking to use more simple, traditional approaches to reduce the impact of our buildings. These two approaches often work in tandem, though can at times contradict each other: for example in the use of highly advanced glazing systems. As we have seen, however, there are a large number of fronts on which action is required, meaning that we need to adopt non-technical changes, such as the way we build. Energy efficiency and double glazing systems are not the only answer, though they do help.

In looking to a new vernacular then, we recognize the importance of such issues as local materials and local control. Also, it means valuing what we have much more, so that it becomes natural to make buildings last and to reuse materials. Jackson, above, shows that our vernacular has arisen without having any long-term objectives and with little planning: it has no sense of future history. Today, however, our future history is very apparent. We know that if we do not change our ways, we will degrade our environment further, and further endanger our society. A new vernacular would be one which has this sense of the future and which seeks to use the best of what we have around us, and limit bad practices so that the local is strengthened and the future not endangered.

5

TRANSPORT AND LAND USE PLANNING

'Let no provincial High Street
Which might be your or my street
Look as it used to do,
But let the chain stores place here
Their miles of black glass fascia
And traffic thunder through'

John Betjeman, 1979

One of the most pervasive tendencies of the last 30 years in developed countries is the elevation of distance to the ranks of a significant and desirable consumer good. We consume distance with an intensity and a fervour that was once reserved for energy and we facilitate the process of consumption by making sure that wherever possible complex journey patterns can be substituted for simple ones, destinations (of whatever kind) can be widely separated and considerable areas of land can be devoted to highways and car parking. The importance of land use changes over time is critical in understanding this societal shift from a (relatively) low energy, space efficient, time efficient model to a space greedy, dispersed, energy inefficient and time wasting model. There is an enormous paradox in this shift over time. Several generations of transport and planning professionals have been reared on a diet of transport–land use interactions. Our understanding of the importance of land use changes in determining patterns of transport demand is as sophisticated as our willingness to do something about it is negligible. Highly trained professionals and the whole apparatus of public and private decision making and investment/disinvestment decision making have moulded a spatial structure at the regional, urban and local levels that builds in the necessity to travel longer distances. Each year we travel further than the previous year and demand more road space, more parking space, more cash and more fossil fuel energy to make it all possible.

In California between 1970 and 1990 the state's population grew by 50 per cent but the total number of miles travelled by cars and trucks grew by 100 per cent. In the period 1972/73 to 1992/94 in the UK the number of journeys that people made went up by 10 per cent but the distances they travelled went up by 44 per cent. Potter (1997) has described this as a 'mobility explosion' and one that has been fuelled largely by growth in medium distance trips (8–40 km):

> 'Growth in travel has been concentrated on medium distance trips. Typically journeys that 20 years ago would have been under 5 kms in length are now regularly 20 kms or further. Many previously short trips have extended to beyond walking distance, which leads to an increasing use of the car for shorter trips as well as the key medium-length trips. The increase in medium length trips also helps to explain the strong growth that has occurred in traffic on trunk roads and motorways in and around our towns and cities. Intended for long distance trips these roads have become swamped by people undertaking journeys that previously involved only local road networks, and some not even car trips at all. Improvements to such roads simply facilitates a further "surge" in trip lengths, resulting in additional capacity being quickly filled . . .'

Potter, 1997, p14

In this quote Potter has identified a key factor influencing one of the most dramatic shifts this century in the structure of the built environment. The built environment is now characterized by more land take, more mobility and greater levels of dispersion and trip complexity than ever before and requires greater distances if we are to do the same things we have always done such as travel to work, school, shops and see friends and relatives. Table 5.1 shows this shift to higher levels of mobility.

Table 5.1 *Average Number of Journeys and Kilometres Travelled per Person per Year in Great Britain*

	Journeys	*Kilometres*	*Average length (km)*
1972/73	956	7189	7.5
1975/76	935	7583	8.1
1978/79	1097	7961	7.3
1985/86	1024	8560	8.4
1989/91	1091	10,425	9.6
1991/93	1055	10,417	9.9
1992/94	1053	10,367	9.8

Source: Potter (1997) page 13

LAND USE, URBAN DENSITY AND MOBILITY

It is almost trivially self-evident that a resident of a large conurbation will travel less than someone living in a remote rural area. Behind this truism, however, lurks a debate about spatial form and structure, sustainability and the built environment that is central to understanding how we might begin to manipulate spatial structures and land use planning to bring about sustainable development and transformations of the built environment that meet wider energy, social, environmental and economic objectives.

Car use in the UK is highest in rural areas and small towns and public transport is used most by people living in large cities. On this basis we might conclude even at this early stage that rural living is intrinsically non-sustainable as a result of its dependence on fossil fuel mobility. Rural areas also supply large numbers of cars that find their way into towns and pollute the residential streets of those who live within walking and cycling distance of their destinations and have a higher level of use of these non-motorized modes of transport and public transport. Potter (1997) has summarized these data for Great Britain (Table 5.2).

Table 5.2   *Modal Split of Journeys (%) According to Type of Settlement, 1991/93*

	Car	Walk	Cycle	Public transport	Other	Total
All London	48	32	1	16	3	100
West Midlands	59	26	1	12	2	100
Greater Manchester	55	31	1	10	3	100
West Yorkshire	55	30	–	14	1	100
Glasgow	43	33	1	19	4	100
Liverpool	43	35	2	15	5	100
Tyneside	45	30	1	19	5	100
Urban Areas Over 250K	56	31	2	8	3	100
Urban Areas 100–250K	59	29	2	7	3	100
Urban Areas 50–100K	61	28	2	6	3	100
Urban Areas 25–50K	59	30	2	6	3	100
Urban Areas 3–25K	61	30	2	5	2	100
Rural Areas	69	23	2	4	2	100

Source: Potter, S. (1997)

Liverpool provides a good illustration of changes over time in the built environment and of the interlinkages between transport and land use. Liverpool has experienced a population decline in the last 20 years as traditional industries and sources of employment have closed or moved away. There has been a 40 per cent loss of jobs in the period 1972–1991 and a 31 per cent increase in road traffic accidents over the period 1985–1991. As jobs have been exchanged for road traffic accidents and Liverpudlians themselves have a lower car ownership rate than national averages, so the congestion and air pollution in the city have deteriorated. Liverpool is a metaphor for the social, physical and environmental failures of urban policies over the last 20 years or so. Employment and population dispersion, relocation and restructuring have robbed Liverpool of its economic base and given it severe environmental problems largely caused by those who have successfully moved away returning by car.

In this period the structure of travel and transport in Liverpool has shifted from a pattern dominated by shorter journeys (under 5 kilometres) to one dominated by medium length journeys. Employment in central Liverpool attracts car-borne commuters from as far afield as North Wales, the Chester area and Southport and has been encouraged by a massive inter-urban and intra-urban motorway construction programme in the last 20 years. Many of the car commuters attracted to Liverpool live in small urban areas (population 3000–25,000) or rural areas with a quality of life that is significantly better than Liverpool itself measured in terms of noise and air pollution. Their lifestyle choices including car dependency illustrate the interdependence of urban and rural areas and the large equity problems associated with relatively wealthy car commuters imposing significant environmental and health problems on relatively poor urban dwellers on the arterial roads into and out of Liverpool.

In the UK there is a strong link between settlement size and distance travelled. In London the average distance travelled per person per week is around 162 kilometres (8500 kilometres per year). In the smallest urban areas this rises to 229 kilometres per week (12,000 kilometres per year). This is illustrated in Figure 5.1.

The graph clearly shows the fall in total distances travelled as settlement size increases and the shift upwards that has taken place in distances travelled between the national travel survey in 1975/76 and in 1992/94. In land use planning terms this empirical relationship draws attention to a number of factors that do not currently receive much attention in the policy debate. Larger urban areas offer a number of efficiency gains in terms of their ability to function at lower levels of total mobility. These efficiency gains can be measured in energy use, demand for new highway infrastructure, public and private costs, pollution, greenhouse gases and accessibility indicators. Land use planning could be utilized to reinforce these advantages by protecting and enhancing quality of life and accessibility in these areas so as to provide strong incentives to remain there or to return there from a rural area. Conversely policies that allow deteriorating air and noise quality, traffic danger and loss of green space will lead to further losses of population as urban residents seek those elusive qualities that are associated with rural and small urban areas. Currently there is little sign of 'intelligent' land use planning in developed countries in the sense that the planning process is clearly focused on enhancing quality of life, controlling pollution and the depredations of motorized transport and returning space to people and social interaction rather than vehicles and fossil fuel mobility.

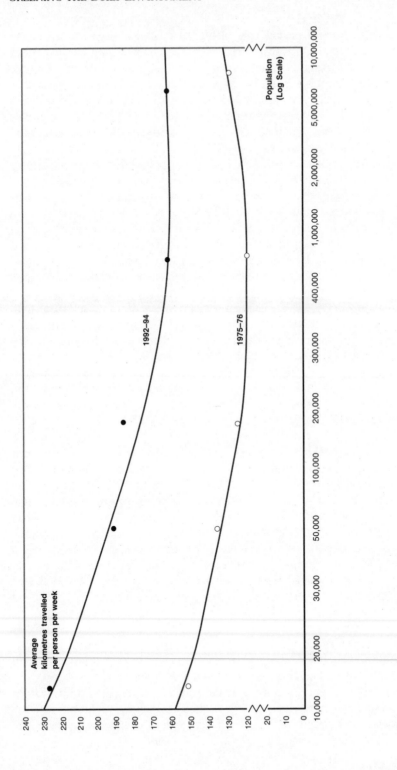

Source: Potter, S (1997)

Figure 5.1 *Relationship Between Settlement Size and Distance Travelled 1975–76 and 1992–94*

There are exceptions to this neglect of land use planning, particularly in North America and the discussion about sprawl and suburbs. In California (Bank of America, 1995) there is a realization that the spread of urbanization and the loss of agricultural land, wilderness and green areas is now acting as a significant additional cost factor in supplying infrastructure to support a low density urban sprawl. As new areas are colonized at some considerable expense for new infrastructure so 'old' areas are abandoned with a sacrifice of all the accumulated infrastructure investments (eg water, sewerage, roads). This process produces very long journeys for commuters and loss of time and large costs that have to be met by new taxation. This is acting as a drag on California's economic performance.

In Calgary (Canada) forecasts of future population growth, increases in car ownership and land requirements have caused alarm and triggered a search for 'the sustainable suburb'. The realization in 1992 that 30 years' more growth would be likely to produce 540,000 more people, 260,000 more houses and 470,000 more cars has led to the development and publication of the Calgary Trans-portation Plan (City of Calgary, 1995). The plan requires that new suburbs should be developed to include community and neighbourhood centres, to be pedestrian and transit-friendly and to provide a rich mix of destinations and facilities (including jobs) within shorter distances than had been the norm in Calgary. Residential densities would rise to at least 17.3 units per gross hectare (from 12.4/ha) and more green space would be provided. Both California and Calgary have realized that unconstrained development of new land for housing and commerce produces significant negative economic consequences which are additional to the problems of pollution, health damage and loss of time.

The link between settlement size and total distance travelled in the UK is mirrored in international data on urban density and annual gasoline use per capita. Newman and Kenworthy (1989) have shown that the low urban densities characteristic of North America and Australia are associated with much higher levels of gasoline consumption than European cities or high density cities such as Hong Kong (see Figure 5.2).

Newman and Kenworthy suggest that there is a critical threshold at a density of around 30 persons/hectare which, as shown in Figure 5.2, coincides with a grouping of European cities (Paris, Stockholm and Hamburg). At lower densities there is a very steep rise in fuel consumption (the Californian problem) whereas at higher densities the reduction in fuel use is much less steep. The nature of the relationship between these two variables should be interpreted with caution. It would not be wise to predict a particular level of fuel use given a particular density or to do this the other way round. Nevertheless Newman and Kenworthy on the basis of their sample of 32 cities have succeeded in encapsulating a major dimension of variability in the international built environment, relating this directly to a central question in sustainable development. They draw our attention to the significance of this in the following ways:

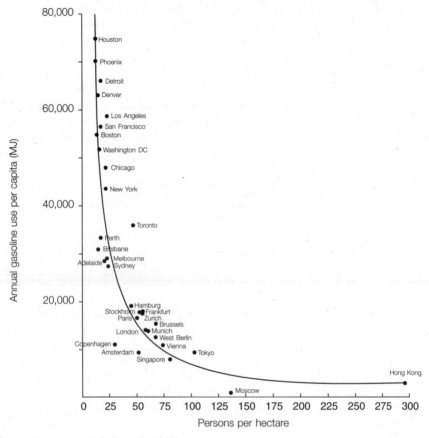

Source: Newman and Kenworthy (1989)

Figure 5.2 *Gasoline Use per Capita versus Urban Density, 1980*

'It means that in terms of transport energy saved or private car use curtailed, the effects of increasing density can be considerable if they move urban areas into at least 30 persons/ha range . . . (the figure) suggests that if cities around 10 persons/ha were able to consolidate and move to densities around 30 persons/ha then fuel consumption could be reduced by half or even to around one third of its low density value'

Newman and Kenworthy, 1989, p 47

The significance for the built environment is even greater than these authors suggest. If we can organize our land use planning system to produce these 'sustainable' densities then the built environment can be manipulated to achieve most of the objectives of international sustainable development including the avoidance of catastrophic climate change (less fossil fuel burning) and less conversion of new land into roads and low density housing (protect and enhance biodiversity). The gains are also to be found in straightforward monetary terms and in equity considerations. An urban settlement at or above the 30/ha threshold can deliver a wealth of goods and services within walking and cycling distances and with investments that are much lower than equivalent investments in highways, car parks and mass transit systems. These settlements will by definition be 'accessibility rich': they will have a number of shops, schools and employment opportunities within a 5 kilometre radius as opposed to the 40 kilometre-plus radius in many dispersed cities or dispersed city-regions. Accessibility rich equates directly with improved equity. Car ownership and use (in higher density cities) are less likely to act as a barrier to accessing the goods and services that are essential to ordinary everyday life in the city.

Higher densities do not involve a sacrifice of quality in terms of green space and other attributes of community life in cities. A US study, 'The Costs of Sprawl', found that a high density planned development could leave over half its land as open space and significantly reduce road and utility investments, compared with a traditional suburban layout. The benefits of higher density developments include reduced costs, reduced pollution and reduced energy use:

'. . . shorter distances would reduce automotive fuel use and air pollution . . . (the cost comparison) found a 35 per cent or $4,600 lower cost per house for site preparation, roads (20 ft wide instead of 30 ft), driveways, street trees, sewers, water services and drainage'

Weizsäcker et al, 1997, p 133

The United States has provided some practical experience of moving in the direction of higher densities and new forms of land use transport planning, guided by principles associated with the New Urbanism movement (Calthorpe, 1993; Katz, 1994). The 'Village Homes' project in Davis, California is based on the encouragement of walking and cycling, abundant supply of green spaces and mixed housing types on narrower streets. People are allowed to conduct businesses from their own homes which in the USA (and the UK) is normally against planning laws. This in turn reduces the need to travel. The narrower streets calm traffic and save money and crime rates are one-tenth of other developments nearby (see Chapter 8 for a detailed discussion of the links between community and the built environment). 'Village Homes' sell much faster than conventional homes and are sold at a premium. These planning and design principles have been extended in the 400 ha Laguna West development in Sacramento, California. This development will integrate parks, lakes, commercial, retail and industrial space with its 3000 homes. Redesigned from a conventional suburban plan it has many innovative features to support walking and cycling and community activities in public open space. Cars have been relegated to 'out of the way' locations and space reallocated to people.

The US examples discussed above and in more detail in Weizsäcker et al (1997) deal with new settlement planning. In most situations this new planning will be targeted at relatively affluent groups who are looking for lifestyle changes involving clean air, reduced crime rates and more community spirit. Just as nineteenth and early twentieth century suburbs offered these groups an escape from the dirty and dangerous city so the twenty-first century escape route will offer relief from both city and suburb. There is a danger in this kind of planning. It ignores 99 per cent of the problem and it panders to well-established principles underlying the provision of better conditions for those who can pay. Weizsäcker et al quoted above see no problem in the higher than average resale value of the houses in Davis, California. Elitist architecture and elitist urban planning in the guise of eco-responsibility run the risk of ignoring and (further) marginalizing the millions of low income or no income/welfare groups in developed societies who live on peripheral public housing estates (very well developed in Liverpool) or in very poor quality high density housing schemes near the centre of cities (characteristic of London). In these situations a totally different approach will be required and one that can cope with the massive task of retrofitting transportation, open space and economic strategies on an often demoralized and crime-ridden community.

The debate about 'town cramming', compact cities and decentralization versus concentration (Breheny and Rookwood, 1993) would be less confused if it were informed by clear equity and environmental considerations running as equals in the search for sustainable city and city region form. Equity consider- ations (see Chapter 7) require an immediate and dramatic improvement in air quality, noise quality, job availability, open space availability and housing quality in urban areas starting with the worst and working from that base. Environmental considerations translated into high quality public transport, housing provision, repair standards and public services will improve the quantity and quality of jobs in urban areas. Strong traffic controls and the reallocation of traffic space to people space will create safe, secure and attractive urban areas and discriminate against the relatively wealthy rural dwellers who have hitherto had freedom to pollute their nearest urban areas. The balance of advantage in quality of life will tip gradually back towards the urban area and away from the rural area in a way that avoids prescriptive planning or social engineering.

In the countryside similar equity considerations would create a different kind of rural area. Planning controls, land use regulations and taxation would release land and buildings for local people, for local enterprise and for a varied community of producers and consumers. The choice of whether to live in a rural or an urban area would be based on a much more level playing field of house prices, job availability and clean air and a lot less on the ability to purchase a good quality environment at the expense of local residents in rural areas and at the expense of those urban residents exposed to the daily tidal flows of rural car commuters. More importantly the countryside needs to be repositioned as a fully functioning working environment where the planning system gives priority to those people who are able and willing to live and work there rather than to those who are wealthy enough to enjoy some aspects of the countryside whilst commuting 20 miles or more to an urban centre. This repositioning need not involve any environmental deterioration, indeed it would be more likely to enhance environmental and social quality (Fairlie, 1996).

Restructuring the built environment in this way is a bigger issue than land use transport planning alone but the latter is central to getting it right since ill-judged land use planning controls currently lock the built environment into a socially unjust and environmentally damaging mould. The restrictions on small-scale housing and employment developments in the countryside damage the interests of relatively low income groups in those areas and the unwillingness to install strong traffic restraints and car parking reductions in urban areas damages the interest of the low income groups there since these groups are more likely than high income groups to live and work near a busy road. The current land use planning system and its underlying principles in most developed countries are, therefore, a structural obstacle to moving in the direction of sustainable development.

LAND USE PLANNING TO REDUCE THE NEED FOR TRAVEL

In 1991 John Roberts produced a report under the title *Trip Degeneration* and in writing about the transport–land use relationship suggested: 'While the great majority of . . . work (has) used this relationship to predict traffic growth from land use, few have investigated how land use can be used to reduce the need for travel and dependency on the car' (Roberts, 1992, p 1). Roberts based his enthusiasm for using the land use planning process as a policy instrument to reduce environmental impacts and energy use on his detailed comparison of Almere in the Netherlands and Milton Keynes in the UK. Almere and Milton Keynes are both new towns dating from approximately 1970 and both with target populations in the range 180,000–250,000. The two cities were planned in very different ways and have different transport and travel characteristics as shown in Table 5.3.

Roberts concludes: 'as the population characteristics of the two cities were found to be very similar, the differences in modal split can be attributed to the dissimilar land use structures, travel facilities and culture of the two places'. Milton

Table 5.3 *Transport Characteristics of Almere and Milton Keynes*

	Almere	Milton Keynes
% Car trips	43.1	65.7
% Bike trips	27.5	5.8
Mean trip length (km)	6.85	7.18
Mean duration of trip (min)	11.0	14.5
% Local trips	74	60

Source: Roberts, 1991, p 14

Keynes was designed around the car as the main mode of transport whereas Almere was designed to encourage as much use as possible of public transport and the bicycle. In Almere a number of measures were introduced in the design stage to control excessive car use including tortuous routes, cul-de-sacs, narrow access roads and humps. These were supported by priority bus lanes, a comprehensive system of segregated cycle tracks and walkways and five railway stations to connect the residents with other settlements and with Amsterdam (25 minutes travel time away). The proportion of local trips made in both cities is also very interesting. A higher proportion of local trips translates exactly into shorter trips, more local trade of economic benefit to the locality and less demand for energy and infrastructure. Almere benefits as a community from its land use transport planning successes.

The implications for creating new settlements are clear. If land use–transport interactions are built in at the design stage with the specific objective of reducing car use and increasing the use of non-motorized forms of transport then car dependency can be reduced. The fact that this approach was not followed in the case of Milton Keynes is symptomatic and representative of a world view of transport and land use that is still prevalent in the UK. This view is based on laissez-faire economics, faulty conceptualization of land use–transport relationships and grossly inadequate assumptions about the costs of supplying facilities for non-motorized transport and public transport and the cost of supplying highways, roundabouts, motorways and car parking spaces. The result is a steep growth in private motorized transport, increased demand for new highway dominated infrastructure and a range of transport, environmental and social problems that are documented throughout this book. The result is also very costly (see Chapter 9 for the economic implications).

FACILITY PLANNING

In May 1997 *The Guardian* newspaper reported the construction of 'the last big out-of-town shopping complex to be built in Britain this century' (*The Guardian*, 29 May 1997, p 11). The Trafford Centre in the northwest of Manchester is adjacent to the M63 motorway and has 10,000 car parking places. It is located at a point where there are 5.5 million shoppers within 45 minutes driving time and is expected to attract 30 million shoppers each year. Nine out of the ten local authorities in Greater Manchester have opposed it because of concerns about its impact on traditional shopping in their city centres. Out-of-town shopping centres have focused attention in the last ten years on the enormous impact of major changes in facility planning (in this case retailing). These changes are social, cultural, economic and psychological but also connected to land use. The growth of large out-of-town shopping centres represents a dramatic shift away from established land use and transport patterns towards new locations on greenfield sites, on the edge of metropolitan areas and in situations where the traffic generation effect is considerable.

Retailing is not an isolated example of this trend. Hospitals are huge traffic generators. The main hospital in Plymouth in southwest England, Derriford, generates 3 million car trips per annum and is the largest traffic generator in the region. It has replaced a number of more accessible hospitals (near the city centre) which have now closed and now causes significant congestion and pollution problems at its new location 8 km from the city centre on the edge of the city of Plymouth. Universities have a similar impact as do business parks and all have followed the same development trajectory in turning to greenfield sites, sites away from public transport routes and difficult for walking and cycling and sites that are well served by car parking and highway provision (at enormous cost).

The last 20 years in the UK have seen a deliberate and expensive shift away from accessible locations towards car-based locations supported by large-scale investments that have been in their turn supported by public funds and heavy subsidies. The provision of 2500 car parking spaces at Lancaster University has been funded entirely by public money (ie taxpayers). At current (1997) prices these spaces have a value of approximately £2000 each. Lancaster University's commitment to supporting the private car has cost £5 million and Derriford Hospital's commitment to 1800 car parking spaces has cost £3.6 million. In both cases these are funds that would have been available for the more mundane purposes of improving educational or health care facilities and have now been deployed in the subsidy of the relatively wealthy members of both communities. Those choosing to cycle or walk to these edge of town locations are not given a subsidy and must cope with the difficulties of a car-dominated and polluted, dangerous environment.

Car parking is an important land use issue (we discuss below the space needs of parking). Like aviation (see Chapter 2) it is a major factor in determining the sustainability or otherwise of the built environment. Generous parking provision is a problem for sustainable development and yet is a desirable commodity. Like aviation it provides a litmus test of commitment to the principles and practice of sustainable development. It is also an important economic issue. One car parking space on level ground, with fencing, surfacing, marking and lighting costs £2000 to construct and £400 per annum to maintain at 1995 prices. Derriford staff pay 20 pence per day towards the cost of this facility and staff at Lancaster University pay £25 each year for the same benefit. The scale of the subsidy to the car user is vastly in excess of any subsidy to the bus, bike or pedestrian commuter and stands out as a remarkably inconsistent policy in a world of free market economics and privatization of transport. It also provides an extremely strong underpinning for a particularly car-dependent built environment.

Potter has summarized some of the land use trends that are made possible by these car subsidies:

'Overall all types of facilities are tending to be more concentrated into larger, but more widely spaced units. Local access to all sorts of services and goods

has declined. This brings us back to the observation made (earlier) that the growth in mobility is due to people travelling further and not more often.'

Potter, 1997, p 61

WHICH FACILITIES MATTER AND WHY?

Potter (op cit) gives a useful breakdown of distances travelled by mode, for each journey purpose per week. Focusing on why people are travelling can point to priority areas for better land use–transport planning. Table 5.4 shows these journey purposes ranked in order of importance.

Table 5.4 *Percentage Breakdown of Distances Travelled by Journey Purpose*

Journey purpose	Percentage
Commuting	18.7
Visiting friends and relatives	18.0
Holiday/day trip	13.4
Shopping	12.0
Business	11.2
Social and entertainment	10.4
Escort	6.9
Personal business	6.0
Education	2.8
Other	0.6
Total	100

Source: Potter, 1997, p 9

Commuting and shopping illustrate some of the most pervasive impacts on traffic generation of all land use changes in recent years. Jobs have largely decentralized from traditional city centres and in some cases away from large metropolitan areas completely. In this respect the UK is only a few years behind the United States. The complex of offices around John Wayne Airport in Orange County, California, formerly used for lima bean cultivation, now surpasses downtown San Francisco as the second largest employment centre in the State. The rise of business parks in the UK in the last ten years, as in Chester and around the M25, has created new centres of employment where 98 per cent plus of all journeys to work are by car and the sites are occupying green belt land or land on the edge of urban areas formerly in agricultural use.

Newcastle City Council's plans include one of the largest ever releases of green belt land to create 'The Northern Development Area' including 2500 'executive' homes and an 80 ha 'prestige' business park (CPRE, 1997). East

Sussex County Council's draft structure plan proposes the release of land for several new business parks in the county including land within the High Weald Area of Outstanding Natural Beauty. Lancashire County Council have plans to develop a new business park in the vicinity of the main M6 motorway junction to the north of Preston adding to the traffic congestion in an area (Broughton) that is already threatened with land take for a new bypass.

Between 1989 and 1991 an estimated 26 million sq. feet of offices (enough for 160,000 workers) were completed in the vicinity of the M25 London orbital motorway. In 1993 some 50 million sq. feet of office space were awaiting construction or planning permission (RCEP, 1994, p 147). The M25 has also attracted retail and leisure activities generating yet more traffic and undermining the purpose for which the road was originally designed. Land use changes on this scale consequent on new road construction carry a double penalty. They add to traffic levels in cases where the new road was expected to produce a reduction in congestion and they render a very expensive road project like the M25 ineffective in delivering its original role. Motorways are a very expensive item of infrastructure and almost certainly the most expensive way possible of delivering children to primary schools, commuters to work or families to shopping destinations.

The August 1997 roads review in the UK gave the go-ahead for the Birmingham Northern Relief Road, a privately financed motorway costing £300 million, and another section of the M66 around Manchester costing £115 million. Both roads will intensify the decentralization pressures on those cities, develop large areas of agricultural land for executive housing and business parks and lead to the abandonment of much expensive infrastructure in the older, inner areas. In this respect the UK is now succumbing to the Californian problem in spite of the mounting evidence that sprawl and urbanization are economically and environmentally unsupportable. The Royal Commission report quoted above expressed concern about developments that follow road construction as in the case of the M40 from London to Oxford and developments that follow bypasses often frustrating the original purpose of the bypass which was to relieve traffic.

Car dependency is high to large out-of-town shopping centres. In addition to the Trafford Centre discussed earlier in this chapter there are three other centres in the UK with over 1 million square feet of retailing and 10,000 car parking spaces: The Metro Centre in Gateshead, the Meadowhall centre in Sheffield and Merry Hill near Dudley in the West Midlands. Mode of travel to these centres is shown in Table 5.5.

The Merry Hill centre has a serious negative impact on retailing in Dudley:

> 'the centre has lost major multiple retailers. There has been an increase in vacancies; there has been a decline of retailing in the centre; there has been a decline in rentals and there has been a marked reduction in shopping flows for pure comparison shopping purposes since Phase 5 of Merry Hill opened. The effects on Stourbridge have been less severe but there has been a major reduction in the quality of retailing in the centre. Rentals have declined and

Table 5.5 *Mode of Travel to Retail Centres (Weekday) (%)*

Mode	Merry Hill	Metro Centre	Meadowhall
Car	84	79	71
Bus	16	16	24
Train	–	4	3
Walk	–	1	1
Other	–	1	–

Source: DoE, 1993, p 30

> *there has been a major reduction in pure comparison shopping trips to the centre'*
>
> DoE, 1993, p x

The damage to Dudley has been catastrophic. It has lost 92,900 square feet of retail floor space between 1989 and 1992 and what is left is described as 'a secondary centre attracting local customers buying low quality or discount goods'. The decline of town centres on this scale is a serious land use planning issue of significance for the future viability of urban areas and the likelihood of a 'doughnut' city along the lines of American cities. Cities with depressing centres, low job opportunity and pollution are more likely to be socially disastrous with marginalized groups living in poor quality environments and dependent on poor quality services whilst at the same time lacking a car to take advantage of the relocated opportunities represented by business parks and out-of-town shopping centres. Land use changes on this scale increase the degree of inequalities in developed societies at the same time as they add to energy consumption and subtract from the available pool of open land. The relatively late in the day retreat from out-of-town shopping centres and defence of traditional city centres in UK government policy in 1995–1996 does not undo the damage done in the previous 10–15 years or deal with the consequences of a large number of projects already in the pipeline. The impact of out-of-town shopping centres and business parks, leisure centres and other dispersed, peripheral activities is to entrench more deeply the psychology and practicality of car dependency. The primary result of many years of auto-centred land use changes is to make a transition to lower levels of dependency that much more difficult and the size of this task should not be underestimated.

HEALTH CARE PLANNING

There are a number of reasons for focusing on health care in the UK as a special case of transport–land use interaction. Health care is still predominantly in the public domain in the UK and is therefore far more amenable to policy intervention than is retailing or business park development. Hospitals are very often the largest traffic generator in a particular city or region and are used by many groups who might not have access to a car, for example the elderly. In spite of these considerations hospitals have centralized and moved out of cities (except London) to a degree that is on a par with retailing and business parks.

Derriford hospital in Plymouth illustrates the land use planning problems generated by the compartmentalized decisions of the health care sector. Derriford has 4000 staff working on site, 1085 beds, and deals with 65,000 inpatients and 82,500 new outpatients each year. It is located 8 kilometres to the north of Plymouth City centre adjacent to the airport and on the main route to Tavistock. Over the last 20 years hospital facilities formerly available in Plymouth itself (Freedom Fields and Mount Gould) have been closed and relocated to the new peripheral site. These former locations were in densely populated parts of Plymouth with ample opportunities for walking, cycling and public transport trips. The new location is effectively beyond walking and cycling range (though a small number of staff do cycle) and is up to 50 minutes by bus from areas of Plymouth to the east, south and west of the city centre. The impact of this locational decision has been to add a significant amount of extra traffic (and health damaging pollution) on the local highway system and to create a demand for additional highway capacity at key intersections or pinch points (eg the Derriford roundabout). At no point did health care planners feed into their considerations the wider land use and transport implications of their choices even though this would have a direct impact on the degree to which staff, patients and visitors could make contact with the hospital. Perhaps even more damning, they did not take any account of the damage to public health that would result from the increased pollution (see Chapter 6 for a fuller discussion of health issues).

In the case of Derriford Hospital decision makers received a report in 1985 (before relocation) which concluded:

> '*The maps of the aged, the unemployed and those without a car show that such groups are concentrated most heavily in those parts of Plymouth that are furthest from Derriford . . . many staff resident in central Plymouth are currently able to walk to work but this will not be possible to Derriford . . . This begs the inevitable question: given the more central nodal position of Plymouth General, must all Plymouth's hospital services go to Derriford?*'

Mohan, 1985

The inability of the planning system in its widest sense to respond to clear information and validated predictions as in Plymouth is a major source of concern for decision making in support of sustainable development. Even worse, the problems created in the 1980s are being replicated in the late 1990s. Kings Lynn in East Anglia is now to have an edge of town new hospital development to replace its current central facilities and once again no account is to be taken of the social and environmental consequences of closing a central location and shifting a heavily used facility to a location that will be accessed primarily by car. Health care decisions made by health care providers have reduced the accessibility of health care facilities in Plymouth and at the same time created a number of planning problems on the highway system and in coping with the demand for car parking spaces. They have also harmed what they are supposed to protect – the public health – by increasing air pollution levels.

These examples illustrates a significant point in land use and transport planning. The majority of key decisions that are routinely made about location and trip generation fall outside of any formal land use planning process. Even where applications for planning permission are made most attention is likely to focus on the design of a roundabout or junction and a very narrow discussion about link capacity. The important issues about the actual location itself, the alternatives that may be available to deal with a particular level of demand for transport and the final balance sheet of environmental impacts and land take are ignored. This is the case for hospitals, schools, business parks and out-of-town shopping centres and is a major structural defect in the land use planning process.

THE DEMAND FOR HOUSING

United Kingdom governmental projections estimate that 4.4 million new homes will be required in England by the year 2016. These projections are based on analyses of the impact of demographic change, smaller household size and more people living alone and represent a major governmental commitment to the now discredited 'predict and provide' approach to national planning. In this case the 'predict and provide' philosophy has been applied to a trend that shows smaller average household size and an increasing level of demand for new housing of a traditional kind. It is possible to predict the trend towards smaller household size continuing whilst varying the ways in which that demand might be met.

The prediction of 4.4 million new homes has been disaggregated to the local level throughout England to give targets for new housing construction which are then translated into planning objectives in the local and structure plan process. The targets are completely inflexible and result in the allocation of substantial amounts of green land to new housing development despite government encouragement to use 'brown' land in existing urban areas. In the case of Lancaster in the northwest of England the local plan is advocating a new residential area, Lancaster Neighbourhood South, substantially on green land and extending the urban area of Lancaster towards the south and the west. The housing development is associated with new road construction and will be a substantial traffic generator in an area where highway capacity is already a problem and will reduce the stock of open/recreational land. The impact of this massive house building programme has not been assessed in terms of environmental damage through material and energy consumption, extra traffic generation, pollution and loss of biodiversity. It stands in stark contrast to the loudly proclaimed sustainable development objectives of government. It removes the flexibility of local initiative and locally derived solutions which are at the heart of the commitment to Local Agenda 21 and like road building in the 1970s and 1980s it simply creates the demand through a supply side solution.

A planning approach based on sustainable development principles would seek to develop a demand side solution through innovative approaches to meeting housing need. These include utilizing existing capacity to the full through a whole range of tax and development incentives to bring into use empty properties, to convert empty office blocks into housing, to redevelop brown land and to convert car parking space into housing space as a strategy to bring life back into cities rather than cars. A combination of reducing the supply so as to meet less than the whole of the forecast demand together with reallocating that supply in the ways suggested above would be more likely to meet sustainable development objectives than the expedient of developing green land on the edge of towns or completely new freestanding towns in rural areas.

CPRE (1997) estimate that 60,000 hectares of land are vacant in urban areas in England and 15–20 per cent of office space is empty. Estimates are presented later in this chapter to show the potential of reallocating 'mobility space' to 'people space' and living space.

LAND TAKE FOR PRIVATE TRANSPORT

Land is a finite resource. The amount of land used for different purposes is a key indicator of the impact of public policies and public expenditure priorities and is a key indicator of progress towards sustainability. The processes that determine land uses are the key to re-engineering the built environment in the direction of sustainable development. The United Kingdom Strategy for Sustainable Development (Department of the Environment, 1994a) identifies land take as an important issue. An estimate of 1.2–1.5 per cent is given for the proportion of land in the UK occupied by roads. No supporting evidence or regional breakdown is given and no definitions of land take are advanced. The area occupied by roads and road related uses depends entirely on the definitions used and on the extent to which parking areas can be included in the estimates.

The estimate of 1.2–1.5 per cent is applied to the whole of the UK and to England (Davies, 1994, Department of Transport, personal communication). Clearly such a broad estimate will be unreliable when applied to components of the whole. In the case of England 1.2–1.5 per cent produces a land take in the range 1603 to 2004 square kilometres (618 to 773 square miles). The mid point of this range (expressed in square miles) produces the figure 695 square miles which is very close to the figure of 690 square miles which has been quoted by the Department of Transport as the area occupied by roads.

The amount of land available for housing, industry, health care, education, retailing, recreation and transport is very much a matter for government, both central and local. There are important linkages between traditionally compart-mentalized policy areas. The development of low density housing in suburban and rural locations reduces the land available for agriculture. The longer distances between these residential locations and urban facilities increases the demand for transport and hence for land allocation for new roads. The decline of traditional industries and transport activities associated with ports, docks and railway sidings releases land in urban areas for new developments associated with urban regeneration initiatives. Manufacturers, distributors and transport industries require increasingly large blocks of land to service their road centred activities and in turn generate vehicle movements that provide the impetus for motorway widening schemes and new roads such as the Birmingham Northern Relief Road (BNRR).

In a German study it was shown that a 150 gram pot of strawberry yoghurt is responsible for moving one lorry 9.2 metres (Böge, 1994) and one 500 gram container of mushrooms is responsible for moving one lorry 65 metres (Böge, 1994, personal communication). Our lifestyles and consumption patterns are dependent on a space-extensive and time intensive organizational system. Lorries are space greedy. They need wider roads to take account of turning circles, they need generous parking areas at every supermarket and loading bay and they need overnight parking and rest areas. Roads designed to take 38 tonne, 15 metre long lorries need more space for their junctions and curves than do roads designed for cars or smaller lorries (Schult and Holzwarth, 1988). Increases in lorry length require more generous road alignments and curve radii and larger areas for vehicle parking. Increases in lorry weight require more substantial structures and road pavements which in their turn demand more of the raw materials of construction particularly sand, gravel, cement and steel reinforcements. Heavier demands on raw materials require greater areas for extraction and processing.

German calculations (Teufel, 1989) reveal that a lorry requires 0.007 square metres of space per tonne kilometre in comparison to rail which needs 0.0025 square metres. The lorry, therefore, requires almost three times as much space to do the same work as the train. Translating these space requirements into the UK context produces a land requirement for road freight of 849.1 square kilometres. This is the result of multiplying the 1992 tonne kilometre figure (Great Britain) for road freight (121.3 billion) by 0.007 square metres:

$$121,300,000,000 \times 0.007 = 849,100,000 \text{ m}^2 = 849.1 \text{km}^2.$$

Teufel (1991) has made similar calculations for passenger travel. Table 5.6 summarizes his results.

The table makes a number of points. Land take is very dependent on mode of transport. Motorized modes are very greedy in their land requirements and there is no difference in this respect between Car 1 (no catalytic converter) and Car 2 (with a catalytic converter). Land take is also closely associated with other

Table 5.6 *Comparisons of Different Modes of Passenger Travel*

	Car 1*	Car 2†	Train	Bus	Bike	Foot
Land use[1]	120	120	7	12	9	2
Energy[2]	90	90	31	27	0	0
CO_2[3]	200	200	60	59	0	0

Notes: * Without catalytic convertor.
  † With catalytic convertor.
  1 Land use is measured in m[2] per person.
  2 Energy use is measured in grams of coal equivalent units per passenger kilometre.
  3 CO_2 is measured in grams per passenger kilometre.

indicators of non-sustainability, particularly energy use and CO_2 emissions. Modal transfer to walk and cycle, for example, offers enormous potential to reduce the impacts measured by all three indicators.

The Umwelt und Prognose Institut in Heidelberg in Germany has calculated that road transport in Germany (the former Federal Republic) occupies 60 per cent more land than the total for all housing purposes (UPI, 1993a). The total land area occupied by roads and parking was estimated as 3800 square kilometres in 1992 or 200 square metres of asphalt and tarmac per vehicle. The total area of the former Federal Republic of Germany was 249,000 square kilometres. The land occupied by road transport uses (3800 square kilometres) represents 1.52 per cent of the total. This is very close to the unsubstantiated figure given for the UK in the Strategy for Sustainable Development (Department of the Environment, 1994a).

The significance of transport's consumption of land lies in comparisons with other major land uses and in the increasing rate with which land is reallocated to transport, particularly road transport uses. Between 1981 and 1985 the amount of land allocated to transport in Germany increased by 25 per cent as a result of 8000 kilometres of new road construction and the construction of wider roads. In Germany, as in the UK, new roads are engineered to much more generous standards in terms of width and curvature/alignment than roads built 20 years ago. The land take of a mile of new motorway in 1994 is likely to be much greater than a mile of new motorway when the Preston Bypass (the UK's first motorway, subsequently part of the M6) was opened in December 1958. German data (Pauen-Höppner, 1987) also show that the daily rate of land take for new roads was 23 hectares or 160 square metres per minute. Swiss data on road traffic and its land take is revealing. Metron (1989) have calculated that the land allocation for road transport is 113 square metres per person and for all living purposes (houses/gardens and yards) is 20–25 square metres per person.

New roads have large land requirements which must often be accommodated in tightly defined 'green' corridors. An example of this is the Birmingham Northern Relief Road. This has been designed as a 44 kilometre (27 miles) motorway link and is a dual three lane motorway for the majority of its length. Total land take for this road is shown in Table 5.7.

Table 5.7 *Land Take for the Birmingham Northern Relief Road*

	Hectares
Road, toll stations and maintenance compounds	536
Motorway service area	22
Stream improvements	11
Temporary diversions	4

Source: Birmingham Northern Relief Road, Environmental Statement, Non-Technical Summary, Department of Transport and Midland Expressway, 1994

The Environmental Statement presented by the Department of Transport and Midland Expressway details land take by section providing a useful insight into the land requirements of major road construction projects. These data are summarized in Table 5.8.

The land take per kilometre of road is 13.729 hectares. For ease of comparison this can also be expressed as 54.68 acres per mile of dual three lane motorway.

Table 5.8 *Land Requirement for Sections of the BNRR*

	Length (km)	Land take (ha)	Miles	Acres
M6 Saredon Brook to Churchbridge	6	80	3.7	198
Churchbridge to Chasewater/				
Burntwood exc service area	6	102	3.7	252
Chasewater/Burntwood to Weeford	9	123	5.6	304
Weeford Island to Wishaw Holly Lane	9.3	111	5.8	274
Totals	30.3	416	18.8	1028

The results of calculations of land take implied by the national road programme (Department of Transport, 1990) are shown in Table 5.9, which refers to England only. The total area of roads completed in the first row (11.47 square kilometres) is enough land for 30,969 housing units. For all three categories of road the number of housing units that could be accommodated on the same area is 275,875 (at a density of 27 units per hectare). A higher density than 27 units per hectare is possible particularly if the need that it is to be satisfied is mainly for single person dwellings as in the UK Government's target of 4.4 million homes.

Given the targets in the UK for additional housing units there must be an informed discussion about priorities for the kind of developments that can take place on land to be released from agriculture. It is clearly illogical to

Table 5.9 *Land Take of the Roads Programme in 'Trunk Roads, England into the 1990s'*

Status of road	Land take (km²)
1	11.475
2	9.303
3	81.398
Total	102.176

Notes: All data from tables in Department of Transport (1990).
1 = Table 1, National Trunk Road Programme schemes completed 25.4.87–31.12.89.
2 = Table 2, National Trunk Road Programme schemes under construction at 1.1.90.
3 = Table 3, National Trunk Road Programme schemes in preparation at 1.1.90.

compartmentalize all the different categories of demand for land and to allow the unconstrained application of 'predict and provide philosophies'. If all the predicted demand for future air travel, housing and transport is to be met in full then serious damage will have been done to the principles and objectives of sustainable development. If the demand is not to be met in full then working limits need to be set and choices need to be made between competing uses. It may well be the case that new homes are more desirable than new roads and, further, that these new homes should be designed in such a way that meet sustainability criteria (City of Calgary, 1995).

The land occupied by roads in the UK does not represent the totality of land that is dedicated to road transport uses. The most obvious addition is parking but considerable areas are set aside for petrol stations, motorway service areas and all the service and ancillary activities associated with maintaining a car dependent society. The space greedy nature of car dependency is often described by reference to the American situation:

'Up to 10 per cent of the arable land in the US is taken up by auto infrastructure . . . about half of all urban space in the US is now devoted to auto-centred transport. In Los Angeles two thirds of land space is devoted to auto use . . . the average car (in Los Angeles) uses up to eight parking spaces daily, each located at different activities. In suburban New Jersey, developers are now required to build 3,000 sq. feet of parking space for every 1,000 sq. feet of commercial office space'

Freund and Martin, 1993, p 19

TEST (1991) developed the idea of secondary land take to include the area devoted to providing the raw materials necessary for the construction of road and rail infrastructure. This would include all the land allocated to the mining and quarrying operations for raw materials used in making vehicles and in manufacturing steel and concrete (and making the cement) used in road construction. This approach is suggestive of a thorough life cycle analysis (LCA) which would take into account land take for these purposes throughout the world and link total land take to a passenger kilometre of car use in the UK. The resources for such an ambitious exercise are not available though there are no technical problems in its execution. The discussion of the vehicle's wider impacts on environment, society and development will continue to be deprived of this 'ecological footprint' component.

PARKING

Parking provision is at the heart of a discussion about sustainability and the built environment. It takes up space and far more of it than is recognized by politicians and planners. It changes the character of the built environment in a very dramatic way. It stimulates higher levels of car use and pollution, particularly of greenhouse gases and it is almost universally supported by politicians anxious to see their town or city increase its competitive edge against its neighbours with a few more spaces than the next town. Parking provision is at least as important as building roads in supporting current levels of car dependency and car use. It is quite clear that if parking provision were reduced then car use would decline (Whitelegg, 1998). Parking is a key element in the built environment supporting non-sustainable tendencies particularly commuting to work by private motorized transport and car-based shopping trips to large retail centres. Policies aimed at reducing car parking provision are crucial in the re-engineering of the built environment. Behavioural changes in choice of mode of transport away from the car are very unlikely indeed in the presence of large numbers of car parking places and the application of 'predict and provide' policies.

Parking takes up a lot of space. The Merry Hill shopping centre to the south of Dudley has 10,000 car parking places and the National Exhibition Centre (NEC) in Birmingham 15,000. A standard parking bay is 4.8 by 2.4 metres; 24 square metres per place is assumed as a planning norm (Tutt and Adler, 1979). Applying this constant to Merry Hill results in a figure for car parking of 24 hectares and 36 hectares for the NEC. The Merry Hill car park could provide housing for 648 housing units, and the NEC 972 housing units. Local authorities supply a large number of car parking places, particularly in city centres. Eco-Logica (1995) estimated that there were over 1 million spaces supplied in this way in England alone and that this number occupied 24.3 square kilometres.

Shopping is increasingly car-oriented and the provision of parking at or near retail outlets an important consideration in planning and development at local authority level. TEST (1989) have documented the average number of car parking spaces by shop type and location. This information is contained in Table 5.10.

Table 5.10 *Average Number of Car Parking Spaces by Shop Type and Location*

Shop type	Location				
	Out-of-town	*Urban, & Out-of-centre*	*District centre*	*Town centre*	*Total*
Purpose built shopping centre	5725	4098	890	857	1940
Retail warehouse	1316	210	766	110	230
Superstore/hypermarket	382	333	423	498	456

Source: TEST, 1989

The Advertising Association (1994) has documented the number of hypermarkets and superstores in the UK. These are defined as retailing units of more than 25,000 square feet, with dedicated parking and removed from traditional shopping centres. The data refer to 1992 and are summarized in Table 5.11.

Table 5.11 *Hypermarkets and Superstores by Country/Regional Grouping, and Selling Space and Land Take for Car Parking*

Country	Number open	Selling space 000 (m^2)	Car parking area	
			(m^2)	(km^2)
UK	776	2769.2	8,492,544	8.49
England	680	2434.2	7,441,920	7.44
Wales	28	97.2	306,432	0.31
Scotland	48	176.4	525,312	0.52
Northern Ireland	20	61.4	218,880	0.22

The provision of car parking at places of work generally represents a significant proportion of total car parking places in an urban area. Private non-residential car parking (PNR) is a major source of concern for urban transport planners and those seeking to achieve a modal shift in the direction of public transport, walking and cycling. This important area of transport policy is not covered by data sources. Hudson and Shoarin-Gatterni (1993) carried out a large-scale survey of parking in London and concluded that 'off street parking information was more difficult to establish and our estimates are subject to some degree of uncertainty'. Occasionally planning documents describe the situation in a particular location. Lancaster has 3815 private spaces compared to a public off-street total of 1715. Cambridge has 40,000 PNR spaces of which 17,000 are in inner Cambridge.

TEST (1984) have made an estimate of the number of firms providing parking spaces. Though very dated it can still be used to provide an estimate of land occupied by car parking for this purpose. As the estimate predates the development of business parks we can assume that there is no double counting of car parking spaces between these two categories. The TEST estimate is based on an analysis of data in the National Travel Survey documenting car drivers' journey to work ending with parking in a firm's car park or private car park paid for by the firm. This results in a national estimate of about 5 million parking spaces provided by the employer (TEST, 1984, p 39). There is no way that this figure of 5 million can be disaggregated into sub-categories such as multi-storey, underground, ground level. It cannot, therefore, be used to quantify land take. Five million spaces at ground level would require 120 square kilometres of land.

Lothian Regional Council (1992) have conducted a survey of car parking which included PNR. Their survey of 16 cities in the UK revealed 97,626 PNR places, an average of 6102 per city. We can use this average to make an estimate for PNR places for England. We will assume a cut off point for city size of 100,000; our estimate will comprise those 53 urban areas in England with a population greater than 100,000 (OPCS, 1984). Thus we can calculate:

$$53 \times 6102 = 323,406 \text{ spaces} = 7,761,744 \text{ m}^2 \text{ or } 7.76 \text{ km}^2, \text{ assuming } 24 \text{ m}^2 \text{ per space.}$$

No data are available to identify the proportion of this total that is surface car parking as opposed to underground or multi-storey.

London merits separate treatment and in any case is not part of the Lothian Region survey. The average number of PNR spaces per urban area in the Lothian Region survey was 6102. Hudson and Shoarin-Gatterni (1993) have produced data to show that central London has 43,464 PNR spaces. If we assume ground level parking this would occupy a land area of:

$$43,464 \times 24 \text{ m}^2 = 1,043,136 \text{ m}^2 \text{ or } 1.04 \text{ km}^2.$$

Given the use of multi-storey and underground car parking in Central London we cannot assume that the PNR total is ground level and no data are available to permit a disaggregation into different kinds of car parking. No data are available on PNR spaces in London outside the central area defined by Hudson et al.

Land take for employee parking at places of work is very difficult to quantify. We will carry forward the estimate of car parking space in English towns with a population greater than 100,000. This is an overestimate because of the problem of disaggregation into different kinds of car parks. We will not include any estimate of car parking space in Central London because of the likelihood that a significant proportion will not be surface car parking and we will not include any estimate of employee car parking in outer London because there are no data. The overall result of these exclusions will be to underestimate land take for car parking.

Education is an important journey purpose and is increasingly important as a traffic generator both for school trips and for higher education. The impact of school trips is felt in all urban areas as levels of congestion rise and fall in time with the rhythm of term time and school holidays. Schools traffic can account for 20 per cent of the traffic volume in the morning peak in urban areas in the UK and much of this demand could easily shift to public transport, walking or cycling. This shift is the subject of a national 'Safe Routes to School' campaign in the UK. The rise in motorized trips to schools and the decline of the alternatives has been documented in some detail by Hillman et al (1990) and linked to serious social consequences for children through their loss of freedom and independent mobility. The size and location of schools is an important variable in the sustainable transport equation and there is a very clear link between size, location and car dependency. Schools that are very large serve a large catchment area and have a higher proportion of staff and children who travel to school by car than in the case of smaller schools serving populations within walking distance.

In January 1993 there were 32,997 schools in Great Britain (Walton, 1994, Department of Education, Darlington, personal communication). The number of parking places at schools is very variable indeed and for the purposes of this exercise we will assume ten parking places per school. This is an extremely conservative assumption given the range of staff size at schools from under 5 to over 100. Car parking standards at schools recommend one space for every two staff plus additional space for visitors. In practice these standards will be difficult to produce and for a proportion of schools parking will spill over onto nearby residential roads. If we assume 24 square metres for each parking space then the amount of parking on school grounds can be evaluated as:

$$32,997 \times 10 \times 24 = 7,919,280 \text{ m}^2 \text{ or } 7.9 \text{ km}^2.$$

Universities are a particularly sensitive barometer of increasing car dependency and one that can be tracked through time by monitoring car parking land take. The University of Lancaster was founded in 1964 on a green field campus site three miles south of the centre of Lancaster, beyond the edge of the built-up area in the countryside. The university has 1665 staff and a student population of 7100 (1992). The student total is expected to grow to 10,000–15,000 by the year 2000. One-third of the students and two-thirds of the staff commute by car. This level of car dependency is encouraged by a clear policy of preference towards car-based access. This manifests itself through car parking provision (2500 spaces) at a considerable cost to the university, and no financial support to public transport. Travel to and from the University generates 3.5 million passenger kilometres per annum and over 700 tonnes of pollutants. The projected increase in student numbers will create a demand, without a change in behaviour, for an additional 1480–3330 parking places (Armstrong et al, 1994). Campus universities (eg Lancaster, Keele, Sussex) are large traffic generators and contribute significant amounts of pollution and congestion to the road network in their areas. The response of British universities to this problem is very weak with most charging very little for car parking places and refusing to implement strategies to reduce car commuting.

Residential car parking provision is difficult to calculate. There are 23,298,374 physically separate households in Britain (OPCS, 1993). The breakdown into type of housing and land take for domestic curtilage parking is shown in Table 5.12.

The amount of space allocated to cars in this assessment of land take is enough to provide for over 1 million new homes (1,035,477).

Table 5.12 *House Types in Great Britain in 1991 and Land Take for Car Parking*

House type	Number	Land-take (km²)
Detached	4,637,909	222.61
Semi-detached	6,703,921	160.90
Terraced	6,718,364	
Total		383.51

Note: the detailed calculations and assumptions in this calculation can be found in Eco-Logica (1995).

A number of transport related land uses have been excluded from these calculations of transport's land take, notably airports, airport parking, social leisure and recreational facilities and business parks. Details of these are presented in Eco-Logica (1995). The land allocated to car parking in all these locations is more than enough to provide for all the predicted 4.4 million homes deemed to be necessary in England over the next 20 years. Clearly it would be unreasonable to reduce to zero car parking provsion at every possible origin and destination for a typical journey but equally it would be foolish to build 4.4 million new homes on 'green' land. The point is that the built environment has more than enough flexibility to manage the demand for new homes, to locate new homes on 'grey' land and in under-utilized buildings and to substitute homes for car parking places on the back of a genuinely effective sustainable transport policy. Indeed a policy not based on these trade-offs and substitution possibilities against a background of demand management is not a policy that can be described as conforming with sustainable development principles.

There are, moreover, global issues that have to be confronted. Our ecological footprints (see Chapter 2) are too large and make it necessary to reduce fossil fuel mobility and land take. Our car dependency is based on global patterns of energy and raw material extraction and transport. Oil, bauxite, rubber, iron, rare minerals for catalytic converters and much more are required to feed car manufacturing and repair. A full audit of the car and its lifetime impact would require a map of its global footprint and this footprint is likely to get much bigger if predictions of alternative fuels come to fruition and we substitute fuels that began their life as crops for fuels that were extracted from under the ground or under the North Sea. The size of the global footprint might well exceed the amount of land allocated to the roads and secondary uses identified in this chapter.

The calculation of the size of the final land take reveals a process of land conversion that proceeds and accelerates in a large number of non-connecting policy areas and institutional responses to travel demand. The whole really is greater than the sum of the parts and the spread of car parking around universities, hospitals and airports demonstrates the close links between land take, higher levels of car commuting and the demands for more road space. The analysis above has revealed the interdependencies of land take for road space and land take for car parking and auto-dependency. If land for car parking is reduced then the cycle can be interrupted and the demand for new road space dampened down as land uses adjust to different patterns of transport supply and better public transport, walking and cycling facilities are installed. Land is a scarce and finite resource and green field developments to maintain auto-dependency are a particularly inefficient user of land. Cars are only used for 2.8 per cent of the time and then often by one person (UPI, 1993b). The rest of the time they are parked somewhere doing nothing. Allocating land to such inefficient uses is bad value for money and bad prioritization given the many pressures on land in the UK in the 1990s.

The size of the forecast demand for new housing and for new traffic suggests that a choice can be made. If we can use the land use–transport planning system to move to lower levels of car dependency (with all its benefits for reduced noise and pollution) we can also win a significant 'space dividend'. It is possible to do far more with our space than we do already simply by abandoning the inefficient policies of the last 70 years that have allocated that space to traffic and parking. This reallocation would release more than enough land to satisfy the demand for new housing and would transform the built environment in urban areas into something far more attractive than parking lots.

Land is a precious resource and when choices have to be made between transport, housing, education, employment, recreation and health facilities we really must ensure that the land requirements of all these activities are compared one with another and with the remit of sustainable development. Where land can be conserved as it can by reducing the demand for transport then transport demands should have a lower priority than (say) health or education. Where universities, schools or hospitals need to expand then they can be encouraged to do so on land previously allocated to parking or on sites with no provision of new parking.

The UK car population in 1992 was 20.631 million. Dividing this total of cars into the total space produces a space requirement per car of 167.6 square metres. This figure very much underestimates the true picture but is large enough to underscore the wider ramifications of car dependency in terms of land take. The result for Germany (UPI, 1993a) was 200 square metres per vehicle. Forecasts of future levels of car ownership (British Road Federation, 1993) indicate a low value of 30.160 million and a high value of 33.713 million in 2020. Applying 1992 space norms (ie 167.6 square metres per car) to the 2020 low estimate implies that we have to find an additional 9.529 million × 167.6 square metres of space if we are to maintain current space standards. This space requirement totals 1597 square kilometres. This amount of additional land is clearly not going to be found, and the only conclusion therefore is that conditions are going to get very much worse for everyone, including drivers, by the year 2020, as the space norm is literally and metaphorically driven down.

Increasing levels of car ownership and an increasing number of trips exact a penalty in the form of increased land demands. Current levels of dissatisfaction with congestion and parking problems are likely to intensify as the pressure on facilities rises. Policy makers and politicians becoming accustomed to think in terms of air pollution and carbon dioxide emissions from transport sources need help to think through the land take implications of pursuing 'business as usual' scenarios.

Land take must be taken seriously as an indicator of sustainable development and as a measure of the gross inefficiencies of the current system of funding and prioritization in transport policy. If the primary and secondary land requirements of transport policies and road programmes were made explicit and were also published in association with forecasts of car ownership and travel demand then the alternatives to car dependency would emerge as much stronger policy options and far better value for money. Land is at the centre of sustainable transport debates. The car-free residential suburb in Bremen-Hollerland will provide high quality housing, better community facilities, clean air and better play conditions for children (Glotz-Richter, 1994). It will need 30 per cent less land than that needed for an equivalent size of development based on the usual norms for car parking and roads.

Land take is also an important European issue. The Trans European Road Network (TERN) proposed by the European Commission is based on a plan to 'complete or upgrade' 12,000 kilometres of routes by 2002 (CEC, 1993). This plan has major implications for land take in all EU countries and serious consequences for rural areas and areas of ecological significance. It would be very appropriate to translate the TERN proposal into both primary and secondary land take estimates and subject this to both a conventional EIA (but for the whole network) and a Strategic Environmental Appraisal (SEA) focusing on wider objectives including greenhouse gases, NO_x reduction, ozone levels, acidification and land take. Reducing the land requirements for road transport is central to the achievement of sustainability and quality of life and there are no reasons why we cannot begin immediately to reduce transport's land take, develop alternatives to auto-dependency and do all this within existing transport budgets and on very short time scales.

POLICY EVALUATION

Pressure on land is a crucial issue in the debate about sustainability and quality of life. Clearly it would not be desirable to meet all the demand in full for the land requirements of current projections for housing, car-based mobility, retailing, tourism and aviation. If all these demands are to be satisfied with no attempt to modify the forces that create the demand or divert that demand then we must come to terms with a land use structure that has more in common with California than with European norms together with the loss of vast tracts of countryside and the spreading of urbanization to a degree that destroys the European concept of the city.

The critical importance of land use has not been lost on successive governments in the UK. In the 1994 Sustainable Development Strategy, the British Government predicted that the size of the urban area 'could increase by over 15 per cent by 2001 compared with 1981 and still further by 2012' (Department of the Environment, 1994a, p 10). The section on land use in this strategy was very clear that development pressures were at least as strong as conservation pressures and that 'land use will continue to be one of the most sensitive pressure points'. The strategy goes further and suggests that the UK land use planning system 'will be a key instrument in delivering land use and development objectives that are compatible with the aims of sustainable development' (para 35.2, p 221). The evidence so far on the effectiveness of that system in delivering sustainable development objectives is poor. Decisions on the Newbury Bypass and on Manchester Airport Runway 2 indicate a firm commitment to strategies that have known traffic generation effects and will add to international greenhouse gas inventories. Fundamentally there is a collision between perceived economic development objectives and environmental objectives. In all planning decisions the economic objectives are given greater priority than any aspect of conservation, nature protection, biodiversity, global warming or local pollution.

The gap between the rhetoric of sustainable development and the evidence of land use change and development is enormous. The Sustainable Development Strategy talks about weighing and reconciling priorities:

> '. . . (development plans and development control) can ensure that the development needed to help the economy grow and to provide people with jobs and homes, takes place in a way that respects environmental capacity constraints and other conservation interests.'

Department of the Environment, 1994a, p 221, para 3.54

There is not one example in the UK of a development proposal that has been deemed to be undesirable because of its impact on environmental capacity. For practical planning and land use purposes the concept of environmental capacity does not exist.

In the UK, Planning Policy Guidance Note 13 (Department of the Environment, 1994b) has emphasized the importance of land use and its impact on transport as a policy instrument to reduce the physical amount of travel:

> 'the location and the nature of development affect the amount and method of travel; and the pattern of development is itself influenced by transport infrastructure and transport policies. By planning land use and transport

together in ways which enable people to carry out their everyday activities with less need to travel, local planning authorities can reduce reliance on the private car and make a significant contribution to the environmental goals set out in the Government's Sustainable Development Strategy'

Department of Environment, 1994b, para 1.3

The planning guidance continues:

'Development plans . . . should aim to reduce the need to travel especially by car, by influencing the location of different types of development relative to transport provision (and vice versa) and fostering forms of development which encourage walking, cycling and public transport use.'

Department of Environment, 1994b, para 1.7

PPG13 is a radical land use planning document which has not been translated into planning practice. The UK land use planning system has proved to be relatively inflexible in influencing major developments that have significant traffic generating characteristics and less useful still in having any impact on existing land use planning structures and their traffic demand. Local authorities on the whole lack the powers, resources and expertise to influence the exact location of new developments and in common with central government are more inclined to encourage new developments of any kind than impose constraints that might have the effect of damaging job creation or losing the development to an adjacent area with a less robust view of sustainable development.

The Dutch experience of land use–transport planning stands in stark contrast to that of the UK. In the Netherlands a specific location policy guides developments to the most appropriate location having taken into account its traffic generating characteristics. This is known as the 'ABC Location Policy'. Haq (1997) has described this system in some detail:

'To reduce total mobility within the Netherlands measures have been aimed at concentrating housing, employment and public facilities and restricting car parking spaces. The implementation of the "ABC Location Policy" in accordance with the Fourth Report on Physical Planning requires labour intensive employment and public services to be concentrated near public transport facilities. Every major housing development is expected to be served by a high grade public transport system and land use plans will need to ensure that new developments are located according to ABC location policy'

Haq, 1997, p 99

The ABC location policy works by matching specific developments to an appropriate location dependent on their traffic generation characteristics. Once designated A, B or C a company must seek out the equivalent location:

- A locations are very accessible by public transport, accessibility by cars is secondary and car commuting is restricted to 10–20 per cent of the total.
- B locations are reasonably accessible by both car and public transport. Situated on a main urban trunk road or near motorway exits. Parking is geared towards business and services with a moderate dependence on motor transport.
- C locations are mainly car oriented and are situated near motorway exits, on the fringe of urban areas and poorly accessible by public transport.

Source: Haq, 1997, p 107

The ABC policy also addresses one of the main concerns of UK land use and development policy. If a municipality does not have enough A locations to attract the large employers then it will either lose that opportunity or have to develop the necessary infrastructure. This neatly overcomes a current obstacle to sustainable land use in the UK which is the enormous pressure to accept any development on the assumption that if a municipality does not accept it, the development will simply go elsewhere. At a larger scale this same argument is the core of the case for expanding Heathrow Airport. If Heathrow does not get permission to proceed with Terminal 5 then the development will simply relocate to Amsterdam Schipol or Paris Charles De Gaulle, and the UK economy will be the loser with no reductions in greenhouse gases. This is a serious threat and one likely to have a powerful impact on the views of the inspector at the Terminal 5 inquiry and on the UK government when the time comes to make the final decision. Measures that remove or dilute this competitive bidding-up process would change the balance of these arguments allowing the urgent case for land conservation and traffic 'degeneration' to be made. This whole situation is analogous to the cold war arms race that dominated global geopolitics from the 1950s to the late 1980s. Progress with sustainable development and the management of finite resources will require the removal and dilution of spatial competition from its decision making pedestal and the restoration of a significant amount of local economic control to guarantee diversity and a measure of independence from the blandishments of the inward investor.

TRAFFIC DEMAND MANAGEMENT

Progress towards sustainable development requires a degree of change in human behaviour that goes beyond the development of sustainable suburbs, compact cities and facility rich neighbourhoods and communities. These all involve physical land use changes and intelligent manipulation of the land use–transport system but this still ignores the bulk of daily travel behaviour and activity systems. The built environment will not change that quickly. Most of the investment that is already in place will remain in place for 50 years or more and new investment will not represent much more than a few percentage points change in terms of new locations for homes or workplaces or new patterns of organization for health care or education. It is necessary, therefore, to influence choice of mode, supply of public transport services and attractiveness of walking and cycling within the constraints of the built environment as it is now. This is the role of traffic demand management (TDM) and its UK variant 'green commuter strategies'.

The objective of TDM is to persuade car users to switch to other modes of transport for daily commuting and (where possible) for journeys carried out in the course of work. Parking strategies have already been discussed in some detail and these are essential to the success of TDM. TDM brings into play the organizational element in structuring the built environment. The built environment will not be re-engineered by the actions of planners and engineers alone but it will be influenced by the decisions made by every large hospital, university, school, city hall and business park. If all these accept a new role in achieving sustainable development objectives within a supportive framework set by central government in their strategies, and local government through Local Agenda 21, then real progress can be made very quickly.

A TDM strategy has been implemented at Derriford Hospital in Plymouth with the intention of reducing the 3 million car trips generated by that site each year (Whitelegg, 1997a). Dealing with parking is critical to the success of the plan and staff car parking charges have been introduced to deter car commuting. On the inducement side of the equation bus services have been improved, cheap travel passes introduced, car sharing arrangements facilitated and bicycle use encouraged. All these steps are contributing to the shift away from car dependency which must involve both a psychological shift on the part of the car user as well as a shift in the design of the built environment.

CONCLUSION: IS THERE A PERFECT LAND USE STRUCTURE?

Much of the debate about land use and transport has focused on an 'ideal type'. The Royal Commission report on transport and the environment (Royal Commission on Environmental Pollution,1994) comes down in favour of the 'compact centralised city' (p 149). This is not very helpful. The vast majority of the population of any developed country already live in something that is very different to this ideal type. It is, for example, totally irrelevant to the need of the population of Liverpool for some dramatic shifts in housing, environmental and open space quality. The importance of land–use transport relationships lies in the sure knowledge that shorter trips are less environmentally damaging than longer, accessibility is more important than mobility and that large developments requiring vast tracts of land for parking (eg airports and shopping centres) are intrinsically non-sustainable because of their energy greedy, space greedy and polluting characteristics. An emphasis on sustainable development takes us in a different direction to that suggested by academic analyses of urban form and structure. It takes us in the direction of how to meet the needs for accessibility without adding to mobility, how to house a population without devouring the countryside in the process and how to arrange shopping, schooling and all other basic everyday activities in a way that minimizes the need to travel. All this can be done everywhere at all times. Designing new towns, new 'urban villages' and new 'growth poles' cannot help very much at all when checked against the legitimate aspirations of the residents of Europe's urban and remote rural areas. Putting into practice these alternative trajectories requires more than a drawing board and a spreadsheet. It requires the restructuring of economic relationships, psychological preferences and the refocusing of planning objectives around environmental and social principles. These are the areas of policy development that are explored further in this book.

6

HEALTH AND THE BUILT ENVIRONMENT

'They are as sick that surfeit with too much, as they that starve with nothing.'

The Merchant of Venice

The main message of this book is that the built environment in the developed world has malign effects on the wider environment, both globally and locally. These effects stem from the structure of our urban settlements, the ways in which resources are used to build and maintain them, and the lifestyles which they encourage and which in turn perpetuate them. In this chapter we extend the analysis to human health and argue that urban development which is environmentally friendly and sustainable, is also conducive to higher levels of human health at lower cost. A built environment which is ecologically healthy will also be an environment which is inhabited by healthy people, and moreover will be able to maintain a healthy population at a significantly lower cost compared to current levels of expenditure on health care in the developed world. A crucial element of the argument is that modern medicine has developed in such a way that much of it is dedicated to repairing people who have been damaged by the environment in which they live. This is a high-technology, high cost, reactive response which neglects causes and treats symptoms. A more rational response would be to change the built environment in such a way that its damaging effects on health were reduced; this would reduce the need for medical care and free resources for other uses. The sort of built environment which does not harm the wider environment, as we have seen, is a low energy, non-car-dependent, socially integrated town or city; it is precisely this sort of urban settlement in which people will find it easier to lead healthier lifestyles and remain free of the illnesses of affluence of the modern metropolis.

CONCEPTUALIZATIONS OF HEALTH AND HEALTH CARE

Modern medicine can be described as scientific rather than intuitive; curative rather than preventive; and individual patient- rather than community-based. It is also technology-dependent, drug-dependent and extremely expensive. It is analogous to an end-of-pipe solution to pollution. Furthermore, in attempts to cure illness the technology used is becoming increasingly complex and intensive in resource use, and some would argue bizarre when considering such practices as trans-species organ transplants. Set against the rising expenditure shown in Table 6.1, the effectiveness of modern medicine in terms of its ability to maintain a healthy population and its return on effort and resources used is questionable. Although life expectancy in the developed world has continued to increase, this has been largely due to the use of antibiotics in keeping older people alive. Levels of illness and time lost from work have been increasing (OECD, 1993).

It is not necessary to go so far as Illich (1975, 1977), who argued that modern medicine harmed general health levels (a process he termed *iatrogenesis*), to suggest that an alternative view of health and health care may be fruitful. Antonovsky (1984) has put forward the concept of *salutogenesis* (the processes which produce and maintain health) as distinct from pathogenesis (those processes which cause illness) as a better focus for health care in that prevention is more effective and cheaper than cure. Contemporary medical research places emphasis on pathogenesis, but even so preventive measures indicated as necessary by this research are left to lower prestige professions such as environmental health, and the medical profession concentrates on treating the illness rather than eradicating its causes. A shift of emphasis towards salutogenic approaches implies a more holistic view of illness and health in which the multi-dimensional nature of both would be recognized. The bases of good health are no secret and include a safe and clean environment, an adequate diet and satisfying work and personal relationships. The interrelationships between these factors indicate the desirability of what Hancock (1993) has termed a socio-ecological model of health in which environment (physical and social) plays an important part. A criticism that can be made of conventional medicine is that it has neglected the environmental causes of illness (and the environmental basis of health) and concentrated on post hoc, expensive and sometimes ineffective cures (Doyal, 1979). It is commonly accepted, for example, that most cancers are environmental in origin, and yet far more resources are devoted to finding a cure for the disease than to discovering and eliminating, or at least reducing, those factors in the environment which cause it.

This is not to say that all medical research is misguided. The bases of health are genetic (biological), environmental, and lifestyle-related. They are also concerned with feelings of well-being, positive outlook, value and status in social networks. There is also evidence that general levels of health are higher in societies with greater levels of equality and social cohesion (Wilkinson, 1996); the basis of this argument is that ill health is in large part generated by psycho-social factors

Table 6.1 *Share of Total Domestic Expenditure on Health (%)*

	1960	1970	1980	1990
Australia	4.8	5.6	7.1	8.3
Belgium	3.4	4.2	6.5	7.9
Canada	5.3	7.2	7.5	9.5
Netherlands	4.0	5.9	8.0	8.4
New Zealand	4.2	5.1	7.2	7.1
Sweden	4.7	7.1	9.2	8.6
United Kingdom	3.9	4.6	5.9	6.0
United States	5.3	7.4	9.2	12.2
OECD Total	3.9	5.1	7.0	7.8

Source: OECD (1993) *OECD Health Systems: Facts and Trends 1960–91*

such as stress, and that in inclusive and cohesive societies these are benign and generate good health. There is an obvious role for scientific medical research in the field of genetics. The grounds for shifting the emphasis towards discovering and securing the environmental and social foundations of health are strong, however. The impact on health levels may be more immediate and the effort involved will certainly be more cost-effective. This has been increasingly recognized in the past 20 years or so, the influential Lalonde Report (1974) leading to the World Health Organization's Ottawa Charter in 1986 and Healthy Cities Project (Davies and Kelly, 1993). All of these have an explicit emphasis on public (as distinct from individual) health and the importance to it of a health-promoting environment. Furthermore, there is increasing evidence that contemporary industrial society is changing the environment in ways which are directly damaging to human health at global and local levels. A socio-ecological approach to health becomes even more imperative under these circumstances.

CHANGES IN PUBLIC HEALTH SINCE THE INDUSTRIAL REVOLUTION

The foundations of the built environment of the developed world were laid down during the Industrial Revolution, largely during the nineteenth century. Industrialization was accompanied by rapid urbanization and the creation of an environment which was highly productive of material goods and, for substantial proportions of the population, human misery. A significant part of this misery was derived from poor health and high mortality rates, largely due to infectious diseases such as tuberculosis, smallpox, cholera and typhoid. The late nineteenth and early twentieth century saw rapid reductions in the incidence of these diseases, reductions in mortality rates and increases in life expectancies. Twentieth century urban dwellers became significantly healthier than their nineteenth century counterparts. Medical science made equally rapid progress in the twentieth century and it is tempting to link causally the two processes. To do so, however, would be to analyse incorrectly the genesis of ill health, and in particular to underestimate the extent to which it is environmental in origin. Indeed, there was a widespread and mistaken view within the medical profession in the later nineteenth century that infectious diseases were spread by 'miasma', or foul air, and the role of other disease vectors was underestimated.

McKeown (1976) has argued persuasively that the major causes of improvements in health in the late nineteenth century in England and Wales were environmental, particularly improved housing and the supply of clean water and public sanitation. These environmental enhancements led to significant reductions in the infectious and water- and food-borne diarrhoeal diseases which were the major causes of death in the nineteenth century city, although as noted above medical science at the time did not understand how. Ironically, a concern for the moral health of the working classes inadvertently enhanced their physical health, since overcrowding was condemned because it meant inadequate separation of the sexes rather than because it increased the probability of the spread of infections (Lowry, 1991). McKeown further argues that health improvements in the twentieth century have been behavioural (especially limitations in family size), dietary (connected with improved living standards) and environmental (again mainly connected to improved housing) in origin.

Ashton and Seymour (1988) have used McKeown's work to argue that since most health is gained, and lost, outside the medical sector, then the most effective way to improve contemporary health levels is to tackle those behavioural and environmental factors which affect health today with the same determination that was applied to their predecessors in the nineteenth century. Some of those factors are still causing ill health today, notably the significant rise in cases of tuberculosis among homeless persons in the UK and America which can be directly attributed to overcrowded and damp living conditions. This is not to downgrade the value of clinical care, especially in reducing the impact of those diseases which cannot be prevented, but recognizes that medicine is only one determinant of public health. The crucial issue that arises in this context is the extent to which contemporary ill health is environmental in origin, and more specifically what the precise links are between particular illnesses and environmental factors.

The commonest causes of death today in the developed world are cancers, heart disease and strokes, and asthmatic illnesses. Infection plays little part in the genesis of these illnesses (although some cancers can be associated with viruses), which can be linked to genetic, lifestyle and environmental factors. To a certain extent, they can be described as diseases of affluence since they are linked to overconsumption of rich foods, excessive intake of alcohol and tobacco and lack of exercise. Changes in individual behaviour are thus an effective means of improving health levels, and indeed public policy responses are most commonly in the field of behaviour modification. This is not surprising, since it is the easiest response and the response which demands least of government and the minimum of more general societal change.

The danger of blaming the victim for his or her illness is that more general determinants of ill health may be ignored. Obesity, for example, can be caused by poor diet, and this can be linked to poverty and lack of knowledge. People may be blamed for their ill health when they are in fact more trapped by circumstances. It makes little sense to separate disparate causes of illness since they interact with each other. Individual behaviour is not just a matter of personal choice, but is shaped by societal processes and the broader environment. Smoking, for example, is one response to stress, and to the extent that today's urban environments are stressful, it can be argued that smoking is in part an environmental problem as well as a problem of self-harming behaviour. A rational public response to smoking as a health hazard would thus include exploration of how to reduce stress in living and working environments. Since stress is also linked to other medical dysfunctions, notably heart disease and mental illness, the benefits to public health generally of reducing stress would be widespread. Similarly, it makes little sense to encourage people to exercise more if cities are so structured for cars that walking and cycling are difficult and hazardous. Sale (1980) has used this example to illustrate the 'double bind' that unless problems are tackled in a holistic way, solutions may be counter-productive:

> 'To build up heart muscle and ward off coronary disease that affect people who don't exercise, people living in cities, where natural forms of exercise have been pretty much done away with, have taken to jogging and cycling. But jogging and cycling along city streets exposes the lungs to about ten times as much air pollution as normal and the activity itself leads to hyperventilation and the inhalation of even greater quantities of pollutants, many of which are known to cause heart disease'
>
> Sale, 1980, p 29

These arguments point to the desirability of a holistic view of health in which all its major determinants are considered together. The importance of environmental factors indicates an ecological approach. The environment is increasingly modified by human activity, and hence a socio-ecological view is necessary which should encompass individual behaviour and the structural constraints within which it occurs. The efforts of medical science, ideally, would be directed towards those illnesses which occur despite a salutogenic physical and social environment.

HEALTH AND THE BUILT ENVIRONMENT

This text focuses on the built environment, but some general observations on the relationships between health and the environment are appropriate at this point. A fuller discussion can be found in Friends of the Earth (1995) and the European Environment Agency and World Health Organization Report of 1996. First, these relationships must be considered at the global as well as the local scale. Damage to the global ecosystem is already having deleterious effects on human health such as increasing incidence of skin cancers as a consequence of ozone depletion. Global warming may result in the longer term in the spread of diseases such as malaria to formerly temperate regions (the consequences of global warming, including health, are discussed in the Second Assessment Report of the Intergovernmental Panel on Climate Change, 1996). The contribution of the built environment to these global environmental processes is thus of profound importance to human health.

Second, the relationships between the environment and health are often subtle and complex, and have become more so as improved technology has enabled us to modify our environment to a greater and greater extent. Furthermore, epidemiological research is fraught with difficulties and the standards of proof which scientific medicine requires are often difficult to obtain. The environmental causes of cancer are generally accepted as being real, but it is problematic to specify these causes because scientific validation is difficult to obtain involving long-term longitudinal, and expensive, research. In the absence of such proof, action to eliminate the sources of the environmental carcinogen is legally and politically difficult. In such circumstances, the precautionary principle should be adopted, as indeed it was in the nineteenth century albeit inadvertently. Public sanitation measures were adopted then, with dramatic effects on public health, in the absence of scientific knowledge of the genesis of many of the more virulent diseases. It was not known for example that typhoid was spread by ticks, but the incidence of the disease was reduced significantly when improvements in hygiene reduced tick infestations. Similarly, reductions in overcrowding as a result of housing improvements reduced the incidence of infectious diseases, although the impetus for the changes came from Victorian prudishness rather than scientific knowledge (Lowry, 1991).

McMichael (1993) has identified three stages in the context of urbanization and human health. In the Industrial Revolution, increased population densities and overcrowding in the absence of basic sanitation produced ideal conditions for microbial infections. This was followed by a second stage in which the provision of sanitation and vaccination led to dramatic health improvements. In the third, contemporary, stage, new pollutants (notably petrochemical based) and new patterns of living have led to new patterns of illness. The fetid sewers and filthy waters of the nineteenth century industrial city were an obvious source of disease, even if medical science at the time had not discovered the exact biological processes at work. Some more recent sources of urban pollution, such as smog, are equally obvious and have damaging and acknowledged effects on public health. There are more insidious pollutants today, however, in air, water, food and our homes which are more dangerous because they are unseen and unrecognized and their effects on health unacknowledged. A holistic, socio-ecological view of health must take account of these new sources of pollution and adopt a comprehensive approach which should include mental as well as physical dimensions and, less obviously, consideration of the health of communities in a sociological sense. We will further argue that cities and towns which are environmentally benign, or *ecologically healthy*, will provide the sort of urban environment which fosters human health. In short, a healthy environment fosters a healthy population.

Cities which are environmentally sustainable provide the best opportunities for people to lead healthy lives. Actions taken to reduce the environmental impacts of our towns and cities will have the additional and welcome effect of improving urban public health levels. In arguing for greater attention to be given to the relationship between urban environments and public health, Cappon (1990) has observed that an ecologically unhealthy city may contain healthy people. This is indeed the case for most present day cities in the developed world, but important caveats are required here. First, there are considerable inequalities in urban health; these are linked to poverty and the uneven impact of bad environments which the poor suffer disproportionately. Second, good health in a damaged environment is obtained at a price in terms of resources devoted to health care. Third, it is probably not possible in the long run to sustain good health in a bad environment, even for an affluent minority, either because of the real cost or because the totality of environmental pathogenesis defeats medical science. General levels of public health can be more effectively raised by creating a more salutogenic environment. Ill health would then be more a consequence of genetics (and thus amenable to scientific medicine) and individual choice of lifestyle.

Hancock and Duhl (1986) have defined a health-promoting city as 'one that is continually creating and improving those physical and social environments and expanding those community resources that enable people to mutually support each other in performing all the functions of life and in developing to their maximum potential'. The World Health Organization's Ottawa Charter, referred to above, states that health promotion must involve the creation of living and working conditions that are safe, stimulating, satisfying and enjoyable, and when applied to urban environments, states that healthy cities should be based on sustainable ecosystems (WHO, 1986). This philosophy formed the foundation of the Healthy Cities programme (Davies and Kelly, 1993). We would strengthen this point by arguing that such cities would by definition be based on sustainable ecosystems. To what extent do our towns and cities, and indeed our rural areas, today provide such a health-promoting environment, and how can we change them if they do not?

CONTEMPORARY URBAN HEALTH – CITY SCALE

Cities and towns can be analysed as units or systems and also in terms of their constituent physical parts, buildings. We have already seen in earlier chapters that at both these levels, contemporary cities in the developed world are responsible for considerable environmental damage. This damage stems from car dependency, low energy efficiency, high resource use and urban structures which have developed as a response to a society driven by materialism and economic growth, rather than considerations of environmental sustainability. Our cities are also very unequal in terms of differing life chances of their citizens, and significant minorities are excluded from the opportunities enjoyed by the majority. They are thus physically, economically and socially unsustainable, each dimension of unsustainability contributing to the other two. In terms of human health, this non-sustainability has negative consequences. Making cities more sustainable across all three dimensions would not only reduce environmental impact but at the same time improve levels of human health both directly by reducing environmental pollution and indirectly by facilitating lifestyle change. There would be benefits at the global scale in terms of reduced greenhouse gas emissions and ozone depletion, and at the local scale by creating healthier towns and cities. Holistic approaches to urban living make solutions to problems easier, since choosing the correct policy options solves several problems simultaneously.

The essential elements of a healthy city are not in dispute. They are a clean water supply, clean air, low noise levels, adequate shelter from the elements, efficient sanitation, and freedom from poverty and fear. To satisfy the requirements for health promotion defined in WHO's Ottawa Charter and later developed in the Healthy Cities project, however, a healthy city would have to be much more than this (Tsouros, 1990). It would have to be an environment in which both physical and mental health was maximized and in which the health of individuals and the health of the community were considered as interdependent. There would have to be a general acceptance of the significance of social and environmental factors in the aetiology of disease so that considerations of health were routine in spheres of public policy outside medical care, such as urban planning, transport and housing. In so far as physical elements are concerned, it would encourage a healthy lifestyle; facilitating walking and cycling as means of transport for example. Opportunities for physical exercise and recreation should be widely and equally accessible to all, and children in particular should have every opportunity to move around safely on foot and by bicycle, to and from school and in association with their peers.

Adequate housing, free from damp and with affordable heating, should be available to everyone, irrespective of income. Non-physical aspects are equally important and in particular the creation of a low stress environment given the links between stress and ill health, both physical and mental. For residential areas this means smaller scale and more varied neighbourhoods in which social networks are supportive but non-intrusive. Rigid segregation on income or racial dimensions would be avoided so that inequalities would be softened and not deepened by the urban environment; inequality itself would be lessened. On a city scale, it means an urban structure which minimizes the stress of journeys to work and shop, to be achieved by land use and transport policies integrated in such a way as to minimize distances travelled. Not least in importance, participation in decision making and the political process would be decentralized and widespread so that everyone feels that they have some control over their environment and a stake in its future. In general terms, the built environment should be structured to reduce inequalities, eliminate the preconditions for racism, be sensitive to the needs of women, children and the elderly, and reduce unemployment.

When our cities and towns are examined today, they fail to match up to the above description and so it is not surprising that despite the huge amount of resources devoted to health services, there has been little improvement in public health. Modern cities are pathogenic in many ways, but perhaps the single most important factor causing damage to urban public health is dependence on the automobile. This has been acknowledged by the medical establishment (British Medical Association, 1997). It is tempting to think that cities in the developed world, at least in North America, the UK and Australia, were designed for the car rather than for people. This has important consequences for human health, both direct such as illnesses induced by air pollution and deaths and injury from road accidents, and indirect but just as significant in the effects of the car on urban form and community. The car poisons, smashes, isolates and stresses people in cities, and has destructive effects on social cohesion and sense of community.

Elsom (1996) has collated comprehensive data on urban air pollution worldwide and its effect on health, and emphasized the role of the car in its generation. United States Environmental Protection Agency data reveal that 60 million Americans breathe city air that has failed to reach federal air quality standards. Car-dependent Los Angeles is the worst case, with air quality failing federal standards on over 130 days per year, reaching a peak of 226 days in 1988. In Europe, too, those cities which rely most on the car for their transport suffer the worst air quality. Table 6.2 shows the sources of airborne pollutants in the UK in 1992 and the overwhelming importance of the car in their generation. London no longer suffers from the sulphurous 'pea-souper' fogs of the 1950s caused by domestic coal burning, but increasing car use has generated different types of pollution including photochemical smogs. It is estimated that the winter smog of 1991, in which concentrations of benzene increased to six times the normal level, caused 160 excess deaths.

Athens has perhaps the worst air quality in Europe; a combination of unfavourable local topography (an enclosed basin), motor vehicles and high summer temperatures creates the *nephos,* a frequent photochemical smog. Hospital admissions for heart and respiratory conditions increase by hundreds when the nephos blankets the city. In 1991, there were 180 days in Athens when air quality failed health-based standards. In Australia, Sydney has suffered from photo-chemical smogs since the 1970s and now has air quality considered worse than New York or Tokyo. The complexity of dealing with environmental issues is illustrated by the role of diesel fuels. These provide more miles per gallon of fuel than petrol and are thus more economical, but are a greater source of PM_{10} particulate pollution. There is now hard evidence from American cities that PM_{10} particulate pollution at levels below current National Ambient Air Quality Standards and World Health Organization guidelines is associated with increased levels of mortality, morbidity and hospital admissions for cardiovascular and respiratory disease (Dockery, 1996). Pollution from petrol has also now been statistically linked with heart disease; research in London revealed that 1 in 50 heart attacks treated in hospital were strongly linked with air pollutants, especially carbon monoxide, which is derived mainly from motor vehicle exhausts (Poloniecki et al, 1997). End-of-pipe solutions such as switching between fuels cannot be seen as long-term or effective solutions.

Table 6.2   *Airborne Pollutants from Transport, UK 1992 (000 tonnes)*

	Road	Rail	Air	Shipping	Total transport	Transport as % of all emissions
CO	6029	12	11	19	6071	90
NO$_x$	1398	32	14	130	1574	57
VOCs	949	8	4	14	975	38
Particulates	215	na	1	3	219	48
SO$_2$	62	3	3	60	128	4

Source: Royal Commission on Environmental Pollution (1994) *Transport and the Environment*

The car not only poisons people gradually over time, it also damages them suddenly and often fatally in road traffic accidents. The World Health Organization estimates that about 250,000 people die every year on the world's roads, more than half of these fatalities being pedestrians and cyclists. Fifty thousand Americans die every year in road accidents, equal to the total number of Americans killed in the Vietnam War. In 1990, 6.4 million people were injured in road traffic accidents in the OECD countries. Despite improvements in car safety technology such as air bags and impact bars, the rate and number of injuries is increasing in some countries, notably the United States and Canada (see Table 6.3). A study of quality of life in cities in the Pacific Northwest of America found that the risk of death by violence was greater from cars in the suburbs than from guns or drugs in the inner city. By fleeing from the violent crime of the cities, the middle classes are increasing their chance of meeting a violent death. The cost of road accidents in terms of human suffering is immeasurable, but attempts have been made to measure the monetary costs. The British Government does this routinely when assessing whether to proceed with road building schemes, and in 1993 arrived at a figure of £10.5 billion for all road accident casualties; this figure covers health treatment, police, ambulance and legal costs, lost output from time off work, and an estimate of individual willingness to pay to reduce risk of death or injury from road accidents. Similar calculations made for the US Federal Highway Administration produced a figure of $580 billion (quoted in Kunstler, 1996, p 68).

Cars also create noise. It is recognized that high levels of noise are harmful to health in a variety of ways. Direct effects include damage to hearing, but there are also more indirect non-auditory health effects via heightened stress levels and disturbed sleep. These include raised blood pressure and greater susceptibility

Table 6.3   *Road Accident Injuries*

	1960	*1990*
Australia	na	28,481[3]
Belgium	78,652	86,240
Canada	90,387	263,140
Netherlands	48,379	52,050
New Zealand	12,306	17,891[2]
Sweden	21,535	22,493
United Kingdom	339,377	347,509
United States	1,422,938	3,453,498[1]

Source: OECD (1993) *OECD Health Systems: Facts and Trends 1960–91*
Notes: 1 = 1985; 2 = 1988; 3 = 1989.

to cardiovascular disease. It has also been observed that the incidence of psychiatric disorders is higher in areas with high noise levels. Noise levels in the developed world have been increasing, mainly due to greater road and air traffic (see Chapter 2 for discussion of noise levels associated with airports). In France between 1975 and 1985 the urban population exposed to noise levels between 55 and 65 dB(A) rose from 13 million to 14 million. In the Netherlands between 1977 and 1987 the proportion of the population claiming moderate disturbance from road traffic increased from 48 per cent to 60 per cent (OECD, 1991). It is estimated that 130 million people in OECD countries are exposed to noise levels in their homes that are unacceptable. Causes of this noise in addition to traffic include increased use of domestic machinery such as power-driven garden machinery; the damage to health due to noise is supplemented by the reduction in exercise consequent upon increased use of artificial power sources.

As well as these direct effects on human health, the car has had more insidious pathogenic consequences through its role in structuring urban form and lifestyles and in particular its effect on a sense of community within the built environment. The dispersed city, at its apogee in Los Angeles, produces long distance commuting and atomistic suburban lifestyles. The frustration created by sitting in a car in a traffic jam, at the beginning and end of every working day, increases the probability of stress-related illness. The effects of a car-dependent and physically fragmented urban structure on community cohesion, and the difficulties of maintaining a vigorous and varied social life, will be discussed in Chapter 8. The health of the community is thus also damaged. A society which is atomised with little sense of community is susceptible to social breakdown and pathologies, such as alcohol and drug abuse, crime and high levels of mental illness. The car is by no means the major agent in this pathogenesis, but is certainly a factor in creating the environment within which it can occur more easily.

Responses to the problems created by car dependence have varied from country to country and city to city. In North America, the UK and Australia the response until recently has been to apply what Sale (1980) has termed *technofix*, that is more technology with its attendant concentrations of science, government, capital and resource use. These types of solution have no long-term prospect of success. For air pollution, technofix has meant developments in engine technology (such as catalytic converters) to reduce exhaust emissions. The California authorities are placing great reliance on this technology by imposing the strictest standards for vehicle emissions anywhere in the world. The percentage of cars sold in the State by the large volume manufacturers which are zero emission vehicles (ZEVs) has been set at 10 per cent by 2003 (the original deadline was 1998, but this was changed in March 1996), and by 2007 all new cars must be ZEVs or use clean burning fuel such as methanol. Honda has already responded by introducing an electric vehicle and will make its California-compliant petrol vehicles available to the rest of the United States.

Increasing the efficency of petrol-based engines reduces emissions per mile travelled, but if the number of cars in use increases or people use their cars more often, then total emissions may increase despite the improvement in engine efficiency. The electric car is seen by some as the ultimate technical solution to the air pollution problem, but misses the point that the electricity to power the batteries has to be generated somehow and will itself raise problems of atmospheric pollution. Daimler-Benz has invested $250 million in the development of a fuel cell car engine, which does not require to be recharged and which may prove more effective than the electric car. Pollution from exhaust emissions is just one of the negative aspects of car dependence, however, and a sustainable, long-term transport solution necessitates a reduction in car use and shifts to more environment-friendly forms of transport, such as buses, cycles and walking. The last two would have the further health-enhancement effect of increasing physical exercise.

Reducing the car-dependence of our cities would entail radical behavioural change and significant change in urban structure. If people are to use cars less, then they must have alternative forms of transport which are efficient and practicable. If people are to cycle or walk rather than drive, then the facilities they travel to – their workplaces, schools, shops – must be closer than at present. This would entail a restructuring of our cities in such a way as to minimize travel. Rigid segregation of land uses, traditionally favoured by land use planners, would have to be replaced by land use mix and a more even spread of facilities throughout the urban area. The 'local' area would have to become more significant to urban residents, and this will not happen unless most of what they need can be found locally. The low population densities of the dispersed suburbs would have to be replaced by higher density residential areas, which make public transport more economically viable and attractive and increase the possibilities for walking and cycling. A city organized along these lines is the core philosophy of the New Urbanism movement in American city planning (see Katz, 1994 and Calthorpe, 1993), although Jane Jacobs was expressing similar views concerning American cities much earlier (Jacobs, 1961). The relevance of cities and towns designed along these lines is that they would create an environment which encouraged healthy lifestyles. Greater opportunities for exercise have already been mentioned, but making the city easier to travel within for more of its citizens would widen opportunities for them to lead healthier lives, particularly the poor.

Diet is an important element of good health, and there is much evidence that the poor eat less healthily than the affluent. Very often, the retail outlets which sell healthy foods are spatially inaccessible to the poor in out-of-town shopping malls and they become dependent on higher price and smaller local outlets selling mainly convenience foods. A higher density, more compact city with a more even spread of retail outlets would increase choice for all households, including the poor. Such a city would also facilitate social contact and non-home centred leisure activity, hence making a full community life more feasible. It would be ecologically healthy in terms of resource use and environmental impact, and healthy for its inhabitants, both physically and mentally.

The multi-dimensional nature of sustainability – environmental, economic and social – has been stressed throughout our arguments. The links between environmental and economic sustainability will be examined in more detail in Chapter 9, but there are important connections between the economic, environmental and public health of cities which should be mentioned here. Most major cities in the developed world have a significant minority of poor households. The degree of their disadvantage is such that the term underclass is commonly accepted to denote such households. A major component and cause of their disadvantage is unemployment. This is wasteful of human resources and imposes an economic burden on the rest of the urban community in terms of social security payments. It is also harmful to public health since there are strong links between poverty, unemployment and illness. Having satisfying work is an important component of good health, mental and physical. We will demonstrate in Chapter 9 that moving towards a sustainable economy creates jobs. The same arguments apply to a sustainable city; it will have less unemployment, less poverty and less illness.

It is worthwhile at this stage reiterating Hancock and Duhl's definition of a healthy city as 'one that is continually creating and improving those physical and social environments and expanding those community resources that enable people to mutually support each other in performing all the functions of life and in developing to their maximum potential'. A city based on sustainable ecosystems would provide just such an environment. As Day (1990) has observed, modern urban life depends upon mechanical, high energy support which creates a hostile and pathogenic environment. Our present cities in which large, monotonous housing estates for the poor characterized by anomie, boredom, alienation and high levels of physical and mental illness, are locked into a mutually destructive relationship with over-consuming and environmentally damaging affluent suburbs, are not sustainable. The route to the sustainable city and a healthy city are the same.

CONTEMPORARY URBAN HEALTH – BUILDINGS

The previous section examined health in contemporary cities viewed as whole systems. This section examines the major physical components of our cities' buildings, and their effect on the health of those who live and work in them. Most people spend at least 80 per cent of their lives indoors, predominantly in the home; the minority who are employed also spend a significant proportion of their lives in their workplace. It is therefore important that the home and the workplace in particular should provide healthy environments. Schools, hospitals and other public buildings should also be designed and built to create a health-inducing environment. The thrust of our argument is the same as that for cities: buildings which are designed and built to be environmentally benign will be healthier for those who use them than contemporary buildings, many of which are both environmentally damaging and unhealthy for their users. Day (op cit) in describing modern buildings writes:

> *'Many of these buildings that form our world, however, do not even rise above their allegiances to dead material – ease of industrial manufacture, material durability or monetary savings at the expense of life-supporting construction and design. Their qualitative characteristics are life-suppressing and their physical, biological and spiritual effect on places and people damaging'*

p 185

Buildings that are constructed to be in harmony with the environment will provide healthier surroundings for their users, both physical and mental, as well as being aesthetically more pleasing than those built without consideration for, and in some cases in defiance of, the wider environment. This is the basis of the *baubiologie* concept in architecture which treats buildings as biological extensions of the people who use them. The building is considered to be a third skin, in addition to human skin and clothes, which has the same functions of protection, insulation, breathing, regulation and communication. Just as health depends upon a healthy 'first skin', so does it depend upon a healthy home.

The role that improved housing, together with sanitation, played in reducing mortality and morbidity in the late nineteenth and early twentieth centuries has already been referred to. Less overcrowding, improved heating and reductions in dampness all played an important part in reducing the incidence and virulence of infectious and respiratory illness. These housing improvements applied particularly to the poorer households who had most to gain. On the negative side, provision of housing for the poor in the last 50 years with the basic amenities of running water and sanitation has often been done on a mass scale to save money, with consequent bad effects for the residential areas built. Many people have been taken out of physical slums to anonymous and soulless estates, replacing community with a bathroom and exclusive use of a lavatory. Physical health may have benefited at the expense of mental health. A clean, brutal environment is not necessarily an improvement on a dirty, friendly one. The community spirit in the former slums provided an important support network that helped people tackle adverse conditions. Strong communities are useful in restricting crime and vandalism and enhancing security. This in turn promotes better mental health with knock-on effects on physical health. The advantages of a holistic approach to housing and health were not recognized in slum clearance programmes and in many of them health levels actually fell rather than rose after rehousing (WHO, 1992). Poor heating and damp housing have not been eradicated, however, and still contribute to ill health.

There are methodological difficulties in establishing causal links between housing and sickness, mainly because both are related to other variables, notably poverty (Bradford Hill, 1965; Ineichen, 1993). This can be used to shift attention to individual behaviour (smoking and diet, for example) as a cause of ill health and away from environmental causes. There is strong evidence, however, summarized by Ambrose et al (1996) and Smith (1989) of at least a statistical association between ill health and bad housing. Poor housing, in terms of lack of heating, dampness, air quality, overcrowding and scale has been shown to be associated with a range of physical and mental illness including tuberculosis, respiratory disease, cancers, stress, anxiety and depression. Given current levels of expenditure on treating people who live in cold and damp homes, application of the precautionary principle would suggest improving housing conditions to be an important part of an effective public health policy. This could also be helpful in meeting targets set by environmental policy. Improving the energy efficiency of dwellings, for example, especially the homes of the poor, would not only reduce energy consumption but also improve the health of those whose homes were better heated and less damp as a consequence.

Attempts to heat homes and keep them dry have rarely been done with the environment in mind. Pressures to reduce building expenditure and the discovery of new materials of lower cost, greater durability and marketable potential have caused building techniques to change in ways which have been commercially profitable but environmentally damaging and harmful to health. The percentage of homes which are now inadequate, in terms of keeping the elements at bay and density of occupation to acceptable levels, has decreased and to that extent we are better housed than in the past. Our present homes, however, present different but no less significant hazards to health. The harmful effects to health of housing in the nineteenth century stemmed from inadequate sanitation, lack of heating, damp and overcrowding. Dwellings were by and large constructed from natural, non-toxic materials such as stone, brick and wood. The structures themselves, especially if built from stone, have often survived to the present day and been refurbished. As people's expectations have risen, so has the demand for cleaner, warmer and more comfortable housing. Housing which conforms to minimum standards is expensive, and hence there have been intense pressures to build as cheaply as possible, especially for low income groups dependent on public subsidy. This has led to the search for cheaper, lower maintenance and more durable building materials to replace traditional products such as stone and wood. Modern industry has responded to this market opportunity and contemporary homes are now built with and contain more and more manufactured rather than natural substances, many being petrochemical based. Wood is replaced by UPVC for windows, synthetic materials replace wool in carpets and plastic replaces wooden furniture and fittings. The market cost of these products, however, does not reflect their real cost in terms of externality effects such as environmental impact, and related to this, their effects on health (Daly and Cobb, 1989).

In order to make buildings warmer, they have been heated more and made airtight to prevent heat loss. When combined with the increasing use of synthetic materials which give off gas at room temperature or below, known as volatile organic compounds (VOCs), this has sealed within them an increasingly diverse mixture of gases, the effects of which on health, singly or in cocktail mixes, were unknown when the materials were developed. Research in the United States by the Environmental Protection Agency into Indoor Air Quality (IAQ) discovered almost 300 VOC compounds in a single building, and over 900 in total (Tucker, 1989). The commonest of the VOCs are formaldehyde, organochlorines, and phenols (see Table 6.4). It is now apparent that these gases are harmful to health, and cause irritation to the skin, eyes, nose and throat, breathing difficulties, headaches, nosebleeds and nausea, and most seriously, some are carcinogens. In addition to these more recent pollutants, buildings can still contain the products of fossil fuel burning such as carbon monoxide, nitrogen dioxide, sulphur dioxide and carbon dioxide.

Not all naturally occurring gases are benign. Radon is a known carcinogen which diffuses into dwellings from the ground, and can become concentrated in badly ventilated buildings. When trapped in a building with inadequate ventilation, these gases, natural and synthetic, produce an unhealthy and potentially lethal environment. The effects of this have been most noticeable in modern offices and public buildings, where people have complained of a variety of recurrent symptoms which has been termed 'sick building syndrome' (Rostron, 1996). These include headaches, fatigue, irritation to the eyes and nose, nausea and inability to concentrate. They may also lower tolerance to other substances to which people are allergic. Research in the United States has estimated that improving indoor environments could reduce health care costs and sick leave and increase worker performance, resulting in an estimated productivity gain of at least $30 billion annually (Fisk and Rosenfeld, 1997). Since VOCs and the gaseous products of combustion are also present in houses, then a similar threat to health exists in the domestic environment.

Sick building syndrome is not caused by VOCs alone; other factors include air which is too hot or too dry, biological agents such as carpet mites and pollen, and particulate matter such as dust and cigarette smoke. Symptoms appear to be worse at higher temperatures, and there is evidence that buildings with air-conditioning are more susceptible than those with natural ventilation. It has proved difficult to associate particular VOCs with specified symptoms because of the complexity of processes involved, but the existence of the syndrome is

Table 6.4 *Volatile Organic Compounds Found in Buildings*

Compound	Health effect	Product
Formaldehyde	Eye and throat irritation; causes headaches, dizziness and breathing difficulties. Possible carcinogen.	Chipboard, adhesives, urea formaldehyde foam insulation (UFFI)
Organochlorines	Eye, skin and lung irritation; cause headaches, nausea, damage to central nervous system and depression. Carcinogenic and may damage liver and kidneys.	Air fresheners, polishes, plastics (eg UPVC)
Phenols	Corrosive to skin, damage to respiratory system.	Disinfectants, resins, plastics, paints, varnishes, preservatives

Source: Pearson, 1989, p 51

now accepted. The precautionary principle indicates greater care being taken with the way we build and the materials we use in the domestic and non-domestic environments. A particular example of sick building syndrome is the Inland Revenue offices in Liverpool (Ward, 1995). These are being demolished and staff moved to other offices because of ongoing problems of dry eyes, sore throats and headaches. Remedial work to the building to solve the problem would have cost £55 million. Conscious of their responsibility to protect public finances and lower absenteeism due to sickness, the Inland Revenue's new offices in Nottingham have been built with the health of the staff in mind. They have also been built with the health of the environment in mind; rather than relying on air-conditioning and heating to manufacture the internal environment, passive solar heating and cooling and the use of appropriate lighting will ensure a healthier working environment and a lower impact on the natural environment.

The threat to public health posed by buildings may be as great today as it was in the Industrial Revolution. In order to make our homes, offices and schools warm and dry we have made them air tight. Many of our homes, especially for the poor, are still damp and inadequately heated with consequent deleterious effects on health. These require to be better heated and insulated. Is it possible to build in such a way that we are protected from cold and damp, and yet can also breathe air indoors that is free from toxic pollutants? The answer is yes, by adopting construction practices that are environment-friendly. In so doing, we will also be creating buildings that are healthy for their users. This argument has been widely expressed elsewhere (for example by Pearson, 1989). Construction should work with the environment, and not against it as with much contemporary practice. It makes no sense environmentally to seal office workers in steel and glass boxes which are overheated by the sun and require air-conditioning to cool them. This is wasteful of energy and contributes to global warming in a spiral of greater and greater environmental damage. The buildings so created also make those within them ill. It is possible to build in a different way that does not cause ecological damage and which also produces healthy indoor environments.

For office blocks, the heat created by machinery and people can be dispersed by using natural ventilation instead of air-conditioning. By allowing the sun to heat air in one part of a building, and have windows open elsewhere, air is drawn through the building, cooling the interior and dispelling stale air. Examples of this system, known as passive stack ventilation, can be found in the UK (the Inland Revenue Offices in Nottingham, mentioned above), France (the Hotel du Departement in Marseilles), the Netherlands (the Nederlandse Midden-standsbank headquarters in Amsterdam), Germany (the Ökohaus in Frankfurt-am-Main) and Canada (the University of British Columbia's C.K. Choi Institute of Asian Research). Passive stack ventilation can be combined with energy efficiency measures (such as high insulation standards, solar gain and combined heat and power systems) and use of renewable and non-toxic building materials (such as wood) to produce buildings which are environment friendly and warm (or cool in summer), dry and healthy for those who use them. These construction practices can also be used for domestic buildings. The technology required is simple and proven, and there are adequate substitutes for the unhealthy products currently used in buildings (Holdsworth and Sealey, 1992; Anink et al, 1996; Thomas, 1996). Cellulose, for example, can be used as insulation instead of urea-formaldehyde foam, and linoleum can be used instead of vinyl-based floor coverings.

The links between buildings and health must include a consideration of mental health. There is now a growing movement in architecture which emphasizes buildings, particularly homes, as healing environments in the fullest sense. Some add a spiritual dimension in this context (Day, 1990) although all emphasize the stressful nature of modern living and the important role buildings can have in reducing stress levels. The idea that architecture can be good for the spirit can be traced back to the Ancient Greeks and was later taken up by Rudolf Steiner, became an important element of Art Nouveau and influenced twentieth century architects such as Frank Lloyd Wright (Pearson, 1995). Twentieth century architecture has been dominated however by function and scientific, rational organization. This produces hard buildings composed of straight lines and right angles which are efficient but unfriendly. They are also designed to separate people from the natural environment and its biological rhythms of night and day, summer and winter. Buildings designed according to organic, ecological principles are softer, with curves, colours and natural lighting. This produces a more restful, healing environment. An excellent, and successful, example of such architecture is the Hundertwasserhaus in Vienna, a social housing scheme characterized by curves, colours and unpredictability.

The built environment, whether considered at the scale of the city or the individual building, will be healthier for people if it is itself healthy for the wider environment. The reasons for this are at one level obvious and at another level less obvious but more important. At the obvious level, increased technology allied with a materialistic society, together with insufficient scientific understanding of the processes at work, has caused the built environment to have an increasingly significant and largely negative ecological impact. This in turn has had a pathogenic effect on human health. At the less obvious level, the built environment has been constructed in a way that ignores complexity and is driven in its development by centralized control. Alexander, in arguing for a system of producing housing that is both efficient in its use of resources and humane in its outcomes, has suggested the biological world as the appropriate model:

> *'In the biological world, there is always an immense complexity; and this complexity comes about as a result of a process of minute adaptation, which painstakingly, slowly, ensures that every part is properly adapted to its conditions . . . The system contains huge numbers of variables, huge numbers of components. And the process which produces it, the living process of adaptation which is typical in all biological systems, guarantees that each part is as nearly 'just right', appropriate to its local conditions, and appropriate in the large, so that it also functions well as part of some larger system than itself.'*

> Alexander, 1985, pp 33–34

The problem with the system that has produced, and continues to produce and modify, the built environment is that it does not adapt to its conditions. If there is a dysfunction, the most common response is to ignore the conditions so that the system can press on regardless, but at greater and greater cost and more resource use. The advances of technology have enabled some people to become rich and to believe that the wider environment is robust enough to withstand any level of exploitation. This is not sustainable in the long term. Centralized control facilitates this process of non-adaptation. If society operated more like a biological system, recognizing and respecting complexity and decentralizing control to the maximum possible, then the impact of the built environment would be less malign, and the health of those living within it would be better with less health care.

ACHIEVING A HEALTHY BUILT ENVIRONMENT

The final chapter of this book will present a full discussion of the difficulties in moving towards a sustainable built environment and possible means of overcoming them. The long-term negative consequences of not overcoming these difficulties will far outweigh any discomfort involved in tackling them sooner rather than later. Similar conclusions can be drawn concerning public health. Modern medicine is becoming more and more expensive. An ageing population and increased dependency on drugs and high technology, are causing upward pressure on health care expenditure which is economically unsustainable. Despite increased spending on health services, general levels of public health are not rising, and inequalities in health are proving to be persistent even in countries such as the UK where most health care is free at the point of delivery (Townsend and Davidson, 1982). A wiser approach to public health would move away from reactive curative medicine and towards preventive, community medicine based on a socio-ecological model of health. The importance of a healthy environment, especially the built environment where most people live and work, in achieving better health for the maximum number, cannot be overemphasized. Health care should be relieved of the burden imposed on it by the unpriced externality costs of other public agencies (road builders, for example) which create unhealthy environments. Health care, in fact, should be more concerned with health and less with finding increasingly expensive and high technology means of allowing people to live in biological maladjustment to the natural environment rather than in harmony with it.

This is not to say that resources should suddenly be shifted from curative to preventive medicine, or that large hospitals with expensive intensive care units should be closed. Those who fall prey to cancer, for example, should expect to receive radiotherapy, chemotherapy or alternative therapies if they ameliorate their suffering, prolong their lives, or both. Illnesses which are predominantly genetic in origin (such as cystic fibrosis) will require scientific medical research to find the means of reducing human suffering. In the long term, however, it makes more sense to tackle health issues by making our environment as health-inducing as possible. This would entail health being considered by all those decision makers who influence the management of our towns and cities, not just those concerned directly with health care. The most effective way to do that is to make our towns and cities environmentally, socially and economically sustainable. By caring for our environment, we are caring for ourselves.

7

SUSTAINABILITY AND SOCIAL EQUITY

'The only things worthy of each are those which are good for all; the only things worthy of being produced are those which neither privilege nor diminish anyone; it is possible to be happier with less affluence, for in a society without privilege no one will be poor.'

André Gorz, 1983, p 8

Outside Oberhausen, in the Ruhr, lies CentrO, Europe's biggest shopping mall. Built on the site of a now-demolished steel mill owned by Thyssen and opened in September 1996, CentrO is a physical embodiment in concrete, glass and steel (and many other non-renewable and high material-intensity resources) of the significance of consumption in the developed world. Described by Newnham (1996) as a 'cathedral to consumption', this DM 2 billion investment is a mixture of fantasy and materialism, cocooning shoppers in a surreal theme park. Shoppers are physically protected from the outside world and socially detached from its problems. Most of the shops, including Charlie's Farm, are under a glass roof to ensure that the seasons are homogenized; the process of parting shoppers from their money is facilitated by keeping them comfortable. Charlie's Farm is a supermarket, where trees with rubber mouths say 'Let's go shopping the American way' in both German and English, there is a collection of plastic farmyard animals (the hens sing), a farmer who fishes and a windmill with revolving sails. Elsewhere in CentrO, lasers project holograms on to water curtains. Shoppers can drink Guinness in an Irish pub, buy sushi or patronize the inevitable McDonalds. For the children there is a pirate's ship.

No more eloquent a statement of the impact of a materialistic culture on the built environment can be found anywhere else in Europe. What is particularly depressing about CentrO is that it is in Germany, where out-of-town shopping centres have been resisted and more care has been taken with the built environment than in the UK or America, the home of the shopping mall. CentrO will inflict serious damage on the natural environment. It has space for 10,500 cars. It is heated in winter and cooled in summer, because most of it is indoors. Planet Hollywood, which gives Germans an ersatz taste of American cuisine, has plans to make hamburgers in Germany and send them to the UK for European-wide distribution; hamburgers sold in CentrO will thus be made locally, sent to the UK, and then sent back to CentrO for sale. This might make sense to Planet Hollywood's accountants in terms of market economics, but it makes no sense in terms of real resource use.

Above all, CentrO's purpose is to maximize consumption. On the first Sunday after it was opened, over 250,000 people visited it even though all the shops were closed due to Germany's strict trading regulations. Even when buying is not possible, CentrO whets the appetite and feeds the fantasy of future consumption. The consumption which sustains CentrO, and which it in turn encourages, is the source of our environmental malaise. This is true not only of the volume of that consumption, but also its distribution. CentrO feeds the materialistic fantasies of those with the income to realize them, but is a physical reminder to those that are poor that they are outsiders to mainstream society. Situated in a region of high unemployment (and indeed located on the site of a demolished steelworks), there is no shortage of poor households who are physically close to CentrO, but economically incapable of buying in it. Shopping malls are welcoming to those with money, but hostile to the poor, especially if they are shabbily dressed or exhibit non-conventional behaviour. Their presence would disturb the comfort of the others and slow down the speed of purchasing.

Just across the North Sea in Gateshead lies the Metro Centre, the UK's biggest shopping mall. Although with less floorspace than CentrO, it has parking for 12,000 cars. On an average Saturday, 100,000 people visit the Metro Centre, 80 per cent arriving by car. Soon after it was opened, the local road infrastructure had to be expanded to cope with the traffic, and yet it can still take up to an hour to get away from the Centre at peak times. Across the River Tyne lie Benwell and Scotswood, two of the poorer districts of Newcastle. Overlooking the Metro Centre and less than a mile away as the crow flies, many of the residents of these adjacent areas might as well live on Mars as far as the Metro Centre is concerned; they may be physically close to it, but their incomes are too low for them to shop there.

The examples of CentrO and the Metro Centre (and many similar shopping centres in America, the UK, France and elsewhere) demand a consideration of the links between environmental damage and the type of society associated with that damage. Issues of equity, both inter- and intra-generational, are particularly important in this context. A fundamental dimension of sustainability is equity between generations. Each generation should not leave to its successor an environment whose capacity to support life has been damaged or an environment within which quality of life is diminished. This does not, of course, preclude passing on to our descendants an environment that has been enhanced. Indeed, given the scale of current environmental degradation, such an enhancement is necessary. Inter-generational redistribution of environmental quality may be a sine qua non for long-term human survival. Within the sustainability debate, consideration of redistribution and equity is invariably extended to cover the intra-generational dimension. It will be argued in this chapter that a precondition for improving our environment is greater social justice within the current human population, and that inter-generational equity will not be achievable without greater intra-generational equity.

Chapter 2 has discussed the concept of sustainability in detail, and it is important to re-emphasize here its multi-dimensional nature. We can distinguish between environmental, economic and social dimensions of sustainability for heuristic purposes, but must realize that sustainability is like a three-legged stool: unless all three legs are present, the stool falls over. Damage sustainability on one dimension, and the other two dimensions will also be harmed. Improving environmental quality will enhance social justice and benefit the economy. Each type of sustainability depends on the other two. Chapter 9 concentrates on economic aspects of sustainability; this chapter considers social issues and the vital part that social equity plays in shaping and maintaining a healthy built environment.

Durning (1992) has highlighted the connections between environmental protection and social equity at the world level, showing that a redistribution of consumption and material living standards from the developed world to the poorest countries is essential for the preservation of the global ecosystem. At a more local scale in terms of the built environment, we will demonstrate that the social inequalities so evident in our cities today are barriers to ecosystem protection, and equally that reductions in social inequalities can be achieved most effectively within an environmental framework. The previous chapter, for instance, argued that ill health was in large part environmental in origin and that the poor were more likely to experience ill health than the rich. Degraded environments are also associated with poor people and hence their health will benefit most from environmental enhancement. By addressing environmental, or ecosystem, dysfunction we are at the same time enhancing public health and reducing social inequality. Furthermore, Wilkinson (1996) has demonstrated that social inequality has an effect on public health independent of environmental factors: a more equal society is a healthier society. A society which cares for its environment, however, will be a fairer and more cohesive society and hence change to enhance the environment will inevitably be linked to improvements in public health. The value of sustainability as a guide to action is that by definition several problems are addressed simultaneously and solutions are reinforcing across different areas of concern.

SUSTAINABILITY AND SOCIAL SYSTEMS

Although intra-generational equity is usually included with inter-generational equity as an important element of sustainability, the justification for this in the environmental literature is often weak or absent at levels other than the global. At the national, regional and local levels, social equality and environmentalism tend to be accepted as complementary and indeed mutually necessary, without justification. This may be because intuitively it 'feels right', but more rational arguments are required if there is to be progress towards sustainability in practice. As well as knowing how in scientific terms natural systems are being damaged and physical carrying capacities threatened, we need to develop appropriate social structures to prevent further environmental degradation. Turner et al (1994) for example justify the inclusion of intra-generational equity on the basis of ethical consistency (having accepted inter-generational equity), but make no reasoned argument linking a fairer society with environmental sustainability. The European Sustainable Cities First Report, commissioned by the European Community, even goes so far as to state that 'There is no logically necessary link between the principles of equity between generations and equity within the present generation.' (Expert Group on the Urban Environment, 1995, para 5.9). Even the literature devoted to the politics of environmentalism gives largely unsatisfactory explanations in this context, although the consensus is that environmental protection depends for its realization on a just society. We attempt here to provide a more satisfactory argument in general theoretical terms. The following section applies the arguments to the specific context of the built environment.

A useful starting point is the attempt by 'deep greens' to draw lessons for the required social and political organization of a sustainable society from natural ecosystems. These have been succinctly summarized by Dobson (1990). Qualities essential to the functioning of natural ecosystems are associated with social and political characteristics of human social systems. Hence species diversity points to toleration, stability and democracy; longevity indicates tradition; and inter-dependence favours equality. A strong exponent of this view is Bookchin, who with respect to the role of hierarchies argues as follows: 'What renders social ecology so important is that it offers no case whatever for hierarchy in nature and society; it decisively challenges the very function of hierarchy as a stabilising or ordering principle in both realms' (Bookchin, 1980, p 36).

Hayward (1995) expresses caution about drawing lessons for society from natural systems, pointing out that decentralists pick on the lack of hierarchy in nature, whereas Social Darwinists come to very different conclusions regarding social systems and natural ecosystems. Both Hayward and Dobson question whether extrapolations from nature to society are justified or helpful. Inter-dependence, for example, is obviously important for all systems, natural and human, but it is not at all clear why this necessarily implies social equality in human societies. It is possible to conceive of a human society which is inter-dependent, functional and unequal; as indeed many contemporary societies are. Others have also criticized the uncritical transfer of natural ecological system properties into the realm of human society, for example in Martell (1994, p 139): 'Ecological stipulations do not necessarily imply egalitarian or pluralist arrangements . . . there are a wide range of problems – for example on justice, equality and liberty – which environmental criteria are not equipped to solve'. And further: 'Ecological imperatives require some forms of social and political response but cannot alone determine them across the board, and structures of a sustainable society have to be judged in terms of traditional as well as ecological perspectives' (Martell, 1994, p 151).

This is a more balanced and appealing argument which accepts that some desirable social goals – social justice, for example – are achievable without consideration of environmental objectives. A society which is collapsing under environmental problems may still be socially just if the attendant human misery is equally shared (although it is probable that social justice is more easily achieved and maintained under less stressful conditions). Ryle (1988) has argued similarly that an authoritarian society could exist in which an elite pursues an ecologically wasteful lifestyle which is maintained at the expense of a suppressed majority living a frugal and sustainable life; such a society could conceivably be environmentally friendly when considered as a whole, but would not be politically sustainable in the long run. To establish a necessary connection between environmental protection and social equity we need more direct and practical arguments than simplistic transfers of system qualities from the natural to the social world. There are important connections between care for the environment and social equity, but they must be specified and demonstrated.

These connections are easiest to illustrate at the international level. It is generally accepted that the health of the global ecosystem depends on a redistribution of material wealth from the developed to the developing world (see Durning, 1992). Long-term global sustainability cannot be achieved if the poor of the developing world attain the consumption levels of the developed world, and more to the point neither can it be achieved if those in the developed world attempt to maintain their current levels of consumption. The material standard of living of the poorest countries needs to be raised, but for global ecosystems and resources to be maintained this can only be done if the rich nations reduce their consumption. Equity and sustainability are thus inextricably linked. Furthermore, in the developing world the poor are more directly dependent upon natural ecosystems and the exigency of poverty instigates environmentally damaging responses. The use of marginal land and deforestation leads to soil erosion and less capacity to remain self-sufficient; the desperate need for industrial employment encourages the acceptance of low pollution standards. Raising living standards allows the poor to follow more sustainable livelihoods. In the developed world, where the links with natural ecosystems are less direct, but no less significant, the connections between equity and sustainability are less obvious.

The key link between equity and sustainability is that of consumption and specifically the distinction between needs and wants (see Young, 1990). Capitalism depends for its continued survival on ever-expanding consumption and the creation within people of *wants*, which are distinct from and not necessary to their basic *needs* for food, warmth, clothing and shelter. These wants are in the main material, rather than non-material and are stoked by the advertising industry irrespective of the capacity of the ecosystem to satisfy them over the long term. They are also stimulated indiscriminately, in those who have the means to satisfy them and within the poor who have not. This is socially divisive and accentuates the gap between rich and poor. Keynes made a similar distinction between human needs, grouping them into *'two classes – those needs which are absolute in the sense that we feel them whatever the situation of our fellow human beings may be, and those which are relative only in that their satisfaction lifts us above, makes us feel superior to, our fellows'*

Keynes, 1951, pp 365–66

In an economy becoming more productive, the latter goods become more widely available and hence less attractive. There is thus continuous pressure on capitalist producers to innovate, or portray products as new and improved. Whether the use value of the products has been enhanced or not is irrelevant; hence the importance of advertising. The social differentiation of consumption is essential to economic growth and hence a consequence of capitalism is social inequality; when coupled with rapid technological change this generates a marginalized, unemployed minority whose labour is not required and who cannot participate in the consumption upon which social status depends. Whilst the majority continue to indulge their wants and are never satisfied, the marginalized minority live with heightened but unsatisfied appetites and some of their basic needs unmet. Those lucky enough to be able to participate in the consumer society are not necessarily any happier. For the majority who have ever-rising material living standards, increasing consumption is accompanied today by job insecurity, rising crime, unsafe cities and environmental degradation. Perhaps the greatest loss for those not subject to poverty is a sense of community or belonging; people seek happiness through consumption and live increasingly private, atomized lives. This situation is not new. Galbraith argued in the late 1950s that ever increasing material production, far from increasing social welfare and human happiness, was bringing increasing problems. It is worth quoting his elegant description of urban America of the time:

'The family which takes its mauve and cerise, air-conditioned, power-steered, and power-braked car out for a tour passes through cities that are badly paved, made hideous by litter, blighted buildings, and posts for wires that should long since have been put underground. They pass on to a countryside that has been rendered largely invisible by commercial art. (The goods which the latter advertise have an absolute priority in our value system. Such aesthetic considerations as a view of the countryside accordingly come second. On such matters are we consistent). They picnic on exquisitely packaged food from a portable icebox by a polluted stream and go on to spend the night at a park which is a menace to public health and morals. Just before dozing off on an air-mattress, beneath a nylon tent, amid the stench of decaying refuse, they may reflect vaguely on the curious unevenness of their blessings. Is this, indeed, the American genius?'

Galbraith, 1958, pp 207–208

Galbraith's main argument was that there was a disparity between the priority given to material, privately produced and individually consumed goods and that given to public services such as education and health. This produced private affluence and public squalor. The environment in an ecological sense received little attention in *The Affluent Society*, although Galbraith discusses pollution in more depth in his later work (see *Economics and the Public Purpose*, 1973). The message that an obsession with material consumption will not lead to happiness, however, is one with which environmentalists would agree.

The social strains caused by inequalities are supposedly eased by economic growth and the social mobility which follows from it. Galbraith (1958) noted that inequality ceased to be a salient issue in the high growth 1950s since both rich and poor benefited from that growth; increasing aggregate output was an easier and less conflict-ridden alternative to redistribution. The burgeoning consumption of the last few decades and the deepening social inequalities identified above now mean that the high growth solution to social problems is untenable. Current economic growth is ecologically unsustainable. In fact the conventional model of economic development whereby a range of problems is solved by economic growth can now be seen to be the source of the problem rather than a solution. The move towards a sustainable economy necessitates a reduction in consumption of 'wants' by the majority and a more effective meeting of the 'needs' of the deprived minority. In a non-material context, it would also mean the unemployed finding meaningful and satisfying work. There is thus a vital link between improving the quality of life of the poor relative to the rich and redirecting society towards more environmentally friendly practices. Environmental damage tends to impact upon the poor more than the rich and the rich have the means in the short run to avoid the consequences of their actions. A sustainable society, in which consumption is reduced and needs given greater priority than wants, would also be a more equal society since needs are less variable from person to person and group to group, than socially created wants. Sustainability implies greater frugality, and this in turn implies greater equality. In terms of conventional economic theory, Daly (1993a) has pointed out, following Joan Robinson, that greater equality of consumption increases total utility, or benefit, since the increase in utility gained by extra marginal consumption by the poor is greater than the marginal decrease in utility due to less consumption by the rich.

Closely linked to inequality is dependence. Richard Douthwaite (1996) describes the dependence of the population of Inishboffin, an island off the west coast of Ireland, on state benefits as a result of the decline of the local fishing and farming economy. The degree of dependence – only 5 or 6 of the 75 households are not totally reliant on state benefits – has attracted attention because Inishboffin is an island, and hence easily identifiable. Douthwaite makes the point that there are mainland populations in many developed countries with similar degrees of dependency, but they are less visible because they are submerged within our large cities in segregated and deprived housing areas. The people living in these areas are not only poor, but also dependent on the broader society to support them. They are not only deprived in a material sense, but are also denied the dignity of fulfilling a useful role in society at large. This is a source of political and social tension because the broader society is obliged to support them but has no economic use for them. Dependence is not limited to the poor, however. Those who have the incomes to maintain an adequate material standard of living can themselves make virtually none – if any – of the products which they consume. Any breakdown in the complex production, transportation and marketing processes which deliver the goods to them would have an immediate impact on the sources of their satisfaction. Most are dependent on large organizations, over which they have no control, for their incomes and for the products which those incomes enable them to consume. Furthermore, the unsatisfying and deskilled nature of most employment in contemporary industrial society leads to greater dependence on consumption as the route to happiness. The affluent are dependent upon jobs they don't enjoy and products they can't make and the poor are dependent upon hand-outs from the affluent.

A society which is characterized by persistent injustice is inherently unstable, inasmuch as there will always be forces at work to remove that injustice. A society which contains within it sharp inequalities in life chances and outcomes will be unstable since the have-nots will wish to progress and the haves will protect their advantages. A society which persistently excludes some of its members from participation in social, economic and political life is unsustainable, because that exclusion has social and economic costs. These issues have been the stuff of political argument since Marx and before, but neither right nor left in mainstream politics seems capable of finding long-term solutions. Socialism and collectivist solutions generally have been widely abandoned since the collapse of the Soviet Union, and yet the apparent triumph of capitalism and the predominance of market-led forces has had little positive impact on the poor and the dispossessed. If anything, the relative position of the poor has deteriorated. This is true at the global scale between nations and locally within our cities. The poor are getting poorer and the rich richer. The dominance of market forces has been associated with a decline in civic responsibility (Knight and Stokes, 1996), that is the willingness of people to devote their energies and time unpaid to the welfare of others through churches, trade unions, political parties and charities. There has also been a decline in more informal social networks such as the extended family and neighbourliness. The denial of both material goods and legitimate means of obtaining them to a significant proportion of a society which measures worth by consumption is an important factor in the generation of crime, as noted by Lansley:

> 'For many youngsters, crime has become a matter of survival in this new society which appears to cater only for the winners . . . Today, denial of the new trappings of consumerism means a denial of full citizenship . . . The result has been a growing lack of community cohesion and a declining sense of social commitment'

> Lansley, 1994, p 50

The glue that has in the past held society together has begun to lose its effectiveness. A society dominated by materialism is not sustainable.

At the urban level in the developed world the response from the middle classes to the urban decay and social pathologies associated with poverty has been to physically escape from them. Encouraged and assisted to do this by the real estate and construction industries, affluent white American households began to flee to the suburbs in the 1950s, a process which accelerated in the 1960s and 1970s. Detroit used to be a city of 1.8 million people, 85 per cent of whom were white; it has now barely a million citizens, three-quarters of them black. Similar processes occurred in Australia and Canada. The result is car-dependent urban sprawl, the environmental consequences of which have already been discussed, in which affluent suburbs exist in association with impoverished largely Black and Hispanic inner cities. The physical segregation of rich and poor itself has negative consequences, eloquently described by Kunstler:

> 'Today the poor in most American cities live only in the context of the poor. The only place they see the other America is on television, and then through a wildly distorting lens that stimulates the most narcissistic, nihilistic consumer fantasies. Since the poor, by definition, can't participate fully in consumer culture, the predictable result is rage at what appears to be a cruel tease, and this rage is commonly expressed in crime. What may be equally damaging is that the poor see very little in the way of ordinary polite conduct, very little civil behaviour... What they do see all around is mayhem, squalor, and disorder, and almost no evidence that it is possible to live a happy life without being a sports hero, a gangster, or a television star'

Kunstler, 1996, p 54

The fastest growing type of urban development in the United States today is the gated 'community', a residential area for the rich protected physically by private security guards as well as economically by price. It is estimated that 28 million Americans now live in such areas (Elliott, 1996, p 15). Over 30 per cent of residential development in southern California is now in this form, one particular example having a wall, moat and drawbridge, and a device that shoots a metal cylinder through the bottom of unauthorized cars. The smooth operation of the market is thus becoming increasingly reliant on force rather than consensus. In the UK, the degree of income segregation in cities is comparable, but the spatial pattern differs because of the historically more significant role of the State in housing the poor; in addition to being confined to inner city areas, substantial numbers are also housed in peripheral public sector estates. A different spatial form conceals an essentially similar phenomenon. Gated developments are now appearing in London. The response to inequality in these countries by the majority has not been to reduce it, but to protect oneself from its consequences. The rich separate themselves from the poor – or are separated by the development industry – by physical distance and security fences. Rich and poor areas coexist in an inefficient and ultimately unsustainable symbiosis. It is inefficient because of the social and economic costs in terms of crime, illness, social breakdown and welfare payments that are associated with an unjust and unequal society.

The strains and cleavages in urban society erupted into violence and rioting in the 1980s and 1990s both in the United States and the UK. With the political victory of the right in the 1980s and the reliance on market-led allocative mechanisms, inequalities have widened (see Figure 7.1). This was predicted, even welcomed by free market theorists, since it would create greater incentives and higher economic growth. The material standard of living of the poor would be raised by the trickle-down effects of this enhanced economic growth, on the principle that a rising tide raises all boats. In fact, this has not happened and the poorest in society have become poorer, both absolutely and relatively (see Barclay, 1995). Parts of our cities have become socially dysfunctional as a result of the concentration of poverty within them. The majority of society may be able to physically separate itself from this problem in gated enclaves, but it cannot protect itself from its wider consequences.

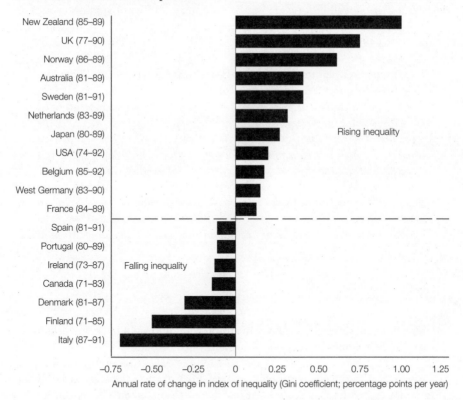

Note: Income inequality has been growing more rapidly in the UK than in other countries (except New Zealand)

Source: Inquiry into income and wealth, volume 1, Joseph Rowntree Foundation (1995)

Figure 7.1 *International Income Inequality Trends*

The political responses to the problem of poverty have been to attempt to ameliorate it through redistributive mechanisms (from the left) or, as indicated above, to rely on economic growth to raise every family's living standards whilst accepting inequalities (the right). Neither strategy has made any significant impact on the low quality of life experienced by an increasing number of marginalized households and individuals in our major cities, and this policy failure has had an impact on the rest of society in terms of rising crime, increased welfare payments and a rising tax burden. One of the key reasons – if not *the* key reason – why policies to tackle poverty have failed is that they have neglected the environmental dimension of sustainability. The key problem in tackling poverty is not how much is produced, nor how that production is distributed, but rather what is produced and how it is produced. The redirection of production (including services as well as material goods) towards needs rather than wants, and its organization to protect rather than degrade the environment, would not only be more socially just but also more environmentally benign. Effective urban policies must take into account social, economic and environmental factors and deal with them together. A coalition of voluntary and campaigning groups in the UK put together an action programme for government in 1996 based on the following assessment:

> '*In bringing together organizations concerned with poverty in the South and poverty in Britain . . . it has become evident how similar are the causes of the issues with which they deal . . . In both cases – contrary to widespread belief – environmental improvement and poverty eradication go together, since the poor almost always live in the worst environments. This has generated new connections between environmental organizations and those concerned principally with social justice: the two aims go hand in hand. And increasingly throughout this process it has become clear how the particular structures and practices of politics in Britain militate against change, whether at an international or community level; and therefore the role that democratic renewal must play in achieving the substantive ends of sustainability and social justice*'

Jacobs, 1996, p 4

This assessment can be applied beyond the UK to the rest of the developed world.

The political strategies of the conventional left and right have one important element in common which condemns them both to failure. They both depend on economic growth, as narrowly defined by mainstream economists, for their success. According to conventional wisdom, this will allow the standard of living of the poor to be raised without harming that of the affluent. The assumption is made that economic growth can proceed indefinitely in terms of resources and without adverse, or at least insurmountable, environmental consequences. This assumption is false. For reasons of common humanity the material standard of living of the poorest countries needs to be raised and this can only be done if the rich nations reduce their consumption. This has profound implications for cities in the developed world, for as we have seen they are not uniformly affluent and contain significant minorities who do not share that affluence. The poverty experienced by the poor of New York or Liverpool is not the same as that experienced by the poor of Calcutta or Rio de Janeiro, but is nevertheless real. Furthermore, a reduction in consumption and a change in lifestyle by the residents of New York and Liverpool who are not materially poor could benefit their fellow citizens who are poor and the poor of the developing world. It would also be a vital element in protecting global and local ecosystems. By reducing the environmental impact of cities such as New York and Liverpool, the problems of poverty, social exclusion and social instability would also be tackled. Reducing unnecessary consumption releases resources for more important purposes, one of which is improving the quality of life of the poor, and reduces environmental impacts.

Within our cities, the majority have managed to segregate themselves from the poor for most of the time. Environmental degradation, however, is more difficult to escape. If environmental damage continues, more strata of society and more areas within our cities will suffer. There are possible parallels here with cities in the nineteenth century, when widespread sanitation measures were introduced only when the disease associated with their absence spread to middle class areas. A major difference with the nineteenth century is that there are now threats to the environment at the global scale as a result of modern urban lifestyles, and these threats affect everyone, rich and poor alike. Technology, political power and money may enable the privileged to protect themselves from environmental decay and the social costs of poverty for a time, but ultimately ecological reality will impose itself irrespective of income. An environmental perspective on urban problems has the great benefit that it considers everyone's interests and hence has a unifying potential in a society riven with conflicts. Moreover, one of the consequences and at the same time preconditions of sustainability is a more equitable society. A 'green' society is also a just society.

THE GREEN CITY AND SOCIAL EQUITY

The major responsibility for global environmental damage lies with the developed world as a consequence of its consumption and waste production. Since the majority of the people living there are urban dwellers then the key to a sustainable global economy will be the values, lifestyles and behaviour of the citizens of the towns and cities of North America, Western Europe, Japan and Australia. A shift towards sustainable lifestyles would have profound implications for the cities and towns of these countries, and previous chapters have examined the contribution the built environment itself can make towards sustainability. In this section we address the issue of the links between social equity and the sustainable city.

At the most general level, material consumption by the majority will need to fall if the global issues of greenhouse gas emission, resource depletion and pollution are to be addressed. This would release resources which could be used for raising the quality of life of the poor, thereby reducing social inequalities. There are also links between environmental impacts and inequalities of power. At the local urban level, negative externalities such as air and noise pollution have a greater effect on the poor and are more easily avoided by the rich. A clear example of the links between social inequalities and environmental quality is the experience of residents of the inner city neighbourhood of East Elizabeth, New Jersey. The New Jersey Turnpike – the busiest road in the United States – runs through the community and Newark airport, America's tenth busiest, is only 1.6 kilometres away. The largest petrochemical complex on the East Coast, which is the seventh largest waste-producing site and eighth largest toxin emitter in the State, is located on the south-west boundary of the community. Nearby, the site of a former hazardous waste incinerator that exploded in 1980 still stands vacant, secured by a 2.4 metre high chain link fence. The damage from these developments will be borne by the global environment, but the effects will be felt most directly in East Elizabeth. Compared to most Americans, the people of East Elizabeth tend to be unemployed, have low levels of health, are unlikely to own a car and do not travel by air. They do not consume much, but do bear the brunt of the consumption of others. Most urban politics are concerned with the distribution of externality effects, positive and negative; the association between power and wealth imposes the negative effects on the poor. Korten has commented as follows on the connections between power, wealth and environmental damage:

> '*although it is true that poor people are far more likely to be found living next to waste dumps, polluting factories and other scenes of environmental devastation than are wealthy people, this doesn't mean that they are major consumers of the products produced in those factories. Nor does it mean that they wouldn't prefer to live in more environmentally pristine settings. It simply means that wealthy people have the economic and political power to make sure that pollutants and wastes are dumped somewhere other than in their neighbourhoods*'

Korten, 1995, pp 30–31

Not only are the wealthy responsible for most environmental damage, but they also use their market and political power to transfer the real costs of their consumption to the poor and less powerful. The reduction in environmental impact of our towns and cities, involving changes in behaviour and urban structure, would not only be intrinsically valuable but also instrumental in improving disproportionately the quality of life of the disadvantaged. Environmental enhancement can form an effective part of policy designed to reduce poverty and increase social equality, but equally that enhancement depends for its realization on a redistribution of power and wealth.

A further link between sustainability and social equity lies in the field of individual behaviour. It has already been observed that in the developing world, poverty makes sustainable living difficult. This also applies in the cities of the developed world. It is very difficult for the poor in our inner city ghettos and peripheral council estates to live a green lifestyle. Market mechanisms, such as buying green products (organic vegetables for example), are not available to those with little purchasing power. These products are usually more expensive and hence not a realistic choice for those on a restricted income who struggle to meet their basic needs. Moreover, the retail outlets where green products are available tend to be located in places inaccessible to the poorer areas, such as supermarkets in out-of-town shopping centres or specialized grocers in gentrified areas. The poor buy second hand products which are often inefficient and more expensive in the long run, but cheap to acquire initially. These products are often environmentally damaging, such as old cars and domestic heating appliances. Poverty channels expenditure towards short-term savings at the expense of long-term losses and poor environmental product performance.

The importance of tackling environmental and poverty issues together is illustrated by Boardman, who describes an initiative in the UK whereby domestic gas consumers were given rebates on their expenditure on gas if they installed a condensing boiler. These boilers cost approximately £400 and thus are beyond the means of the poor. Boardman describes this as a 'reverse Robin Hood approach; the money has been raised from all consumers, but distributed solely to richer households' (1994, p 122). The capital expenditure required to obtain new gas condensing boilers or solar panels, which yield long-term energy savings, is possible only for those with sufficient income. That income enables them to live more economically in the true, sustainable, sense of the word. It is also not realistic to expect a single mother struggling to feed, clothe and house her children in a run down, dirty and crime-ridden social housing scheme to worry about sorting her refuse and taking it to the nearest recycling centre, let alone saving the planet. She will have, understandably, different priorities connected to the immediate and basic needs of her children. Her limited means will force her into short term calculations, greater long term expense and behaviour patterns which do not take into account environmental considerations. Making our cities sustainable must involve improving the quality of life of the poor, not only for their sakes, but for wider reasons of social and ecosystem health. Improving the incomes of the poor will diminish environmental damage if it makes it easier for them to change their lifestyles and live in a more environment-conscious way.

The specific mechanisms of urban non-sustainability and how the built environment can be made more environmentally benign have been discussed in earlier chapters. Changing our towns and cities in these ways would not only benefit the environment in the widest sense but also contribute towards greater social equity and increase the effectiveness of poverty programmes. Indeed, we can say that the solutions to environmental and poverty problems are inseparable because the degree of social change necessary to achieve sustainability can only be accomplished by a society characterized by consensus and social justice.

Two of the most ecologically damaging aspects of modern urban living are car dependency and low energy efficiency of buildings. The changes required to render our towns and cities more sustainable centre on a significant shift towards the use of public transport, bicycles and walking rather than cars, and large increases in building energy efficiency. These changes will benefit poorer households disproportionately and hence reduce poverty. Although car use is widespread in terms of numbers of users, it is more restricted in terms of particular social and economic groups. The corollary of these statistics is that public transport is the province of the disadvantaged and becomes a second class service. Investment and priority are given to car users and the attendant infrastructure of roads, flyovers and interchanges. Overall levels of accessibility fall for everyone as congestion causes average speeds to fall, but the poor and other non-car using groups are particularly disadvantaged. Facilities will be located for the benefit of the majority and hence will be most accessible to car users and least accessible for public transport.

A city which places greater emphasis on public transport is a more equal city, since by definition public transport is available to all. Improving its quality in terms of frequency, reliability, comfort and network expansion will benefit everyone, but particularly non-car owners. We may contrast cities such as Vienna and Amsterdam with Los Angeles or London. Vienna has an integrated public transport network of buses, trams, underground and surface railways. Tickets are transferable between all of these, and many stations are multiple interchanges. It is easy and cheap to travel almost anywhere in the city. Cars are not prohibited, but most people who have cars choose to use them less because of the quality of the public transport available. The buses, trams, S-bahns and U-bahns are as a consequence used by a cross-section of Viennese society and from this point of view can be considered as being socially integrative as well as efficient for transport and environment-friendly. Since public transport is used by rich and poor alike, there is a consensus to support it and invest in it.

By contrast, using public transport in American or British cities where it is largely unsubsidized and with respect to buses patronized mainly by the poor and immobile can be an unpleasant and occasionally dangerous experience. When a service is provided largely for the disadvantaged, it inevitably becomes second class. Falling investment levels can lead to safety problems in terms of maintenance, and late night travel can become risky from crime as experienced on the New York subway and London underground. There are also health considerations since air pollution would be reduced by a shift away from car use and again the benefits would be felt more by the poor, the young and the elderly. In addition to these we can add the significant effect that such a shift can have in terms of social integration and equity. High quality public transport increases general levels of mobility, but especially those of the poor. It increases social contact between different social and economic groups, whereas the car isolates people, socially and physically. It gives a wide range of people a common interest in maintaining a community asset. For all these reasons, public transport has the potential for raising the quality of life in our cities for all citizens, but perhaps more importantly it can do this disproportionately for the poor without harming the majority.

The most environmentally friendly transport modes of all are walking and cycling. Bicycles and footwear are non-polluting in use, and consume few materials in their manufacture. Walking and cycling are also generative of good health. In the context of social equity they are available to rich and poor alike. Unfortunately, many towns and cities in the developed world, particularly in North America, the UK and Australia, are decidedly difficult to walk and cycle in. Suburban sprawl and zoned land uses require long distance travel for commuting, shopping and social purposes, and the roads constructed for the cars necessary to overcome these distances are hazardous for pedestrians and cyclists. Urban areas planned and built to have mixed land uses, higher densities and more evenly distributed services would require less travel, fewer cars and would be suitable for more walking and cycling. They would be less polluted, quieter, more socially mixed and provide an urban environment in which rich and poor had more even access to the services they require. Rich and poor would be more likely to encounter each other in non-threatening situations which would facilitate social harmony.

Earlier chapters have described the environmental impact of buildings and emphasized the significance of wasteful energy use. A key to more sustainable building practices and use is the adoption of energy efficiency measures such as better insulation, fuel efficient technology and creative use of solar gain. As with the shift to public transport, improvements in energy efficiency in our buildings would be of especial assistance to poorer households. As far as domestic heating, cooking and lighting are concerned, environmental and poverty policies can be mutually reinforcing. We all need to eat, keep warm and dry and hence expenditure on food, heating and lighting is relatively income-inelastic. The poor therefore have to spend a higher proportion of their income on basics than more affluent households. The poor, in fact, spend more of their income in relative terms but less in absolute terms on domestic energy consumption. Moreover, their homes tend to be less well insulated, have fewer modern heating systems and they get less heating for the money spent. It is estimated that in the UK there are at least 8 million homes which are uninsulated and inadequately heated, most being the dwellings of poor households (Boardman, 1991; later estimate given in Jacobs, 1996, p 128). Pressures on their budgets lead to economies and often the failure to heat their homes properly with the attendant health risks and potential damage to the dwelling through damp (Hutton and Harmon, 1993). A possible response to their difficulties is to subsidize their heating costs, as was done in the UK in 1995 to counteract the imposition of VAT on domestic fuel.

This is a short-term, end-of-pipe solution, which is environmentally wasteful since it encourages consumption without increasing efficiency. It makes far more sense to ensure that all buildings, domestic and non-domestic, the homes of the poor and the rich, are effectively insulated and heated with the most efficient technology possible. This will be of greatest benefit to the poor who may be able (perhaps for the first time) to heat their homes adequately without increasing

153

their expenditure or physical fuel consumption. The effect on their quality of life would be dramatic in terms of comfort, health and reduction of anxiety. Achieving this will entail significant capital expenditure quite beyond the means of the poor themselves, but not beyond the means of society as a whole. Research has shown that although building energy efficient housing is more expensive in capital terms, over the life cycle of a dwelling it is cheaper and imposes a significantly lower environmental burden (Smith et al, 1995, 1997).

This research is being reinforced by practical experience of improving the energy efficiency of housing for poorer households. Scandinavian countries have a good record of building energy efficient housing and are at the forefront of the application of new and effective technology in this field. A particularly good example is the Skotteparken project to be found in Egebjerggård, in Ballerup (Denmark). One hundred flats have been built with extra energy efficiency features, including extra insulation, low-emission glass, heat recovery from ventilation, solar panels and combined heat and power. These measures increased the capital cost of the development by 8 per cent. Completed in 1992, 50 per cent savings on energy use for heating and hot water have been obtained which has meant that total running costs to the tenants (rent plus heating and hot water) are no higher than more conventional schemes despite the higher capital cost.

An equally impressive example of retrofitting existing dwellings as distinct from new build is Easthall in Glasgow, an area of post-war council housing suffering from problems of poverty, unemployment and social exclusion. To magnify the tenants' problems of income deficiency, their tenement flats were built in the 1950s to very low standards of energy efficiency: no double glazing or central heating, poor insulation, and a reliance on open fires and electric heaters. It was estimated in the early 1990s that it would cost about £40 per week to heat each flat to an acceptable level of comfort. Not only was this beyond the means of the tenants, but if it had been achieved would have been extremely wasteful of energy, most of the generated heat escaping from the buildings. The tenants could not afford to heat their flats sufficiently anyway, most heating only one room at a time, which caused condensation, discomfort and ill health. Through their Residents' Association, however, the tenants decided to do something about their cold and damp homes. Drive and organization led them to apply to the European Community for financial assistance under the Energy Demonstration Fund, designed to stimulate investment in energy efficiency. Their bid was successful and, supplemented by cash from the landlord, Glasgow District Council, about £32,000 per flat was spent on improving the energy efficiency of 36 flats in the area. Solar panels, central heating, and extra insulation were installed and the balconies were glazed over. The returns have been remarkable, those tenants using the new heating and ventilation most efficiently reducing their heating bills from £40 to £7 per week. This level of improvement would repay the initial capital investment in about 15 years (or less if real energy prices rise). The achievements at Easthall, plus examples from elsewhere, have encouraged Glasgow Council to shift its housing investment strategy such that since the mid-1990s 60 per cent has been devoted to energy efficiency. This has enabled the Council to make a direct attack on poverty as well as reducing the City's environmental impact.

The £32,000 spent on each flat in the Easthall scheme represented a level of investment way beyond the means of the tenants themselves. The investment would not have occurred, however, without their initiative. Furthermore, the benefits of the investment have extended beyond the direct savings in energy use, improvements in domestic comfort and personal health. The fact that much of the credit for the improvements lies with the tenants themselves, in the guise of the Easthall Residents' Association, has had non-material benefits in terms of community empowerment and self-respect. The link between poverty and dependence has been referred to earlier, and in deprived areas such as Easthall many of the material improvements required to improve quality of life can be effected by the tenants themselves, with some assistance, rather than being imposed by external agencies. This includes not only initiative and organization as in Easthall, but also doing the actual work when accompanied by appropriate training. When this occurs, the income generated by the improvements remains in the local area. Unfortunately, in most cases of physical refurbishment of deprived housing areas the work done is contracted out to firms who use outside, already trained, labour. Much of the environmental enhancement of these areas, such as improvements in energy efficiency, could be done by the residents themselves. The most valuable resource in deprived areas is the people, a resource which is currently left unused. The spare time available to the unemployed, for example, could be used to cultivate allotments on derelict or unused land. This would improve diets by providing fresh vegetables, enhance health through physical exercise and improve the environment by making 'green' use of urban space. Perhaps most importantly, it would replace unoccupied time with useful activity.

If action to improve the environmental and social conditions in deprived areas is left to outside agencies, public or private, the evidence indicates that the effects are minimal and short term. Sustainable improvements require the involvement of the people living in these areas, both in the planning and the implementation stages. The success of the Easthall project depended on such involvement. Sustaining a healthy environment requires a healthy community at the local level. This means a community which is socially cohesive, democratic and participatory. It should have control over its environment and responsibility for its care. Given the training and skills, people from the community will be more effective in doing so than outsiders who have no immediate stake in it. This is particularly important for the poorer communities, since they have the most degraded environments and the least resources, other than themselves, to improve them. The importance of community to sustainable development is discussed in greater detail in the next chapter.

The most important link between care for the environment and social equity derives from the move towards a less consumption-oriented society. The consumer society is propelled by the manufacture of wants as much as the products which are supposed to satisfy those wants. A consequence of this is a social system driven by competition and envy, a society of winners and losers. It is possible to conceive of a society in which more attention is given to non-material sources of satisfaction once the basics of material needs are met. These include, for example, the development of skills, both manual and non-manual, artistic and practical; the cultivation of a greater diversity of human relationships beyond the nuclear family, whose primary purpose today is as a consumption unit. Such a society would impose a far smaller burden on the natural environment and would not be rent by the social and economic fissures to be found in the modern city. Material consumption would be lower, but quality of life higher and more evenly distributed. The physical form of an environmentally benign city has been defined above and in earlier chapters: high density, public transport- and pedestrian-oriented, mixed land use, dedicated to public space rather than private. Physical form does not determine behaviour, however, and there is no guarantee that such a city would exhibit social cohesion and equity. Proximity does not on its own produce community. Such a city, however, would certainly have a lower environmental burden and would at the least make it easier for society to be fairer in terms of the distribution of quality of life. The changes required to achieve sustainability are mutually reinforcing; a just society will facilitate care for the environment and vice versa.

LIFE IN THE GREEN CITY

What would a city which developed according to principles of environmental protection and social equity look like? What would life be like in a city which was non-polluted, had a low environmental impact and provided a high quality of life for all its citizens? The elements of such a city have been discussed in earlier chapters and there are examples already of some of these elements in existing towns and cities; Vienna's transport system and domestic heating in Denmark have been described above. What would a town be like which had all these elements together and how would it redistribute life chances in a fairer way?

The New Urbanism movement in American architecture and planning has produced guidelines for sustainable urban environments which are based on higher densities, mixed land uses, and greater dependence on walking, cycling and public transport (see Calthorpe, 1993 and Katz, 1994). This would involve the end of the suburbs/city dichotomy, and its replacement with decentralized concentrations of urban development. The dominance of the central city as a centre of employment would be replaced by a redistribution of jobs to more scattered centres within residential areas of higher population densities than existing suburban sprawl. People would live nearer to their workplace and most of the services they need on a day-to-day basis, and would thereby be able to walk or cycle for most of their journeys. There would be no out-of-town shopping centres accessible only to car-owning households. When longer trips were required, the linking of these mixed-use neighbourhoods by efficient and cheap public transport would make frequent use of the car unnecessary and second best. Referred to by Calthorpe as *transit-oriented developments*, these neighbourhoods would provide more or less equal access to jobs and services for all their residents, rich and poor alike. Rich and poor alike would also benefit from the unpolluted air and the reduction in risk from death or injury by car accidents.

Developments such as these would not only be mixed in terms of land uses; they would also be mixed in terms of income groups and provide dwellings at a range of prices and rents. All of the dwellings would provide warm, dry and healthy living space with minimum impact on the environment and at low whole-life cost. Quality homes would be affordable for all. The rich have been fleeing from our cities because they have become undesirable, and in some cases uninhabitable. Neighbourhoods as described above would be attractive to the more affluent households. The negative externalities currently associated with the poor would not be present and hence mixed income neighbourhoods would not deter those conscious of property values. Indeed, with an emphasis on preserving the quality of public space and architecture (the parks, squares, shopping centres, libraries and schools) which are for everyone, as well as private space, the neighbourhood could become a cohesive community in which at a minimum behaviour would be civil and which would have the potential for a richer community life than offered by the atomized and private consumption-centred life which dominates contemporary suburbia. The fact that most journeys would be made on foot or by bicycle means that people would meet more often in public spaces on a casual basis. The presence of people on foot in these public spaces, day and night, would make them more secure and less attractive for crime. The absence of heavy traffic would make them quiet and pollution-free. The poor might have less money, but this would not mean either social or spatial exclusion. Their incomes might be low, but this would not be further compounded by the disadvantages of a degraded and polluted environment. Such neighbourhoods would provide a physical environment designed to enhance and sustain quality of life in the broadest sense, material and non-material, individual and community.

Our present towns and cities have developed to nourish consumption and growth, and as such are inevitably unfair and unsustainable. They are incapable of satisfying fundamental human needs, and are inhuman in their scale and the lifestyles they provide. We are, however, left with the enormous physical and capital investment that they represent and it could be argued that for most people to live in the type of neighbourhood described above is unrealizable except in the very long term. Fixed capital in the form of the built environment is continually being destroyed and rebuilt according to capitalist imperatives, but with little consideration to waste avoidance and recycling. With ingenuity it should be possible to reuse the existing built environment whilst at the same time redeveloping according to environmental and egalitarian principles. Commercial and industrial buildings can be converted to residential use to create mixed-use neighbourhoods and reduce the need to travel. Derelict inner city land can be used for residential or public open space uses. There is no reason why our urban areas, new and existing, cannot become more civilized, humane, socially cohesive and environmentally benign.

8

COMMUNITY, SUSTAINABILITY AND THE BUILT ENVIRONMENT

'Those are only happy who have their minds fixed on some object other than their own happiness; on the happiness of others, on the improvement of mankind, even on some act or pursuit, followed not as a means but as itself an ideal end'

John Stuart Mill, *Autobiography*, 1873

Mill wrote these words more than 100 years ago; the notion that human happiness is not to be found in individual gratification is not new. The recent growth of support for communitarianism (Etzioni, 1993), a concern for duties and responsibilities as much as individual rights and for greater social cohesion, represent a revival of Mill's philosophy. They are a reaction to the social breakdown, rising crime and increasing social pathologies of the 1980s and 1990s, consequences of a society in which the emphasis is heavily on 'me' and not 'we'. While many in the developed world – indeed the majority – became materially better off in the Thatcher–Reagan years, it is arguable whether they also became happier. The power of self-interest to motivate human activity and to stimulate economic growth has been proved beyond doubt, but the accumulating physical wealth and accelerating consumption were accompanied by social exclusion, alienation, insecurity and environmental damage.

In the late 1980s, an attempt was made to quantify a broader concept of quality of life that would encompass non-material elements and collective as well as individual sources of human satisfaction (Daly and Cobb, 1989). Known as the Index of Sustainable Economic Welfare (ISEW), the updated index for the UK produced by the New Economics Foundation and Friends of the Earth shows a decline from the mid 1970s, with gross national product showing a steady rise over the same period (MacGillivray, 1997). People's disappointment with their failure to become happier as they became richer has statistical support, even if direct causal links are more complex. The communitarian movement articulated by Etzioni (op cit) has become increasingly significant in the political context, and was influential in the electoral campaigns of Clinton in America and Blair in the UK; the success of those campaigns would indicate that the message has a wide appeal. Communitarianism has been largely applied in the fields of social and economic policy, but has not as yet embraced environmental issues. This is somewhat surprising, since a sense of the common good over and above individual interest and a concern for the non-material as well as the material as components of human contentment and fulfilment, are intrinsic to environmentalism.

We have discussed the impact that the built environment has on the natural environment, and how the concept of sustainability is vital in moving towards a more benign configuration of the former. Since the built environment is a product of human activity, it is necessary to analyse the type of society that has produced the particular and harmful form we have of it today. By providing a link between societal characteristics and the malign elements of the built environment, the way forward in terms of social change towards a more sustainable future will be signposted. There are complex links between the built environment and society, and both are contained by and must ultimately respect the natural environment. What sort of society is it that gives so little consideration to caring for the natural environment, and so little thought for the future? What sort of society will embrace different values and behave in different ways?

The key to answering these questions is the concept of community. This is not a new concept and is one to which lip-service is often paid. It is also too often used carelessly and in an undefined way. When allied with the concept of sustainability, however, it becomes a powerful tool for analysing where we have gone wrong with respect to the environment and changing for the better. In this chapter, the concepts of sustainability and community are examined together; in particular, an attempt is made to define the essential elements of a *sustainable community*. This is then linked to the built environment and it is argued that a sustainable built environment can be achieved and maintained only by a society composed of sustainable communities. It will be further argued that a sustainable built environment will itself nourish and encourage lifestyles associated with sustainable communities; there is a two-way relationship between behaviour and the environment. The long-term health of the natural environment is inextricably linked to the long-term health of the social groupings living within it. A symbiosis exists between natural and social processes and this is most effectively understood through the concept of sustainability.

THE DECAY OF COMMUNITY

There is a large and long-standing academic literature on the notion of community; sociologists have considered the structural elements of community, social psychologists the effects on individuals of living in small, close-knit groups, and geographers have attempted to place community in a physical and spatial setting. The consensus across disciplines is that community has become less relevant over time in describing societies in the developed world in the sense that people are less attached to and dependent upon small social groups and evaluate their welfare from an individual rather than a social perspective. People's material needs are met through the formalized and impersonal mechanisms of the market and large public bureaucracies, and their social needs (in the general sense of human contact) are satisfied in the workplace or increasingly sublimated by passive electronic means of entertainment. There is less and less requirement for people to organize themselves into groups to satisfy their needs, material and social. This has the further effect that people have less attachment to place or locality – their neighbourhoods become more dormitories than the physical setting for interactive social groups. People lead more individualized and home-centred lives, and over the years have become less and less engaged in civic affairs.

The American sociologist Robert Putnam (1995) refers to the cohesiveness and quality of social relationships as 'social capital'. Social capital is essential for people to be able to cooperate and achieve common goals, and Putnam argues that the loss of social capital has negative consequences in terms of increased social pathology and crime. He ascribes the diminution of social capital in America to the influence of television, but the increasing levels of materialism and widening social inequalities discussed in Chapter 7 are also significant in harming social cohesion. The neighbourhoods within cities which formerly gave structure to urban life and counteracted the anonymity of large populations have weakened as social phenomena, and now even small-scale rural society has lost much of its former cohesiveness. This has been seen as a source of regret by some, allied to nostalgia for a lost lifestyle, and as a trend to be welcomed by others, linked to notions of inevitable change and progress. Despite its absence, or at least rarity, from contemporary social relationships the concept of community remains vital in understanding the social dimension of sustainability. We must re-address community, but from a new perspective. At its simplest, our argument is that a society which does not care for itself as a functioning whole will not care for the environment which contains it. A society in which individuals place their own selfish interests before those of others and before the common good, will begin to suffer strains and structural failures which will threaten its long-term survival as a social unit. The long-term survival of society may also be threatened by the degradation of the natural environmental system. These social and environmental threats to the long-term survival of society are intimately connected. A society which develops lifestyles and structures that produce and maintain consensual social cohesion from generation to generation will also be aware of the importance of the natural environment and will live in ways that respect the long-term integrity of the natural world.

We need therefore to consider what form of society will be most likely to guarantee its long-term survival in social and environmental terms. What social arrangements will produce and maintain a high quality of life for the maximum number of people? We require a form of social organization that provides cohesion, permanence and flexibility. Cohesion must be consensual if it is to last, and is dependent upon inclusion, participation, justice and equity.

161

Permanence implies flexibility, since social structures must be able to adapt to changing circumstances. Social cohesion implies community, and permanence implies sustainability. The combination of the two points the way to the forms of social organization that will be required. The absence of community and a lack of concern for the future are evident throughout the developed world. They are connected to, and are indeed the cause of, many of today's social and environmental problems. These include inner city decay and the growth of a permanent underclass, inequality, environmental degradation and problems of public health. They also include the isolated and socially destructive lifestyles of the affluent in our car-dependent suburbs, lifestyles which cause environmental problems and which are in stark contrast to those of the poor.

The Industrial Revolution transformed both social life and the built environment. The most noticeable change in the former was an increase in scale and pace, leading to a more atomized society held together by formal and market relationships rather than social bonding associated with cooperation and locality. The size of human settlements increased and the number of impersonal social contacts that people experienced increased commensurately. Despite these changes, however, some urban neighbourhoods managed to retain elements in their social life of cohesion, connection and mutual support. These were largely working class areas in the older parts of cities, classic examples being Bethnal Green in the East End of London as described by Peter Willmott and Michael Young in the 1950s (Young and Willmott, 1957) and the North End in Boston described by Jane Jacobs (1961).

These areas were characterized by a multiplicity of social, family and economic connections which were mutually reinforcing. Extended families were contained in the area, and provided support in times of need across three and sometimes four generations. People tended to be born, live and die in the same area, leading to a stability and continuity of social networks. Most of the working population had the same or similar employers and work, giving rise to a commonality of interest outside the home and a solidarity in the face of poverty and exploitation. Life was hard in material terms, but rich in social terms; there was a community of interest and a feeling of community. These areas were by no means rose gardens, however. The poverty was hard and associated with underachievement and restricted cultural horizons, and illness and early death were common. The built environment had features connected with the good and the bad elements of social life. There was a high density of population and an intermixing of land uses and services. Travel to work was short and social interaction across a range of activities high. People rarely had to leave the area for their needs and developed a high degree of attachment to their neighbours and their neighbourhood. On the negative side, the housing was poor and overcrowded, the hygiene basic and the environment polluted and unhealthy. The relationship between people and the environment was viewed as one-directional, the latter impacting more on the former than the other way round; given the generally low living standards and car ownership in these areas, this was appropriate at the time. The built environment provided the context for a healthy social life, but also a threat to people's physical health. The response in the post-war period to this threat threw out the baby with the bath water by providing a built environment that was physically healthier in the short term, but which damaged the elements of community cohesion.

The post-war period of urban development and redevelopment has been dominated by a planning philosophy of tidiness, land use sorting and car dependence. The wholly admirable desire to rehouse families from slums was unfortunately unaccompanied by any conception that a healthy and vibrant neighbourhood is more than bricks and mortar. The important issues of land use and transport planning and their effects on the built environment in terms of sustainability, were discussed in detail in Chapter 5; here we concentrate on the social effects of change in the built environment in the post-war period and in particular on the degree to which community has been rendered less and less important. In the UK, the old working class neighbourhoods were largely destroyed in physical terms by slum clearance and their inhabitants removed to new areas of subsidized housing on the urban periphery, often remote from their original locations. Young and Willmott describe how the rehousing of families from the slums of Bethnal Green to large, homogeneous council estates in Essex 25 miles away produced an immediate and substantial improvement in housing conditions, but also destroyed the social cohesion and rich social interaction typical of the East End. The residential densities were lower, the air was cleaner (at least for the time being), the houses bigger, drier and more comfortable, but something important had been lost from the fabric of people's social lives. The built environment was less varied, the journey to work was longer and the number of different social contacts significantly reduced. The extended family became geographically dispersed, and the attachment to neighbours and to neighbourhood was severely impaired. Young and Willmott discovered that just two years after moving out to Essex from Bethnal Green, their survey respondents had reduced contacts with their own or spouses' relatives from 15 to 3 per week. Many of the migrants were pleased with their new houses and bathrooms, but found their new life lonely.

The movement to the suburbs was not restricted to the families involved in slum clearance; what the poor were doing (or rather having done to them) via bureaucracy, the affluent were (or thought they were) doing through choice. The history of post-war urban residential change, especially in North America, the UK and Australia, is the history of the suburb. Cities have historically (and in many European cities still do) provided opportunities, freedom, choice and an improved quality of life which can be contrasted to the cloying restrictiveness and inward- and backward-looking character of rural communities. The suburbs are physically attached to the city, but in social terms are not of the city and do not provide the greater opportunities historically linked to urban life. The history of the suburbs is one of the decay of social cohesion and communal life. It is also one of increasing environmental damage; the two sets of processes are intimately connected. We have created a built environment which is both socially and ecologically destructive. These trends are at their maximum in the United

States, crudely but eloquently described by Kunstler as 'crudscape' (Kunstler, 1994, 1996). They are also present elsewhere in the developed world; there has been a widespread rejection of cities as acceptable living environments and a flight to lower density, scattered dormitories. This migration has been techno-logically enabled by the car and has been associated with more general societal change connected with a rise in materialism and individualism, and a decline in a sense of community. People have become richer in material terms, but are not more content. This can be directly associated with the isolation and emptiness of a society without community. The rapidity of environmental change has now revealed these changes to the built environment to be unsustainable.

VALUES, SOCIAL LIFE AND THE BUILT ENVIRONMENT

Few would disagree with the assertion that society has become more materialistic in the post-war period; with the significant increase in consumption that most people in the developed world have enjoyed, an increase in contentment may also have been expected. There is little evidence that the latter has occurred. Furthermore, instead of examining the absence of happiness from a fundamental and wide-ranging perspective, we have attempted to obtain it by consuming more on the assumption not that we have enough material things and should be looking for other sources of satisfaction, but rather that we do not have enough of them. The assumption that we will be happier with two VCRs instead of one, or the latest model instead of a perfectly serviceable but barely obsolete one, seems ridiculous but has been profoundly influential. Associated with materialism has been a steadily increasing accent on individualism, based on a misreading of Adam Smith's philosophy that the common good can be maximized through the pursuit of self-interest. This was given a boost in the Reagan–Thatcher years, summarized neatly by Thatcher's claim that 'there is no such thing as society, only families'. The shared goal of society – or at least the goal assumed by politicians to be commonly shared – became economic growth, and longer term considerations of environmental protection and social contentment and cohesion, were dismissed as the concerns of minority pressure groups. The contemporary built environment is a physical manifestation of that society. It is an expression in concrete and brick, tarmac and steel, of the selfishness and short-sightedness that characterize our lifestyles; it does not reflect a concern for the common good, or the importance of non-material elements of human happiness. It does not provide a setting in which people can live in contentment and lightly on the Earth. Margaret Thatcher was wrong to aver that there was no such thing as society, but she would have been right if she had said that we have lost our sense of community.

The pursuit of self-interest without countervailing measures inevitably results in an unequal society. The effects of this inequality on the built environment and on sustainability are examined in detail in Chapter 7. Here we concentrate on the loss of community and the relationship between this loss and the built environment. More than half of all Americans now live in suburbs; Clinton was the first suburban president, in that more than half of those who voted for him were suburban dwellers. The movement of people out to the suburbs has also been the experience, to lesser or greater degree, of most other developed world countries. This has been associated with, and has been instrumental in achieving, the increase in material consumption noted above. The suburb has proved to be a highly efficient urban form for maximizing consumption and increasing the intensity of materials and energy use (discussed in Chapters 3, 4 and 5). An important element of this has been connected with the car industry, since although many suburbs were initially established and expanded through the mechanism of public transport (notably trains and trams in the late nineteenth and early twentieth centuries), and most still depend in part upon public transport, in the latter half of the twentieth century they have become increasingly dependent on the car. Cities such as Detroit and Coventry became economically dependent upon the car industry at the same time that it was transforming their physical structure and, in the case of Detroit, draining its core of life. The suburbs have proved effective at maximizing household material consumption in a more general sense, and have simultaneously contributed to changing urban social life for the worse. It is no accident that a materialistic society should have produced a built environment which facilitates consumption and makes a non-materialist lifestyle difficult.

The typical suburb consists mainly of houses. There are few social facilities, the commonest being retail establishments. The suburbs contain few workplaces integrated into residential areas; most of the working residents are commuters, mainly by car, either to central city areas or to expanding centres of employment in peripheral locations. The development of 'edge cities' in America, where the affluent and their employment have moved out of the existing cities to more dispersed, low density locations outside the jurisdiction and tax raising reach of the city authorities, has not reduced car commuting. Langdon (1994) has described in detail how social life has been damaged in the American suburb. The journey to work can be long, frustrating and stressful; this reduces the time and energy available for socializing once home is reached. The physical layout of the suburbs has often been designed using the principles of traffic engineers, which isolate suburban dwellers within their own particular enclaves. Travel within suburban areas without a car is difficult and sometimes impossible because of the distances involved and the lack of public transport. These factors together make social life outside the home difficult and satisfaction is sought through other means: consumption. The commonest location for social interaction is the shopping mall; the most frequent non-domestic social contact is associated with more consumption.

The suburban home is an ideal repository for material goods, one of which, the television, can provide the varied contact with the outside world that the local physical and social milieu cannot. America has developed into a society of channel hoppers and video watchers, isolated in cars to and from work, and isolated in homes away from it. Travel to work becomes an individual activity, only misery and frustration being shared. The separation of home and work, enabled by the car, reduces much of the day to unproductive time. Furthermore, by living in the suburbs at long distances from their work, people become detached from, and escape from, the problems of the districts where their employment is located, often in the inner city, and the overall cohesion of the urban community is reduced. In the United States, the fragmented nature of local government also means they escape any financial burden in terms of financial support for the poor. In the UK where local government structure is more rational in a spatial sense, a similar objective has been obtained by the capping of local authority expenditure and the dominance of income tax restriction on the political agenda.

People are isolated in their cars and alienated from the wider community by their cars. The construction of urban motorways to accommodate the car creates physical barriers within cities, and deepens any socio-economic divides that are already present. Car ownership is not universal, and car owners and non-owners (the latter being predominantly poor, old, disabled or disadvantaged in some other way) become antagonists in urban management. The low density, dispersed city, made possible by the automobile, is a physically and socially fragmented city. Its day-to-day functioning creates stress, and people retreat to their homes for relaxation and relief. Paradoxically, the car-dependent society is more private and home-centred, and less social, than society before mass car ownership. The mobility promised by the car has proved difficult to obtain and keep. The barrenness of much suburban life is encapsulated in this quote from an American living in Lisle, Illinois, a western suburb of Chicago:

> 'For a while, the people in the subdivision used to get together to take care of the sign at the subdivision entrance and the landscaping round it. Then the house next to the entrance changed hands, and the new owners started taking care of it themselves. That was pretty much the end of organized neighbourhood activity.'

quoted in Langdon, op cit, p 17

Such isolation places strains on the social unit that does continue to operate: the nuclear family. The pressures of providing for the emotional and human contact needs of suburban dwellers falls heavily on the nuclear family; the social interaction of the family members is predominantly with each other outside of work and school. The nuclear family is being required to perform beyond its capabilities. Its primary function is child rearing, and the suburbs are often quoted as the ideal environment for bringing up children. They are low density and distant from the pollution and crime of the city. They offer security and predictability. A contrary view, however, is that the suburbs are a very bad environment for children. They reduce their independence because safe travel demands a car, and for most of the time they are restricted to the immediate home area, which is often only a cul-de-sac. The extended family has been geographically dispersed, so inter-generational assistance with child care is difficult. This places further restrictions on the parents in terms of their own social needs. The suburbs offer little stimulation since they are monotonous, both physically and socially. Children see their parents, adult neighbours who are like their parents and other children like themselves. The children of Bethnal Green in the 1950s had decrepit school buildings, little equipment and few books, but a far more varied experience of life than the contemporary suburban child. The suburbs are dull, lacking in social life and conducive to conformity.

Langdon has observed that many Americans enjoy a high standard of living, have obtained their dream house in an exclusive enclave and yet feel a sense of unease that they are not happy when they should be. This often stimulates a move to a bigger house and a more exclusive suburb, a signal of progress; this does not remove the unease, and by promoting mobility further undermines the growth of any sense of community. At the level of the individual family, the suburbs are becoming economically and socially unsustainable. Rising housing and commuting costs place greater burdens on household budgets, and in a society which measures success by consumption, progress at work becomes important. Husbands work longer hours and become less capable of devoting energy to non-domestic social life and neighbourhood interaction. Two incomes become necessary to maintain the mortgage, motoring expenses and other consumption, and women who don't wish to work outside the home have to. Those that do not work are condemned to a life of social isolation, coffee mornings and unassisted child care until their exhausted husband comes home. It is not surprising that the divorce rate has risen. Hutton (1997) has observed that the growing insecurity associated with flexible labour markets and an increasingly marketized society has highlighted the lack of social support mechanisms in the modern suburb, and notes that in Australia's suburbia a new phenomenon is the marginalised, divorced middle-aged man, living alone, without the old structures that might have integrated him back into society. It is no coincidence that Australia has one of the highest suicide rates in the world.

The suburbs do not make up all the built environment, however. The cities still provide homes for millions of people and there are still rural towns and villages. In the latter, at least, we might hope for some elements of community to have survived. Unfortunately, the decay of community has become almost universal. In the inner city, the flight of the economically comfortable has left behind the weak and the disadvantaged. Suburban dwellers may be social isolates, stressed and discontented, but at least they have physically comfortable homes, some sense of security and a place in broader society even if it is not fulfilling. The unemployed, the single parent and the disadvantaged ethnic minorities have none of these things. In the past, working class urban residents faced hardship, but they did live in communities; there were mutual support networks and a sense of social belonging which helped them cope with the ordeal of poverty. Today's urban poor still face the hardship but in addition have to cope with social breakdown, high levels of crime and a hostile and unforgiving society. Instead of solidarity and mutual support, the poor have begun to prey on each other since the weak make the easiest targets. This is illustrated by this quote from an unemployed man in Preston, Lancashire:

> *'On these estates now, if you leave your house you've got to leave somebody in it. And that's it . . . If I go out, it's either me or my missus has to stay in. If you both go out there's 99 per cent chance of getting robbed. They stand on the corner and watch you.'*

quoted in Lancashire County Council, 1997, p 130

As far as they are concerned there is indeed no society, but no family or community either. Their social environment can be brutal and their physical environment is almost always polluted and dangerous. The irony is that their low incomes, low levels of car ownership and lack of travel outside their neighbourhood mean that their ecological footprint is relatively light. They are the victims of non-sustainability, not its cause. The suburbs, by contrast, are the cause of immense environmental damage through high levels of consumption, car commuting and land take. The conventional wisdom is that the poor are a drain on society and a threat to the long-term sustainability of public finance. Put another way, the existence of a non-productive underclass is a threat to low taxation and continued over-consumption by the more fortunate. The real threat to sustainability comes from the suburbs, not the inner city, and from the rich, not the poor.

Perhaps it is not surprising that community has atrophied in the inner city and the suburbs given the scale and stress of contemporary urban life. A more likely environment in which a sense of social cohesion and reinforcing social interaction might survive is the rural milieu of small towns, villages and scattered farms. As Webber (1964) predicted, however, we all have urban lifestyles now, whether we live in the city or the country. The advance of communication technology, the depopulation of the countryside as farming has become dominated by agribusiness and lost its demand for labour, and the growth of villages which are little more than dormitories for urban commuters, has reproduced in rural areas an individualized and home-centred social life similar to that found in the suburbs. The lack of connection between many rural dwellers and the local economy further weakens any sense of social belonging with neighbours and can produce divisions within rural society as affluent incomers (commuters and the retired) use their greater economic power to obtain housing at the expense of locals. In the UK over the last 20 years, up to 100,000 people per annum have abandoned the cities and towns to seek a mythic rural life and in so doing have destroyed what they have tried to find. Between 1991 and 1994 alone more than 1.25 million people left the UK's six largest urban areas.

Large swathes of Berkshire and the other Home Counties could now more accurately be described as 'rurban' rather than rural. Rural areas now resemble cities in terms of the nature of their social life; it just takes place at lower densities. In the more remote areas out of commuting range, the decay of local services as population falls and demand thresholds are not reached, causing reliance on more centralized provision, is socially damaging. The closure of the village shop is the loss of a regular local meeting place; the closure of the village primary school lessens the opportunities for people to meet in non-domestic circumstances; and the falling population makes it more difficult to sustain the village cricket team. In addition to the fall in quality of social relationships and the loss of social capital, these changes have been environmentally damaging. The loss of local services and activities increases travel, almost all by car, and causes pollution and the depletion of non-renewable resources.

THE DESIRE FOR COMMUNITY

The loss of community has not gone unnoticed or unmourned by those responsible for the regulation of urban development. Post-war planning philosophy in the Anglo-Saxon world has contained a strong anti-urban element which has been reflected in decentralization policies and a misguided attempt to recreate within built-up areas a version of a cohesive bucolic village. The origins of this can be traced back to Ebenezer Howard's Garden City, which attempted to merge the best of town and country. When applied to the post-war world, with all the attendant social and technological change in the preceding 50 years, the end result has been the merging of the worst, not the best. We have ended up with all the least desirable features of urban social life, but at lower densities. Instead of Webber's 'community without propinquity' we have produced 'propinquity without community'. We live next door to each other, but we are not good neighbours – unless good neighbours are defined as those who mind their own business.

The planners' mechanism to revive community was the neighbourhood unit, the building brick of the British New Towns, but also applied in America. As a means of delivering services in a spatially equitable way, this proved to be a useful tool. As a means of reshaping urban social life, it was hopelessly misguided and unrealistic. Communities are not created by bricks and mortar, but by the willing cooperation and sense of mutual identity and interest of groups of people, reinforced and maintained by frequent social interaction. The built environment can be shaped in such a way as to encourage and assist community formation and maintenance, but it cannot create community. In post-war Britain, the New Towns were the jewel in the crown of the planning system, but the attempt to create urban neighbourhoods as local communities failed under the impact of the growing materialism and individualism of the post-war economic boom. The economy of the 1950s grew in direct proportion to the decline in the richness and complexity of social interaction. As material consumption rose, Putnam's social capital atrophied. Consuming things replaced social activity and building neighbourhoods was futile as an attempt to rescue the latter.

The private sector has placed an equal faith in the neighbourhood as the most effective way to extend the residential environment. Since the objectives of

169

the developers have been different from those of the planners, however, they have more cause to be pleased with the results. As a source of profit, housebuilding and neighbourhood development have proved to be enormously profitable. Since the developers have not been concerned to create real communities, but rather to circulate capital as rapidly as possible, the rapid expansion of the suburbs has been an immense success for them. The privately owned suburbs (in contrast to the peripheral public sector estates) have been a triumph of marketing over planning.

Langdon (1994) has illustrated how the American housebuilding industry uses sophisticated marketing techniques to maximize sales and profits. One of the most effective of these techniques is market segmentation, which when applied to suburban growth has produced exclusive developments, often described in the promotional literature as villages or communities (the developers themselves refer to these developments as 'pods', a term which, not surprisingly, does not appear in advertising blurb). These developments offer seductively attractive physical environments which are exclusive in every sense of the word. They are difficult to get to and from without a car, and they exclude the poor by price. They are homogeneous by virtue of price and income band sorting and are inward looking. Narrow targeting at particular income groups also results in a very fine-grained and sharp degree of income segregation, necessitating frequent moves as income rises follow career progression; this allows little scope, or indeed incentive, for the investment of time and emotional energy in the development of close social ties in the neighbourhood. It also reduces the opportunities for interaction with people from different income and social backgrounds. These 'urban villages' may be physical neighbourhoods, but they are not communities; nor do they form part of a wider community. They are essentially dormitories and spaces for material consumption. They are also a form of built environment which is immensely ecologically damaging.

The public sector has been less careful in its fashioning of residential areas, presumably on the grounds that the residents of public sector housing have to take what they can get. Furthermore, resources have been more limited for the construction of subsidized rented housing and considerations of cost minimization have taken precedence over user satisfaction. The consequence has been the development of large, often peripheral, public sector housing developments with little attempt to create any sense of community. Facilities have been sparse, employment largely absent and the lack of community accepted at first as the price to be paid for getting the maximum number of people out of the slums as quickly as possible. The emphasis on numbers of dwellings, with scant attention paid to the quality of the residential environment as a whole, exacted a longer term price. The peripheral estates became anonymous and intimidating environments, the dumping grounds for those who were found surplus to society's requirements. Transplanted from their decrepit, but socially supportive, former neighbourhoods, the tenants became alienated from themselves as well as from the wider society which had rejected them. The consumer society which had contributed to the destruction of community passed them by, and in an attempt to improve their physical environment, deprived them of their most valuable asset, their integrated and supportive social networks. At least their ecological footprint is light; by their lower levels of consumption they are contributing more to the attainment of sustainability than the middle classes in the suburbs.

SUSTAINABLE COMMUNITIES

Elements of social life within the contemporary built environment are unsatisfactory and incomplete for the affluent and threatening for the poor. Furthermore, the negative features of social life can be linked to features of the built environment that are ecologically damaging. The link is provided by materialist and individualistic lifestyles. There is a need to move towards social relationships which provide more cohesion and fulfilment, and which encourage more environmentally friendly lifestyles. The two key elements here are a shift to a more cooperative social organization which allows people to place more emphasis on common goals, and a prioritization of environmental care as one of those goals. Society will have to be less a collection of large numbers of competing individuals and agencies, each following materialist objectives, and more a large number of locally based communities who have a broader view of what constitutes quality of life. These communities in turn will cooperate with each other in the pursuit of wider common goals. A socially healthy society and a healthy natural environment are mutually dependent, and if achieved would change the nature of the built environment. This in turn would nurture sustainable lifestyles and protect the natural environment.

These are fine words, but they require definition. What are the essential elements of a sustainable community? Cohesion, permanence and flexibility were mentioned earlier. Cohesion is derived from the sharing of common goals and the willingness to make individual sacrifices to achieve those goals. These sacrifices can be considered as rational and in everyone's long-term interest if they are instrumental in maintaining social harmony and achieving environmental protection. The short-term pursuit of self-interest can likewise be considered irrational and ultimately self-harming. Permanence refers to the retention of the best from generation to generation, and in a changing world requires flexibility. Sustainable communities must be able to adapt and resolve conflicts. They must therefore be inclusive, participatory and democratic. To provide stimulus, they must also be diverse. These things are difficult to create and maintain; sustainable communities would place demands on their members, but they would also enrich them and give shape and purpose to their lives. They would also enable them to live in harmony with the natural environment.

Community as so defined could not be more different from the so-called communities of our suburbs and cities. Life in the contemporary suburb is in some ways easy and makes few demands. Neighbours demand little beyond non-interference and perhaps humanitarian assistance in an emergency. Unless the neighbourhood is threatened by some catastrophic development such as a new road or sewage plant which would affect property values, suburbanites do not have to go through the bother of organizing or even mixing with neighbours. Once in their homes, they can relax with the products of the electronic age which provide passive entertainment. Yet life in the suburbs is also hard and creates stress and dissatisfaction. Suburbanites endure the loss of hours every week sitting in traffic queues. They are stressed when they reach work and stressed when they get home. Passive entertainment on its own is ultimately unsatisfying. Dependence on the nuclear family alone does not provide the richness of diverse human contact which would improve all relationships. Many suburban dwellers live stereotyped and monotonous lives that dull the mind and are much less than they are capable of. The suburbs are about conformity and an unwillingness to change. The organization of suburban residents into homeowners' associations may be more about the wish to impose uniformity and protect property values than organize a vibrant social life. The urban poor, whether in the inner city or on the peripheral housing estate, also lack community. Segregated from the mainstream of society in large, anonymous blocks, their spatial concentration is not a source of solidarity and mutual support, but a perpetual reminder one to another of failure and exclusion. Their social relationships are characterized more by anomie than connection and cohesion, and the nuclear family has broken down under the stress of poverty and lack of work. Lack of confidence, low expectations and failure are transmitted from generation to generation (Wedge and Prosser, 1973).

A shift to a community-based form of social life is thus vital if we are to live fuller, more satisfying lives. The form of built environment which would facilitate such a shift would also be more sustainable. It would enable people of diverse backgrounds to meet frequently, informally and for different purposes, including accidentally. It would permit more walking and cycling. It would be higher density, and more mixed in terms of land uses, activities and income groups. There would be more actively used public spaces and people could spend less time in the home if that was their choice. Many would choose to do this if public spaces were safe, attractive and interesting. At the most local scale of the street, this would mean creating neighbourhoods in which the streets were not only means of travel, but also meeting places. Langdon (1994) has described in detail how roads in American suburbs make social interaction difficult by creating physical barriers between neighbourhoods for those without access to a car. The roads are designed to accelerate automobile travel and are built wide with gentle curves so that the line of sight for the driver is not impeded. This makes them more hazardous for pedestrians to cross. Moreover, low residential densities mean longer distances for people to travel and the pavements along the roads are seldom used by pedestrians; chance encounters are therefore rare. Suburban roads are solely communication routes between places and not locations of interaction. Their primary purpose is as a conduit for cars.

Appleyard (1981) studied the relationship between traffic levels and social interaction in San Francisco streets and found that on those streets where traffic levels were light (200 vehicles per hour at maximum) the degree of interaction was high and there was a sense of attachment to neighbourhood. By contrast, on streets where traffic was heavy (maximum 1900 vehicles per hour) neighbourliness was much lower and people thought of their apartment or their block as home, and had little attachment to the neighbourhood. Those who lived on streets with the lowest traffic levels had three times as many local friends and twice as many acquaintances as those on the most heavily trafficked streets. The physical layout of streets is also important. Cul-de-sacs, for instance, are safe environments for children and enable interaction between those living within them, but do not necessarily encourage more general social interaction because they are cut off from other areas. They also offer little privacy beyond retreat into the home. Ideally, the physical setting should both facilitate socializing and provide people with privacy should they require it. The degree of choice of interaction should also be maximized and not restricted to a small group of people, for example those living in a particular cul-de-sac. There is no ideal structure for residential areas, but experience suggests that rectangular grids provide maximum connectivity, slow down traffic levels (because of the frequent intersections) and dilute traffic on individual streets, and also provide opportunities for people to walk and cycle and to meet by chance. They do not guarantee neighbourliness, attachment to place and a sense of community, but they do facilitate them.

It could be argued that the arguments above are false in the same way that the attempts to create communities in the neighbourhood units of the 1950s and 1960s were futile. Changing the built environment cannot of itself bring about social change. This is true, but the comparison is superficial. In the first place, we now have a more sophisticated understanding of the complex links between the built environment and social behaviour, and a firmer grasp on the sort of environment which would favour sustainable communities. Our present neighbourhoods may have had the purpose of instilling a sense of community, but we now see that their physical form, and the broader urban structure within which they are set, actually helped to produce the opposite. We have ended up with a series of socially homogeneous, inward-looking and largely inactive set of dormitories. There is little interaction within these neighbourhoods and little between them either. The mechanisms of housing provision and allocation, market and bureaucratic, have sorted the urban population into homogeneous clusters, and then placed these clusters in space so as to make communication between them difficult. This makes any sense of common interest at the city-wide level difficult since it is difficult to appreciate the problems of others if contact between diverse social groups is rare. Secondly, change to the built environment will have to be accompanied by fundamental changes in attitude and values with respect to lifestyle and the natural environment; indeed, the former cannot occur without the latter. We recognize this, but we must still think about what form of built environment would be consonant with sustainable communities.

SUSTAINABLE COMMUNITIES AND THE BUILT ENVIRONMENT

Kirkpatrick Sale (1980) has argued that a meaningful community has to be small to function effectively, and suggests a few hundred people as being the optimum size. In terms of everyday living, this is true; we cannot hope to be intimate with more than a limited number of people. Our built environment already consists of settlements with populations of hundreds of thousands or more, however, and we need to consider how we are to live within these urban agglomerations and how they are to be governed and managed. Community is important, but it has to be considered at more than just the local scale. It is more than 30 years since Jane Jacobs argued strongly for town planning to focus on the neigh-bourhood, or street level, if our cities were to be socially rejuvenated. Our arguments with respect to locally based communities follow hers closely. She also placed neighbourhoods within the city-wide context, however, and added more formal levels of organization and administration at the district (sub city) and city level. These are necessary for strategic planning and the disbursement of funds.

The notion of community in the sense of giving priority to the common good applies at all spatial levels. Local neighbourhoods have a community of interest with other neighbourhoods, and districts within the city have a community of interest with other city districts. The city as a whole can be considered as a community in the sense that all its inhabitants have a common interest in living in a sustainable and life-enhancing environment, and the city can only be considered healthy if all its parts are healthy. Just as a local neighbourhood requires cooperation within to be cohesive, so successful strategic planning requires the cooperation and consent of different neighbourhoods and districts. The city should be considered as a hierarchy of communities, and a community of communities. Each is diverse, and each connected to others both socially and physically. Local communities may interact more within themselves than outside their boundaries, but these boundaries will be porous, and the communities outward-looking. The social and physical structure of the city should maximize connection between its diverse parts, not minimize it, whilst at the same time ensuring that people can obtain as many of their needs as possible locally. A city will inevitably be mixed in terms of ethnicity, income, age and social class. This diversity can be a source of strength and stimulus if the different groups understand the others' needs and viewpoints, or it can be a source of conflict if they do not. Understanding is facilitated by contact, and hindered by isolation. Our communities and cities should be mixed, not segregated, if they are to be sustainable.

The importance of locality and neighbourhood, and how these can be placed in the wider urban context, have been considered by Blowers (1993, Chapter 9). Blowers tackles sustainability at the city region level and outlines a broad blueprint for different areas (inner city, suburbs, rural) at different spatial scales. The building brick of sustainability throughout is the mixed land use, pedestrian-based neighbourhood, linked to other areas by efficient mass transit. Blowers emphasizes the land use aspects (see Chapter 5) but the community dimension is equally important. The essential role of the local community in achieving sustainability has been recognized elsewhere, most notably in Agenda 21 from the Rio Earth Summit. This placed great emphasis on the important function of local authorities in reaching global sustainability objectives (UNCED, 1993). It was stated earlier that moving towards a sustainable built environment would be impossible without a change in values and lifestyles. This can only happen from the bottom-up as a conscious decision by people at the local level, and cannot be imposed from above by government. One of the most important roles of local authorities in the future is the education of their people in environmental issues, and responding to their initiatives to achieve sustainability. These initiatives, if they are to be successful, must come from local communities, aided where appropriately from above.

Gilbert et al (1996) give examples of how local communities have initiated projects to enhance their local environment. All have been assisted by their local authorities and other government agencies, but the long-term success of the projects has been dependent on the involvement of local people acting together. Greenpoint-Williamsburg, in Brooklyn, is one of the poorest and most polluted parts of New York. Cooperation between local people and New York City has resulted in the establishment of the Environmental Benefits Program (EBP); this involves the local community with the City's Department of Environmental Protection in identifying pollution problems and developing solutions to these problems. The EBP is partly funded by the fines levied on polluters in the area, revenue which previously disappeared in general local government funds. The involvement of the local community not only improved the effectiveness of pollution control by the City, but also helped to enhance community cohesion and self-confidence.

Other examples of the link between local communities and sustainability are given in Rajan (1993), including the 'ecovillage' of Tuggelite in Sweden. In contrast to Greenpoint-Williamsburg, Tuggelite is the product of middle class initiative. The project began in the 1970s when a small group of professionals (doctors, teachers, librarians) got together to build a small community which would live in a more cooperative and environmentally friendly fashion. Each element – cooperation and care for the environment – was considered essential to the success of the other. The end result, completed in 1984, is a group of 16 houses with a communal centre, the latter housing the boiler, laundry, kitchen, nursery and activity room. The houses are highly energy efficient, have composting toilets and attached greenhouses. The success of the scheme depends on a high degree of cooperation, but the residents also have their own private space. The main stimulus to the project was the desire to be more ecologically minded, but its success has depended upon the willing cooperation and continued social cohesion of those involved.

A significant proportion of the UK's poorest families live on the large, soulless housing schemes located on the periphery of the major towns and cities. These areas have presented chronic social and economic problems since the 1960s. In the 1980s and 1990s the poorest households became increasingly concentrated in these areas and excluded, spatially and socially, from the rest of society (Power and Tunstall, 1995). Until the last few years, the policy response to these problem estates was to spend public money in various ways: physical refurbishment, house improvements, landscaping, door-entry control schemes and so on. The view that the core of the problem was physical design became very popular with Margaret Thatcher, who lavishly funded research by the geographer Alice Coleman to find statistical correlations between design features and social malaise, and further funded experimentation (at even greater expense) with physical modification of actual housing estates. These solutions have not been and could not be effective since the cause of the problems lay mainly in the processes which generated poverty and concentrated poor people in bad housing, not on the effects that bad housing had on people already socially and economically disadvantaged.

More perceptive policy responses now centre on the families living in deprived housing estates, and involve giving them control over their environment to shape it in ways that suit them and meet their needs. The large estates have been split into smaller management units and the tenants given control over management and improvements. This recognizes that the success of a residential area depends on the people living within it and the quality of their social relationships (the local social capital) more than its physical design. If they are a cohesive unit, interact in mutually supportive ways and are participatory in controlling their affairs, then they will form a successful community. This then empowers them to shape their environment to suit their needs. Lacking power and influence as individuals, they can achieve much more acting together. There are many examples within British public sector housing where tenant-centred projects have transformed estates previously condemned as beyond hope; these include Craigmillar in Edinburgh, the cooperatives in Glasgow and Liverpool, and many more. A study of social rented housing in the North of England by Cole et al (1997) concluded that while housing management, design and maintenance were important to residents, more crucial to their contentment was the ability to live happily with their neighbours.

Drawing on many years of experience working on policy solutions for deprived estates in the UK and northern Europe, Power (1996) has concluded that the most effective have been those that not only empower the residents but also link them to the wider community through local governmental support and efforts at social inclusion, emphasizing Jane Jacobs' arguments concerning hierarchies of communities. Furthermore, through cooperation and being given the responsibility for looking after their areas, tenants have become aware of wider environmental issues: issues that they would almost certainly never have addressed while taken up with their own problems as disempowered individuals. These include energy efficiency, pollution, waste and recycling, and public health. Many public sector dwellings in the UK have very poor thermal insulation, which places pressures on domestic heating budgets and is associated with ill health.

Examples are given in Chapter 7 of how energy efficiency has been tackled by tenants' groups, benefiting them physically in terms of warmer homes, and economically in terms of reduced fuel bills and in some cases employment when tenants are employed to carry out some of the work. They have also benefited socially in terms of community cohesion. Environmental issues are essentially issues affecting everyone, and as such are best tackled in a collective way. Collective organization is a step towards prioritization of care for the environment and is important in the strengthening of community cohesion.

Community, like sustainability, is a comprehensive and integrative concept. By giving community development priority, a range of problems can be tackled simultaneously and more effectively through mutual reinforcement. The important links between health and the built environment were discussed in Chapter 6; equally important is the development of health within a community context, since a cohesive community is less stressful for individuals, more supportive and hence more likely to generate and maintain high levels of public health. This has been recognized in the UK by the decision to establish a nation-wide network of Healthy Living Centres (Scott-Samuel, 1997). These will be locally based and will place emphasis on physical, mental and social well-being. An important element of these centres will be that people will address health issues together within a shared sense of community. Facilities such as fitness gyms will be provided, and leisure activities involving exercise such as walking and cycling will be organized. Mental and social health will be developed through cultural and educational activities, including concern for local environmental issues. Good health is seen as multi-dimensional and its maintenance dependent on self-esteem, social support and community cohesion as well as purely physical factors.

A particularly good example of the importance of community to sustainability is given by Pearce (1996), who describes the revitalization of the village of Husa in Sweden. Developed in the eighteenth and nineteenth centuries to exploit local copper resources, the fall of the copper industry precipitated a steady fall in the village's economic fortunes and by 1979 the population had fallen to 90, the only shop had closed and the school was threatened. At this point the villagers got together to write and perform a play reflecting Husa's history and uncertain future. This proved to be a turning point in the village's fortunes, for the success of the play demonstrated to the villagers that they could achieve much more acting together as a community than they could as individuals. The shop was re-opened, the local authority was persuaded to keep the school open, and 15 cooperative enterprises were established to address the village's employment, infrastructural and social needs. These included the development of skiing facilities to attract tourists, a museum to record the village's history, a sawmill, new housing and sewerage improvements, a nursery and a village hall. Individual enterprises have also been established, including a goat farm, bakery, pony trekking and restaurant. In 1990, a village association was set up to coordinate developments and provide an element of strategic planning, and the population had risen to 160. The key features of this success story are community action, participation (25 per cent of all adults are involved in at least one cooperative), inclusiveness (anyone can attend meetings of the village association) and self-sufficiency and the use of local resources and enterprises. Local links are reinforced by economic and social contact, and development is not seen as solely economic. Husa is now economically and socially secure, and is aware of the importance of protecting the local environment. Developments are small scale and appropriate to the local ecology, and future plans include a local organic garden and composting scheme.

The next chapter will explore the links between the modern economy and sustainability, including the effects of globalization on local communities. As a bridge to this discussion it is useful to stress the connection between a successful local economy and a strong local community, and the threat to both posed by contemporary economic organization. Local communities and economies have been destroyed by global movements of capital, with devastating effects on the built environment in terms of abandoned and decaying infrastructure. One response by the people living in such abandoned localities has been to construct a local economy suited to their own needs, for instance by breaking dependence on outside agencies through Local Exchange Trading Schemes (LETS) and Credit Unions. Such schemes increase the interactions between local people (strengthening community) and provide them with locally based employment, income and services (strengthening the local economy).

What these examples illustrate is that for the transformation of our built environment to be more ecologically benign depends upon changing the manner in which we relate to each other. A sense of community – that is, caring for each other – is a vital prerequisite to caring for the environment. A society based on materialism and gratification of individual short-term interest will not only be exploitative within itself and of its weaker members, it will also inevitably exploit and degrade the environment. The built environment such a society produces will reflect that lack of care. By becoming more community-minded, we can shape the built environment to respect natural ecosystems and to provide a context for community to be sustained from one generation to the next. Moreover, community is not just a social concept. The decline of community and social cohesiveness has been one factor in driving individuals into consumerist lifestyles, with all that means in terms of economic growth and environmental impacts. For a community to be successful and sustainable, it needs to integrate social, economic and environmental systems. The beauty of sustainability as a guide to action is that it shows how such integration leads to success on all dimensions. The next chapter shows how a sustainable economy depends upon a sound community and care for the natural environment.

9

A NEW ECONOMY AND THE BUILT ENVIRONMENT

'Economists know the price of everything and the value of nothing'

Anon

'The leaders and institutions that promised a golden age are not delivering.
They assail us with visions of wondrous new technological gadgets, such as
airplane seats with individual television monitors, and an information
highway that will make it possible to fax messages while we sun ourselves on
the beach. Yet the things that most of us really want – a secure means of
livelihood, a decent place to live, healthy and uncontaminated food to eat,
good education and health care for our children, a clean and vital natural
environment – seem to slip further from the grasp of most of the world's people
with each passing day'

Korten, 1995, pp 18–19

Our built environment is the physical result of economic decisions and the involvement of individuals and organizations in the economy. Chapter 7 looked at the CentrO Shopping Centre in Germany and discussed the social impacts of such a development. As a modern temple of consumption, CentrO is the outcome of a fairly simplistic economic supposition: if we build it, people will come and spend lots of money. The impact on the wider environment through pollution, materials use and energy use, and on the immediate built environment through land use and transport generation is not considered. Looked at in this way, we can see that our economy and the type of decisions it promotes will have a great impact on our built environment. This means that if there are problems within our built environment, then at least part of the blame must be laid at the door of the economy. Following this through, if we need to remedy these problems to produce a sustainable built environment, then we need to adjust the economy and make it sustainable.

Our modern towns and cities are the result of industrialization and the growing dominance of the market over our lives. Even in the past, it was the necessity of trade which led to towns and cities building up around established markets. Our great cities such as Venice, Lisbon and London prospered as centres of international trade and as entrepôts for various empires. It was, however, the economic forces of the Industrial Revolution which forced or encouraged people to leave rural areas for the dark satanic mills of our towns and cities and transformed the populations of different countries into predominantly urban ones. The demands of employers were the first major influence on this new built environment: they needed workers and workers needed housing, and this produced a mass building programme that has persisted from Georgian times almost to the present day.

As industrialization has progressed, the economy has attained pre-eminence in our lives. The material has eclipsed the spiritual. Perhaps the greatest change came at the end of the Second World War when governments turned to rapid economic growth to expunge the devastation wrought in Europe and beyond. For many, this preoccupation with market forces has proved lucrative and society now sees economic growth as the dominant paradigm, and the market as the natural place in which to meet our needs and conduct our affairs. Yet it was not always like this. Market forces were originally seen as a means to gain what we needed as individuals, but they have come to be an organizing principle, meaning that the market has institutionalized our behaviour such that we can only act as individuals rather than as part of a community or other social group. Instead of using the market simply as an efficient means to exchange goods, we have internalized its ideas and altered our behaviour accordingly. Wilkinson makes the point that:

> '. . . the self-interested individualism of the marketplace spills over into other areas of social life. If we come to know ourselves through the market, then we behave as if its motivations were inherent deep within us. The nature of public life changes and human interaction becomes dominated by the asocial values of the market.'
>
> Wilkinson, 1996, p 145

This change in society has had profound implications for the built environment. As the nature of our public life and of human interaction has changed so our demands on the built environment change. In the previous chapter, we discussed the importance of community to sustainability and the built environment. A community is the mortar which binds together the physical aspects of the built environment and informs our notions of a sense of place. Without this, our built environment loses its ability to meet the true needs of its inhabitants and becomes a soulless place. The existence and strength of a community depends upon the maintenance of social values; values which have had little part to play in modern day capitalism. The economic principles of the free market were promoted most obviously by the governments of Thatcher and Reagan. However, the free market policies unleashed in the 1980s mean that we are all *'committed to facing whatever adventures may befall us on our predetermined developmental journey. The future rigours of that expedition may cause us one day to look back upon the Thatcher years . . . as a time of high humanity, temperance and clemency.'*

Seabrook, 1996

It was Margaret Thatcher who promised to make the UK 'a more abrasive, less cosy place' and famously declared that 'there is no such thing as society'. Without society, there is no community and without this little to hold our built environment together. According to George Soros:

'Unsure of what they stand for, people increasingly rely on money as the criterion of value. What is more expensive is considered better . . . What used to be a medium of exchange has usurped the place of fundamental values, reversing the relationship postulated by economic theory . . . Society has lost its anchor.'

Soros, 1997, p 2

The adoption of the mantra of economic growth has dramatically sped up changes in society and has turned us into consumers. Consumption has become the main instrument of economic policy and the main way in which people increasingly seek happiness and declare their individual worth and status. Our built environment has metamorphosed to reflect this fact and increasingly resembles a temple of mass consumerism.

Consumption necessitates the use of raw materials and energy for production. Once we have taken part and entered into the game, we then need more products to justify these first steps, and are encouraged at every turn to go further. For example, average home size has risen in the developed world even as family size has shrunk. In the United States, between 1949 and 1990, floor space requirements per person for new houses doubled because as Gopal Ahluwalia of the US National Association of Home Builders puts it, 'everybody wants a media room, a home office, an exercise room, three bathrooms, a family room, a living room, and a huge, beautiful kitchen that nobody cooks in' (Owens, 1994). Increases in house size, increases in levels of car ownership and use, increases in the number of consumer goods and shops we 'need' to satisfy our wants, all affect the built environment. All these things require more land, increasing rates of extraction of natural resources and rising levels of energy use. All this puts more and more pressure on the natural environment.

As we come to behave more and more as creatures of market forces, so our reliance on other forces, such as social networks, decreases. For example, while we once might have relied on an extended family or neighbours to provide childcare or baby-sitting, these options are no longer available to many people. Families are often scattered geographically and communities broken, in part because of the impacts of market forces. The lack of such options means people must use the market to provide for such things, increasing their reliance on it (through an increased demand for money). This further limits their ability to step outside the market to provide for their own needs. The result is a vicious circle of increasing dependence and an increasing breakdown of non-market forces.

Our consumption-based economy also creates social problems within the built environment. Planning decisions, land use policy and a growth in levels of transport all tend to impact more heavily on the poor, as was demonstrated in Chapter 7. While it is the poorer members of society who usually bear most of the costs of economic growth, they are normally the ones who see the least benefit through employment and regeneration, so are the least able to use the economy to alleviate their situation. A lack of social or community structures means they cannot find other ways to meet their needs, and this compounds their poverty.

If, as Korten noted at the start of the chapter, our economy is not providing for our basic needs but offering us only illusory pleasures, and if the result of our economic activity is a built environment which seems only to reinforce unsustainable patterns of resource consumption while undermining its own social fabric and damaging the natural environment at a local and a global scale, then we need desperately to look for a new economic model which will be sustainable and which in turn will produce a sustainable built environment that provides for our real needs.

To become sustainable, our economy needs to be one which considers these wider social and environmental costs as a part of its thinking so that consumer decisions reflect full benefits and costs of each particular product. We also need an economy which works within and promotes the shared values so important to each individual community. Shared values work best within local areas, less so across continents. Therefore it is important to ensure we support a locally based rather than a globally based economy. It is within our local area that we have control over how we work. Outside of this we have no such control and as economies increase in scale from local through national, international and finally to global, it becomes harder and harder to ensure that they behave responsibly and within the bounds set by individual communities and groups of communities. In practical terms this means rooting economic activity much more firmly in the local environment. Greater levels of economic activity must take place within a single area, rather than between areas and regions. The end result should be a more vibrant built environment with a more stable and sustainable economy in which we can live and work. Finally, we must look away from the concepts of growth and consumption and seek satisfaction in other areas. In part this will come from reinvigorating our communities. Alongside this, however, it will come from our towns and cities which have long served as centres for culture, art and education. By exploring these avenues maybe we can meet our needs more completely than from interminable excursions to out-of-town shopping centres.

PROMOTING LOCAL ECONOMIES

Globalization – our increasing reliance upon global trade and global markets which are dominated by a small number of large corporations or trading blocks – has tended to be seen as the inevitable consequence of the free market and competition, and as the most efficient and therefore cheapest means of providing us with what we want and need. In a bid to be efficient and to promote international trade and therefore economic growth, countries are steadily reducing tariff barriers and freeing up capital so that it can move around globally in search of the best return on investment. Political ventures such as the European Union (EU) and the North American Free Trade Area (NAFTA), as well as global counterparts such as the World Trade Organization and its investment equivalent the Multilateral Agreement on Investment (MAI), have as their prime concern the facilitation of international trade. Other concerns are almost always secondary to this.

For example, under MAI, governments will be less able to use investment policy to pursue social, economic or environmental objectives, and transnational corporations will acquire new powers including the freedom to move capital and profits unhindered by policies which bind domestic companies. Furthermore, it will place corporations on an equal or higher legal footing with governments; for example corporations can sue governments for non-compliance with MAI, but governments have no similar right. One can be fairly certain that corporations will use instruments such as MAI to roll back environmental and social laws which may restrict global trade. The President of the US Council on International Business (USCIB) wrote in a letter to senior US officials on 21 March 1997, 'The MAI is an agreement by governments to protect international investors and to liberalise investment regimes' and 'We will oppose any and all measures to create or even imply binding obligations for governments or business related to environment or labor [sic].' (McAllister, 1997). Instruments such as MAI will make more common court challenges over environmental regulations and prohibitions. For example, the Ethyl Corporation is currently suing the Canadian Government for a breach of NAFTA, because the Canadian Parliament has banned MMT (a fuel additive) on health and environmental grounds. The Ethyl Corporation argues that such measures are 'tantamount to expropriation'. NAFTA has an environmental 'sidebar' governing environmental protection, yet MAI has no such concerns, meaning that such legal actions are likely to become more common and governments robbed of some of the power they need to take forward sustainability (McAllister, op cit).

The global economic system was supposed to bring an interdependence between nations and increased security and prosperity. Too often, however, it has led to dependence of communities on market forces which have little regard for hardships which economic processes such as relocating factories might cause. Communities are either dependent upon outside agents for their food, products and services, or else rely upon other communities continuing to buy the food, products and services they provide. Such dependence is the result of economic specialization which encourages one region or city to become a centre for one industry or other. The Single Market in the EU is accelerating this process of specialization as companies take advantage of free movement of capital and a lack of tariff barriers. According to David Owen, an economist at Dresdner Kleinwort Benson in the City of London, single market reforms and the move to Monetary Union will produce greater concentrations of industries in certain areas. The consequence of this is that:

> 'Instead of being evenly distributed within each country, firms are likely to huddle together in clusters of excellence and expertise, irrespective of national barriers . . . It could mean that no longer will every country have, for example, a car industry and a financial centre. There is likely to be room for only one of each within the monetary union – as in the United States, where car production is heavily concentrated in Detroit, finance around New York, carpet manufacturing around Dalton, information technology around Silicon Valley and agriculture in the mid-West.'

quoted in Atkinson, 1997, p 4

The study suggests, for example, that car production would concentrate in Germany, light machinery in Italy, plastics in Portugal and cement production in Greece. The end result is one of a few 'honey-pot' areas, and a mass of communities with little or no industry, high unemployment and rising inequality. It means having more Liverpools and Detroits; more cities left high and dry when the industry they relied upon for so long either moved or went under. Such concentration and specialization of our economies is therefore unsustainable. Once an area is committed to its specialism it is hard to readjust and reinvigorate the local economy which can truly serve local needs. It also means increasing levels of transport across increasing distances (Whitelegg, 1993), as people will need to 'import' into their area everything they have ceased producing in order to specialize in their particular field. Such trends are exacerbated by the global free market, because international companies will often move capital and production elsewhere in search of lower labour costs, lower regulatory standards or to help them access new markets.

These harsh realities mean that local communities are compelled to compete ruthlessly with each other for inward investment, and often have to provide generous tax breaks and sacrifice all other concerns – such as the environment – in the quest for job creation. This sacrifice puts further pressure on the surrounding built environment. For example, according to Jim Gill of English Partnerships (the organization responsible for industrial development and urban regeneration in England) it is naive for local government to offer large international companies brownfield sites to entice them into an area, as these companies have a particular 'mindset' which means building on the edges of towns and cities on greenfield sites with good motorway access. His view was that it is very hard not to sacrifice environmental considerations in the quest for inward investment and economic growth (Gill, 1996). Reliance upon large outside companies can often mean bowing to their demands, which can involve the use of green sites and the construction of new roads. Such developments encourage other greenfield development, greater levels of car use, more road building and an increasing level of environmental damage. Subsidies offered by governments to encourage such developments mean that taxpayers' money is being used to fuel unsustainable practices. As we shall see next, such development practices are also of limited use to, and may even damage, the local economy.

LOCAL ECONOMIES, RETAILING, LAND USE AND CONSTRUCTION

Globalization and the destruction of local economies is also leading to our towns and cities becoming increasingly homogeneous, with the same shop fronts and products found with monotonous repetition between towns, countries and even continents. This is done in the name of choice and job creation yet, paradoxically, such chains contribute little to the area they settle in. Commercial developments such as arcades, retail parks and shopping centres are often promoted by developers and planners as ways to strengthen our local economies, yet sites at such developments are unaffordable to local firms, and in any case, prime units are usually only offered to national chains and often at low rates. Because people's choice of where they shop now depends upon the presence of certain stores, developers need such stores to relocate to their mall. The result is a self-fulfilling prophecy. Local firms remain in traditional town centre locations whilst larger stores move into out-of-town arcades. Shoppers are attracted to these arcades at the expense of traditional shopping areas. Because of the political support given to retail parks local authorities, who are keen to bring investment to an area, often waive all or some of the local taxes payable and are generally supportive of planning applications made for the development.

Developers are therefore encouraged to build out-of-town centres on greenfield sites leading to the built environment slowly encroaching into the surrounding countryside. Even if such developments are in town, or on brownfield sites, they will require large investments in infrastructure: in particular large amounts of land for roads and car parking. The provision of free or subsidized car parking amounts to a significant subsidy for car use (Litman, 1996) and does little to enhance the look of an area, while road building only encourages greater levels of car use and further damage to the natural environment.

After all the effort, however, it is unlikely that the local area will benefit. Local people get to have more national and international chains located on the edge of their town, but the employment creation of such developments is limited. Developments are often accompanied by press releases from developers and the local authority emphasizing the new employment being generated through construction of the site and through employment at the stores. These claims are usually repeated in the local press yet rarely materialize. Research suggests that a supermarket will need to increase turnover by £250,000 to create one extra job, whereas only £50,000 is needed to create a job in a local corner store (New Economics Foundation, 1997). This means that if the end result is less trade for local stores and more for large chains, the employment effect will be negative.

There are only two ways such developments can boost rather than depress a local economy. The first occurs if the park is of such a size that it attracts shoppers from a substantial hinterland and the increase in trade is enough to boost overall employment levels. Even if this occurs, however, the development will still see the closure of local stores and will be at the expense of other local economies. The success of the enterprise will also be based on large-scale environmental damage with greater levels of land use and increased levels of transport leading to greater pollution and the need for new roads. The second option is if consumers themselves can be encouraged to spend more and more often. However, local stores would still suffer because the site of consumption has been changed. Furthermore, greater levels of consumption necessitate increasing levels of material and energy intensity within society which is unsustainable.

Despite the negative social and environmental consequences of such developments, they tend to be seen as vital elements of our modern economy, and it is this which determines how our built environment develops. Areas are seen as economically backward if they do not have at least one such development, when in reality the economic benefits are mixed. The problem is that our economy is based on increasing levels of economic growth which must be supported by increasing levels of consumption. This being the goal of society, individuals in turn take it as their goal, and the built environment evolves accordingly. Planners and government officials facilitate such development in the belief that it will bring the employment demanded by the local community. If, however, the benefits prove fleeting, the effect is irreparable. Such developments have knock-on effects with surrounding land being taken up by further development. New roads cement relationships between the consumers and the particular retail park which cannot easily be undone, and once a town centre deteriorates past a certain point, there will be little that can revive it. Furthermore, once people become accustomed to a certain kind and a certain level of consumption they resent it being threatened. Shopping becomes a right because we feel it as an innate need. As Schor notes, 'Over time, people become habituated or "addicted" to the level of consumption which they are attaining. Goods which are originally experienced as luxuries come to be seen as necessities' (Schor, 1995, p 74).

The current trend is for less local stores and greater levels of spending at out-of-town shopping centres. A study of UK shopping habits has shown that the top four trading locations, judged by turnover and profitability per square foot were all out-of-town shopping centres over 1 million square feet (9.3 hectares) in area. Out-of-town centres already account for a quarter of all retail sales and this is likely to rise to a third by the end of the century. The report concludes that town centres will survive but will shrink in size and increasingly cater for poorer people who cannot afford to travel to more luxurious or distant sites (Mintel, 1995).

One point not considered above is the respending effect of different types of employment. Large chains tend to 'export' money out of the area, whereas local firms are more likely to recirculate it within the area. A study by the Institute for Local Self Reliance in Washington, DC showed that for a typical McDonalds outlet, 74 per cent of the store's expenditure left the community, 9 per cent had no clear destination, and only 17 per cent remained in the community (Sale, 1980). Similarly, when constructing new fast food restaurants and 'drive thrus', fast food chains such as McDonalds tend to use outside work crews which are 'parachuted in' to build a building of a standard design and type. Using the same crew over and over again with little variation in the design means that costs are saved with the construction time, from availability of the site to completion and revenue generation, being an average of nine days (CIRIA, 1997). However, it provides little benefit to the local community short of giving them a new burger bar to take their children to. This method of working is not peculiar to the fast food sector, but is an approach used by many large companies and large construction firms.

It is widely recognized by the industry that medium-sized local-based firms are important for a healthy construction sector, as they provide stability in local areas, help train apprentices and are of a sufficient size to handle most work. Market trends show, however, that the number of construction firms is falling, while the average size is increasing (MacGregor et al, 1995). This means that construction is increasingly becoming the concern of a small number of national and even international companies. These companies have little local accountability and provide little lasting employment to an area, so that when a recession hits they simply withdraw, shedding their self-employed labour and cutting their losses, and when the recession ends they are slow to recruit again and provide the employment and stability that people and communities need. In short, our construction industry, like many others, is losing its base in the community, and our communities are losing the support these firms gave.

If local firms and local labour are used in construction projects, then local communities and economies are strengthened rather than weakened. Studies conducted show that it is often difficult to create local employment through the use of construction projects, because the work is often of a temporary nature. However, through supporting local firms, existing local jobs can be safeguarded and valuable training opportunities provided for local people. It has also been shown that employment can be provided through concentrating on building refurbishment and renewal (MacGregor et al, 1995). Such work is cyclical and is much in need, given the importance of making houses more energy efficient and the poor condition of much of the housing stock in the developed world.

Directing work to local firms ensures that the money circulates much longer within the community, rather than leaving with a remote construction firm once any building work is completed. Large, distant firms have no concerns for a local area, save those which assist its profit-making activities. However, local firms have a greater duty of care to an area and are more likely to make better informed longer term decisions that assist the locality. A good example of this can be seen in the financial sector. Through loans and investment, the banking industry invests in and supports our economies, and the way banks choose to invest can strengthen or weaken our local economies.

In the UK, over 3000 bank branches (about one in three) have been closed down by the main high street banks. These closures have affected our smaller and poorer communities leaving many without easy access to banking. Bank of England statistics show that one in seven residents of Birmingham now have no local access to a bank (Conaty, 1995). This problem is heightened by the fact that banks are increasingly reluctant to invest in problem areas, because nowadays their principal interests lie in currency speculation, insurance and stockbroking. The ways in which a bank can abandon a local area and promote its downfall, and how community banking can help promote and support an area, are all amply demonstrated by a close look at the South Shore district of Chicago. In the 1950s, the district was considered one of the better neighbourhoods of central Chicago. However, by 1970, white flight had produced a swift turnover in the population and the area had become 70 per cent black. Most of the area's banks moved out with the white population, leaving only three banks for a population of 78,000. Two of these were later closed by the government regulator, leaving only the South Shore Bank, which itself sought to move but was denied permission by the regulator. It had already changed its lending policy: of the $33 million deposited in the bank, only $120,000, or 0.3 per cent, had been returned as loans to its customers living in the area. As Douthwaite notes, 'Chicago's banks had made a self-fulfilling prophecy: because they expected the area to decline they refused to lend in the area, thus making it certain that the predicted decline would occur.' (Douthwaite, 1996, p 151).

However, in 1973 South Shore Bank was taken over by a small group of bankers committed to serving the needs of the community. Mortgages became available, and the bank began to lend money for renovation projects in the area. Some 25 years later, the bank had financed the renovation of more than 10,000 residential units – over a third of the total in the district – placed 3500 people from its job training programmes and assisted over 150 new firms. Furthermore, the bank has not been out of profit since 1983 (Meeker-Lowry, 1995; Douthwaite, 1996). Following its success, other US banks are now investigating the possibilities of community banking and South Shore has helped set up a bank in Arkansas which aims to support rural communities and small towns in the state through channelling 'financial and informational services to local economies independent of large, distant corporations.' (Gryzywinski, 1996, p 153).

Locally based banking is an important part of a locally based economy. The alternative is to continue moving towards a global economy in which regions and countries concentrate only on what they do best. This, however, will reduce the self-sufficiency of communities and nations and push wage levels and environmental standards down. The absurd finale of such a policy is described in the novel *Snow Crash* by Neal Stephenson:

'This is America . . . this country has one of the worst economies in the world. When it gets down to it – talking trade balances here – once we've brain drained all our technology into other countries, once things have evened out, they're making cars in Bolivia and microwave ovens in Tadzhikistan and selling them here – once our edge in natural resources has been made irrelevant . . . – once the Invisible Hand has taken all those historical inequities and smeared them out into a broad global layer of what a Pakistani brickmaker would consider to be prosperity – y'know what? There's only four things we do better than anyone else

music
movies
microcode (software)
high-speed pizza delivery'

Stephenson, 1993, pp 2–3

Before we reach such a situation, we should take stock of our position and remind ourselves just how ludicrous some of our transactions really are. Instead of this ongoing specialization and monotony, we should promote diversity through strengthening local economies. We depend upon the economy to provide the stability and resources for maintaining a healthy built environment. Our economy provides the employment and capital needed for development, and a stable economy allows effective planning for the long-term needs of an area. There is no doubt that these objectives can be better met if local communities are able to provide for more of their own needs. As the Rocky Mountain Institute (RMI) states:

'In every town, many goods and services which are purchased out of town are, or could be, produced and/or marketed locally. Such greater self-reliance means more than saving money. Without a strong local economy, there is little basis for strong regional, and ultimately national, commerce. In this sense, a lasting recovery on Wall Street must begin on Main Street'

RMI, 1995, p 128

TELLING THE ECOLOGICAL TRUTH

The conventional model of economic growth tells us that we live in a prosperous progressive society, and that growth has brought about large-scale gains. For many, this may seem true, yet the price of this growth often goes unnoticed. The lesson of ecological economics is that our economy must internalize environmental and social costs within day-to-day transactions. This is not just idealistic green thinking, but makes sound economic sense, because we cannot have a strong, stable economy able to meet the needs of society without stable foundations. New economic thinking shows explicitly that our economy needs the support of natural and social elements if it is to prosper. New measures of wealth such as the Index of Sustainable Economic Welfare (ISEW) or the World Bank's Wealth and Genuine Savings Indicators show clearly that ignoring these elements simply means hiding real costs which can actually be greater than the much vaunted gains from economic growth. ISEW calculations suggest that our economy is actually running backwards as external costs begin to outstrip actual benefits (Jackson and Marks, 1994; World Bank, 1995; New Economics Foundation and Friends of the Earth, 1997).

Damage caused by our economy is apparent across the globe, but nowhere are the social and environmental costs more visible than in the built environment. To correct this we need an economy which can create employment, increase social welfare and safeguard the environment at the same time. This requires a recognition that employment and environmental challenges may both be:

> *'symptoms of the same defect in our present pattern of economic development: an inefficient use of resources, represented by under-use of human resources and over-use of environmental resources . . . the only viable and lasting solution may be a strategy that addresses both concerns at the same time.'*

EU, 1993

It is critical that we recognize that it is within our power to control the form of the built environment. As was made clear in Chapter 2, if we choose, we can have a built environment which is sustainable, which fosters a high quality of life amongst its residents and has a vibrant economy able to meet people's needs equitably while protecting and enhancing the environment. To achieve this built environment, we first need to choose sustainable development as the model for our society and the course we wish to embark on. Once we have done this, we must then put in place the steering mechanisms needed to point us in the correct direction. As Redclift notes:

> *'To achieve sustainable development we should look no further than our own behaviour, and the economic and social institutions we have constructed which need to be radically overhauled. We are accustomed to speak about bequeathing the environment to future generations, but frequently balk at the idea that we are also bequeathing social institutions with which to manage the environment. It can only be achieved by incorporating a knowledge of the consequences of our behaviour into the behaviour itself'*
>
> Redclift, 1996, pp 1–2

The steering mechanisms and the changes needed in our economy are set out below, but first it is important to look at the costs we impose upon ourselves by not choosing sustainable development and continuing on as before, regardless of all the warning signs.

The Environmental Costs of our Economy

Mainstream economics tends to ignore natural resources (classified as 'land') as an element of production, and usually concentrates on labour and capital. Over time our economy has become more capital intensive and less labour intensive, because capital intensive processes tend to use energy and raw materials to replace expensive and 'inefficient' labour. This shift towards more energy and materials intensive forms of production has come about because we undervalue both the raw materials (the source) which are the essential productive input and the planet's capacity to absorb (the sink) our pollutants and waste that seem to be an unavoidable consequence of our economy. Undervaluing these functions leads us to waste precious resources and abuse the planet's assimilative capabilities, and locks us into more and more damaging forms of behaviour.

Our built environment takes its qualities from this behaviour. Undervaluing the natural environment has encouraged forms of building which are materials and energy intensive and which have high levels of obsolescence. Buildings designed with no consideration of environmental issues are usually cheaper than those built with high environmental standards. If financial considerations lead us to construct buildings of lower environmental standards, then money will be saved in the short term, but ultimately we are damaging the long-term strength of the economy through squandering the natural capital on which it depends. On top of this, we have very low rates of reuse and recycling within society in general and the construction industry in particular because such practices are seen as costly and therefore unviable (Liddell et al, 1994). It is more economically efficient using conventional costings to extract new material from one hole whilst burying old building materials in another. The only recycling in this instance is the eventual end use of all these quarries as landfill sites in their own right.

Undervaluing natural resources has also encouraged increasing levels of transport, with goods travelling increasing distances, and people relying increasingly on motor transport for commuting, shopping and entertainment. This fuels demand for more roads and more parking spaces, and a gradual pushing back of the built environment into the surrounding countryside. Undervaluing the role of our rural environment means that our built environment spreads outwards not because we have run out of space but because we have used available space inefficiently. Financially it often makes more sense to develop greenfield sites than to bring old abandoned sites back into use.

The way in which economic policies affect land use policies and practice can be clearly seen in the built environment; perhaps one of the worst examples is Detroit. The advent of the motor car led to the rapid growth of Detroit and economic dependence upon the automobile. Detroit's population quadrupled in only 20 years, rising from 280,000 in 1900 to well over 1 million by 1920. By 1950, its population was 2 million and city planners were building roads and setting aside land for commercial development and housing for an expected population of 8 million. Such profligate use of land came about because of the city's embracing of a car-culture, yet this culture has also been its downfall. Before the Second World War most factories were located along railroad lines and most housing clustered around railway stations, but as road transport grew, factories relocated out of inner city areas to greenfield sites, and suburbanization led to a mass exodus of workers to better quality homes. Today the population is down to 1 million, and in the past two decades has fallen by 32 per cent. Factories and housing for the affluent tend to be located outside of the city boundaries in neighbouring boroughs, meaning that the city authorities have little tax income to spend. The outflow of industry and people has left the city with a rash of abandoned housing and deserted industrial sites, much of it contaminated land which developers find to be too expensive to clean up on conventional accounting mechanisms.

These are the physical impacts and costs of inefficient and wasteful economic policies, but there are also social costs to be dealt with. The percentage of poor in Detroit has doubled from 15 per cent in 1970 to 32 per cent in 1990. Infant mortality rates are three times higher in Detroit than in the neighbouring suburb of Warren. Forty per cent of the residents of working age in 'Motor City' do not have a car, but mass freeway construction has left poor public transport links so that those still living in Detroit have trouble commuting to neighbouring boroughs for work (World Resources Institute, 1996).

These mistakes stem from the economic system's preoccupation with financial capital, economic growth, land speculation and road construction. By excluding other costs from the financial analysis, policy makers unleashed a chain of events that have produced at least as many costs as benefits. Internalizing such costs within our economy would have ensured the decisions made did not hide future costs but took them into consideration. The end result would have been less urban sprawl, less abandoned land, and a less fractured community.

THE SOCIAL COSTS OF OUR ECONOMY

The Industrial Revolution itself marked a massive change away from production by small-scale artisans to production by factories and machinery. But these factories were still heavily reliant upon labour. Today, however, the typical factory only needs a few people to run it, most of the work being done by machinery. The impact on our towns and cities is a growth in underemployment and a rise in associated social problems. For those of us not at the sharp end of this, the replacement of human by machine is mirrored in our homes by our fascination for and use of so-called 'labour-saving' devices. We are prepared to spend our hard-earned money on these devices because we see it as more efficient to use our money in this way rather than use our time/labour.

Within industry, investment in new machinery is an important part of remaining competitive, and price signals encourage the use of more machinery and less labour. Thus, when a company takes on workers it is taxed more, yet when it sacks workers and replaces them with machinery, it is allowed to offset the cost of this machinery against tax. This outlook, coupled with the rapid technological advances in our society, presents us with a situation in which economic growth and technological change are not being accompanied by a growth in employment. As David Orr has stated: 'The emphasis on production leads to the ever greater use of ever more scarce resources in order to conserve labour that has become abundant' (Orr, 1979, p 80). The end result may be a 'new phase in human history' in which: 'fewer and fewer workers will be needed to produce the goods and services for the global population . . . Already, millions of workers have been permanently eliminated from the economic process, and whole job categories have shrunk, been restructured or disappeared.' (Rifkin, 1995, pp xiv–xv).

The effects of this lack of employment are increasingly obvious within our built environment. In agriculture, the replacement of labour with machinery has robbed villages of much needed employment, and has promoted a drift to towns and cities in the search for work. Houses vacated are bought up by richer commuters whose lack of contact and involvement with the community often turns these areas into sterile places with little cultural life and whose car-based community causes environmental damage and pollution. Within our towns and cities, lack of employment is creating a permanent underclass gathered in sink-estates. UK research shows that as few as 22 per cent of people in social housing have employment (Burrows, 1997). Many others on such estates are on low wages or are underemployed.

However, an economy which recognized the importance of human resources would not find it more efficient to replace labour with machinery or technological processes that are capital, materials and energy intensive. Instead, we would seek to use all our assets equally. Investment and technological change are both imperative for a healthy economy, yet investment should aim to reduce material and energy intensity and utilize human resources. Such a policy would help us solve the wider problem of how to help those in society suffering from the effects of underemployment and inequity. Lower levels of unemployment will help us to tackle problems of deprivation and poverty prevalent in large parts of our built environment. Such problems fuel vandalism, crime and fear of crime, and reduce overall quality of life. Provision of employment can provide people with the financial security they need and bring them back into society. By doing this, the bonds of society and community can be strengthened and not worn down over time.

The physical shape and nature of our built environment will also be changed if our economy ascribes more value to labour resources. Construction practices will begin to value materials more highly and use them efficiently. Comparatively lower labour costs will encourage the redevelopment of traditional crafts in our buildings, while architects will turn away from the use of materials and designs of high embodied energy, and instead use materials which are more locally sourced or are of lower embodied energy. Reliance upon cars and lorries is also likely to decrease as costs rise, allowing us to reclaim the spaces we have progressively given up to the automobile and the lorry. Such changes will change the layout and nature of our built environment, making it more sustainable.

LINKING ENVIRONMENTAL AND SOCIAL CONCERNS

Genuine wealth comes from economic policies which are concerned with financial, natural and human capital. For the built environment, conventional financial perspectives encourage developments that squander our natural resources and ignore associated social costs. Large-scale road building is seen as good for the economy, yet if it leads to a deterioration of the environment and causes social problems such as the breakup of community, then it may actually reduce the wealth of our society.

If one looks at our modern buildings – especially industrial and commercial buildings – one can see that they utilize technologically advanced materials which are materials and energy intensive. While the construction industry is still a labour intensive one, more technologically advanced building methods are often less labour intensive than traditional ones. The use of system building methods, mass produced components and the specification of materials such as sheet steel and poured concrete instead of timber, straw, stone or brick reduce our reliance upon labour. Such choices are seen as cost effective, but they are non-sustainable socially and environmentally.

Our current accounting practices are incredibly wasteful in use of materials. Buildings often have criminally short lifetimes, it being apparently more cost effective to tear one building down, landfill its remains and then use fresh materials to construct a replacement. The financial capital needed for this process must be used and recirculated as quickly as possible to generate the required profits. Furthermore, the expected level of profit increases and the payback period decreases as speculators demand more and more from their investments. In order to meet such financial demands developers lean more heavily upon the social and natural environments which bear increasingly disproportionate costs yet do not share the benefit. For example, the value of a modern office building has little to do with the materials and energy used in its construction, but depends heavily on its rent earning capacity. The *real* cost of the development is therefore obscured, but a small number of developers and companies become rich at the long-term expense of the built environment (Ambrose and Colenutt, 1975).

DISCOUNTING THE FUTURE

Developers are encouraged to think of short-term profits rather than the long-term consequences of their actions because our financial system actually discourages long-term investment through the practice of discounting. Discounting is used in financial assessments to calculate the most effective use of capital in investments. The application of discounting often leads to short-term policies, because the cost-yardsticks used discourage spending more money now to save more in the long term. It is equivalent to saying that benefits or costs to people next year matter 5 per cent (or whatever the rate is) less than current benefits or costs. Daly and Cobb compare discounting practices to killing the goose that lays the golden egg for the short-term gain while being blind to the long-term consequences:

> *"When is it economically rational to kill the goose that lays golden eggs?" Any exploited species (fish, timber, etc) managed on a sustainable-yield basis is like a goose that lays golden eggs in perpetuity ... Folk wisdom says never kill it ... [Discounting] says to kill it under certain circumstances ... (that is) discount the income stream of the golden eggs at the rate of interest and if that discounted sum is less than the price you could get for the cooked goose today then you kill the goose. The fact that individual capitalists are made better off by killing the goose ... does not alter the fact that society has lost a perpetual stream of golden eggs.'*
>
> Daly and Cobb, 1989, pp 155–56

Within the built environment discounting works against the adoption of construction practices designed to provide long-lasting buildings. Instead, costings on new buildings are typically made over a 60 year lifespan and investors are unable to look beyond such a time period because as time increases so does investment uncertainty. House buyers have no personal interest in planning for such lengths of time because they may not be alive or their needs may have changed, but financial signals do not encourage them to look forward in time and plan accordingly. Those seeking commercial property see little point in thinking long term because the future is too uncertain beyond a certain point. The end result is that it becomes cost effective to build up to or below this 60 year limit, rather than specify a design and set of materials which will last much longer. Discounting also works against the adoption of high energy efficiency standards. Against current cost-yardsticks, energy efficiency can be shown to make good financial sense, but financial gains are limited because our investment system downgrades the worth of savings made in the future.

One UK study found that energy efficiency measures could reduce overall building costs by £11,000 (or 10 per cent) over the standard 60 year period. However, under the discount rate of 8.0 per cent – which is the rate recommended by the UK Treasury for long-term investment analysis – the savings gained over the 60 years come out at £1100. This would mean an investor would only be prepared to spend an extra £1100 to save over £11,000 across 60 years (Smith et al, 1995, 1997).

For consumption generally, discounting discourages spending more on products which will last longer or use less energy. This in turn discourages manufacturers from designing and producing higher quality products. Within the construction, automotive and electrical industries, much has been made of 'design for demanufacture' and the taking apart of old buildings, cars, washing machines at the end of their product life. Consideration of demanufacture at the design stage can dramatically reduce future costs of reuse and recycling, but discounting practices work against such an approach. While a washing machine might sell for £200, after a product life of 20 years it might only have a resale value of £20. The present value of this resale is only £7.50, meaning that it is only worth spending this much extra to extend a product's lifetime or to build in features which would make components easier to reuse or recycle (Simon, 1997). Economic cost-yardsticks show that it would be cheaper to invest this £7.50 in new production involving the manufacture of new products of short lifetimes.

Even when there is a realization that current economic policies have future costs, discounting artificially reduces the size of these costs, allowing them to be forgotten and left for a future time. However, as the examples of East Elizabeth (see Chapter 7) and Detroit have shown, future costs are often considerable and go beyond our ability to pay. By leaving problems to the future, we increase rather than reduce the cost; even small insignificant costs mount up over time. A prime example of this is the problem of contaminated land. In the UK alone it has been estimated that there are as many as 75,000 sites affecting over 100,000 hectares. Clean-up costs are put at between £10 and £30 billion (ENDS, 1991). Through a lack of concern or understanding about the environment, industrialists and planners – of the distant and none too distant past – have promoted profit without concern for future costs. One has only to think of Love Canal in the USA to see that when the chickens come home to roost on contaminated land, the cost is often too much to bear. Passing the buck to future generations in this manner is obviously unsustainable and ought to make no economic sense. That it apparently did is a damning indictment of our present economy.

We must avoid the temptation to use the built environment as a storage area for these hidden costs and instead deal with problems as they arise. We should therefore be prepared to make decisions on a more long-term basis and be realistic about the future. Buildings which will stand the test of time, and land use policies which will reduce our impact on the environment should therefore be promoted.

Discounting, however, is not the whole problem, but merely a symptom of the failure of our society to recognize the importance to the economy of environmental and social issues, and speaks volumes of how unsustainable current practices are. A prime concern of sustainability is the stability of future generations, yet discounting practices discourage us from considering this. It is therefore clear that discounting 'contradicts the most basic principle of sustainability, that the rights of future generations are as important as those of the present.' (Expert Group on the Urban Environment, 1996). A more sustainable economics would include the social and environmental costs within its pricing structure, which is one of the goals of ecological tax reform.

ECOLOGICAL TAX REFORM

Ecological tax reform (ETR) involves a restructuring of our taxation system so that the environment takes up a place on the economic balance sheet (Weizsäcker and Jedinghaus, 1992) and is 'probably . . . the most realistic instrument for approximating economic costs to the "ecological truth"' (Weizsäcker, 1994, p 128). Such instruments will be important for changing the pricing signals which have so damaged our built environment and can therefore help in steering society towards more sustainable forms of behaviour.

The other advantage of ecological tax reform is that it allows governments to shift the basis of taxation away from labour. This means that indirect labour costs would fall making it more profitable to lay off stocks of materials, kilowatt hours and barrels of oil than to lay off people. Because of its ability to encourage employment as well as protect the environment, ecological tax reform 'is increasingly taking on the mantle of a social policy rather than an environmental one, a switch in bias that reflects the judicial and ethical component of sustainable development' (O'Riordan, 1997, p 3). Table 9.1 shows a possible list of relevant winners and losers and provides some indication of how the built environment might change with ecological tax reform.

On the whole, the construction industry would be a beneficiary of ETR (Gee, 1997) because it is a labour intensive industry, though material and energy costs within the industry would rise considerably, which would necessitate a change in methods of construction and in the type of materials used. Over time the face of the industry would also change as it responded to price signals and began working in new ways appropriate to these signals.

By making materials use more expensive, the aggregates and quarrying industries would contract as products became relatively more expensive and demand fell. Higher prices would encourage the use of longer lasting materials, and the construction of longer lasting buildings. Similarly, it will become better financial sense to refurbish rather than demolish buildings and ensure that the lifespan of materials in use is extended. This will lead to planners, developers and architects adopting a longer-term outlook and considering how an area, the needs of users and the suitability of a building might change over time. Buildings more easily adapted to fit different uses would be seen as desirable.

At the same time, the reuse and recycling of construction waste would become more attractive financially and markets would expand. Changing price signals will express better the future financial opportunities to be had at the end of a building's lifetime from the sale of old materials. Instead of being seen as a burden, old properties will be seen as containing useful resources with ready markets. Similarly, derelict sites and run-down buildings in our built environment would be seen as useful sources of materials – 'quarries' within our towns and cities rather than hazards and eyesores – which could either be developed or 'mined' for their resources. Construction methods which allow these resources in buildings to be re-accessed will therefore be seen as good business practice,

Table 9.1   *Winners and Losers from Ecological Tax Reform*

Winners	Losers
Construction:	Construction:
Traditional forms of construction;	'Advanced' construction methods;
Vernacular based architecture;	Tower blocks and skyscrapers;
Renovation;	Demolition without reuse and
Forms of construction which enable	recycling;
reuse of materials and recycling;	Greenfield developments;
Land reclamation;	Road building;
Tram and railway construction;	Energy intensive forms of building;
Pedestrianization and cycleways;	Materials intensive forms of building
Labour intensive forms of building;	
Use of renewable materials in building	
Extraction and materials:	Extraction and materials:
Some small quarries serving local	Quarrying – especially superquarries;
needs;	Cement extraction and manufacture;
Aggregates reuse;	Mining;
Recycling industries;	Less use of synthetic materials;
Sustainable forestry;	Iron and steel extraction and
Greater use of natural materials	production;
	Metals extraction and production;
	Plastics production
Utilities:	Utilities:
Renewable energy generation;	Fossil-fuel based energy generation;
Energy efficiency products and	Energy intensive products and
techniques;	techniques;
Water efficient products and	Water intensive products and
techniques	techniques
Transport:	Transport:
Rail freight and travel;	Road haulage and transport;
More locally based forms of	International and global forms of
distribution	distribution
Other:	Other:
Locally based production and	Internationally based production
consumption;	and consumption;
Service oriented consumption;	Product oriented consumption
Most manufacturing industries	

while those which 'lock' materials together into a structure will be seen as short-sighted and naive. This means that current practices such as the use of cement mortars which bond bricks together strongly so that they cannot be separated and reused will fall out of favour. This may result in a partial return to using bonding agents such as lime-based mortars, but the change will also provide an opportunity to the construction-products industry to come up with new bonding methods which better suit modern building practices. Possible new ideas in this area were discussed in Chapter 4.

Construction processes are often wasteful of materials because it is usually too expensive to use labour to allow more efficient materials use. This will be reversed under ETR, with the result that materials use will be more efficient and the amount of waste generated by the construction process will fall. Employment potential will also rise.

ETR will also promote changes in the types of building and building form in the future. Higher energy costs will encourage the use of materials with lower embodied energy values. The result will be lower levels of use of synthetic and processed materials such as plastics, metals and concrete, and an uptake in the use of such diverse materials as timber, 'glu-lam', straw, thatch and rammed earth. It will become prohibitively expensive to build large skyscrapers and buildings reliant upon 'advanced' construction techniques and expensive materials. Instead, there will be a return to more traditional, appropriate forms of architecture and this will inevitably affect the look of our built environment.

Taxes on quarrying, mining and extraction generally would increase the relative cost of raw materials and encourage more careful use. This would promote more traditional craft-based ways of using materials such as stone and slate because such methods are more responsive to the material in use and seek to use it appropriately and sparingly. Under current methods of working, stone and slate mines produce large quantities of waste because the market will only pay for regular-sized blocks or tiles in order to cut down on labour costs in building. Under ETR, however, the labour cost is reduced in comparison to the material cost, which will encourage a return to craft-based methods which can make use of irregular-sized stone and slate. An example is the stone shake, a traditional roofing material in Scotland. The cutting and fitting of shakes is a craft which has almost died out owing to the availability of other cheaper materials (Ecological Design Group, 1996). ETR could encourage the rejuvenation of such practices.

NEW ECONOMICS AND ENERGY USE

Rising energy costs will also encourage more energy efficient buildings, as businesses, organizations and householders react to changes in price. Energy efficiency is already financially viable, but changes in the tax regime would mean efficiency is taken for granted and is an integral part of any new building. Within existing buildings there will be increased demand for renovation and retro-fitting of energy efficiency measures. One part of ETR calculations assumes the use of a portion of ETR revenues to fund an energy efficiency programme for lower income households. This would ensure that rising costs were not inequitable in their impact. Furthermore, if such a programme were implemented, jobs could be created amongst the long-term unemployed and thus tackle existing social problems at the same time (Tindale and Holtham, 1996; Barker, 1997).

Even in the current financial climate, energy efficiency makes financial sense and is a good employment creator in terms of jobs per pound spent. ETR can only multiply the financial gains in this area. Energy conservation creates jobs not only in the manufacture and installation of products such as insulation and double-glazing, but also in the respending effects of the savings people make in their energy bills. The UK has poor standards of insulation in much of the housing stock, leading to one of the lowest standards of energy conservation in the developed world. Even in modern housing, standards are well below those of other countries. However, such a situation could be remedied through a national energy conservation programme. If paid for by the government, ideally from ecological tax revenues, the estimated cost is £15.5 billion, which would create 500,000 job-years of work (or 50,000 jobs for ten years). This works out at a net cost of £23,000 per job-year. Other studies put the costs of energy efficiency at as little as £9000 per job-year created (Taylor, 1992).

In England, Newark and Sherwood District Council plans to harness this job creation power to provide local employment. The Council is actively pursuing a wide variety of strategies ranging from autonomous housing (ie housing capable of meeting its own energy and water needs and dealing with its own waste) to energy efficient renovation. One programme involves the creation of a cyclical maintenance programme spread over 15 years for the refurbishment of the council's housing stock (much of which has already been refurbished to very high levels of energy efficiency). A long-term programme such as this is needed if lasting employment is to be created. The whole programme costs £16.4 million and involves the installation of full house central heating to an anti-condensation specification/design, the fitting of controlled ventilation, the retrofitting of insulation in roof spaces and cavity walls and the repair of 'design defects'. As well as the direct benefits of improving efficiency and reducing condensation, the Council estimate that wider benefits include the creation of 639 person years of employment, a reduction in unemployment benefit payments of up to £5.7 million and – because of making dwellings more healthy places to live – an avoided expenditure of £14.4 million by the local Health Service (NSDC, 1995a). More up to date figures suggest that the economic benefits could be even greater (Pickles, 1995, Newark and Sherwood District Council, personal communication).

The Newark and Sherwood programme shows how energy efficiency can go hand in hand with job creation. Current energy provision policies centre around the provision of new power stations to meet rising energy demands. Through seeking to reduce demand, that is demand side management (DSM), energy can be saved, financial savings made and jobs created. DSM is a concept pioneered by Amory Lovins and encapsulated by his idea that it is more cost effective to produce 'negawatts', that is to reduce demand, than to constantly seek to match increasing demand with greater supply capacity (Lovins, 1991).

A study of energy investments by US electricity utilities found that efficiency measures could satisfy demand for electricity at a lower cost than traditional supply side options. The authors concluded that an investment of $3.1 billion in demand side management programmes would reduce the need for the construction of power stations to provide an extra 50 terawatts of electricity and generate an extra 75,000 jobs (Goodmans Group, 1992). A Dutch study into the potential employment effects of increasing energy efficiency so as to meet international CO_2 targets, concluded that potential gains of a demand side management programme were twice the level of those in the US study (WWF International/CECET, 1995). This difference is partly accounted for by the large difference in energy prices between the two countries. Because the Netherlands has higher energy prices, the financial gains and the respending effect from energy efficiency measures are likely to be even higher. DSM is important for the built environment because it will encourage greater energy efficiency and provide much needed employment to implement efficiency programmes. Just as ETR would make us see derelict buildings as valuable 'quarries' of materials ('nega-quarries'), so DSM policies coupled with ETR would make us take a fresh view of the built environment and seek out ways of reducing energy consumption.

NEW ECONOMICS, TRANSPORT AND LAND USE

Globally, transport contributes 30 per cent of the world's carbon dioxide emissions (ECMT/OECD, 1993) and within the built environment, motor vehicles cause congestion and pollution, which have negative effects on health and damage our overall quality of life. Even understanding this, governments have often allowed new road development because of the presupposed economic gains stemming from extra mobility. There is little evidence, however, that road developments have a positive economic effect, with a growing body of research suggesting effects can be negative or lower than gains from alternative planning and development strategies.

One frequently cited reason for road building is that better access to road transport network provides companies with better access to goods, services and new markets. Road construction is often justified as being good for the overall economy, through aiding the movement of goods and services. As Whitelegg notes 'There is simply no evidence of the claimed link between access and employment or economic prosperity' (Whitelegg, 1993). Road construction and increasing levels of road haulage are just as likely to harm as well as stimulate the economy, because road infrastructure also provides the means for outside firms to extend their activities into new areas and potentially put local firms out of business. In other words, the overall level of economic activity is likely to stay the same, yet goods will travel further: increasing costs and only benefiting road haulage firms, whilst rising fuel consumption will exacerbate environmental problems such as global warming (Whitelegg 1993, 1995).

The urban spread which results from encouraging road transport can significantly damage the economy. New roads lead to increased pressure on surrounding land, which will in turn produce greater traffic levels, congestion and the demands for new or wider roads (Headicar and Bixby, 1992). Road building is expensive and heavily subsidized, but investment will be wasted if it only creates a new imperative for more roads which will themselves lead to more demand. These mechanisms are set out in Figure 9.1 and show clearly how the provision of roads, urban sprawl and economic problems are linked together. Significantly the relationship is a dynamic one, creating a vicious cycle of futile development.

In contrast, investing in public transport has been shown to bring greater benefits to the economy. In Portland, Oregon the new light rail system has not only been successful in reducing car use, it has also been the catalyst for rejuvenating the downtown area of the city. Before construction the area accounted for only 5 per cent of the city's retail trade. That figure is now 30 per cent (Arrington, 1993). As well as producing better economic performance, investment in rail or light rail infrastructure produces more jobs than road building. A study by the German Road League and the German construction union IG Bau Steine Erden found that investing DM100 billion on roads would yield only 1201 to 1630 person-years of employment as compared to about 1880 job-years in railway construction or 1992 in local public transport such as light rail (Renner, 1991). These figures do not include the jobs generated in operating the public transport systems which are often considerable. Furthermore, investment in public transport leads to a greater respending effect within the local economy, which will further boost the economic benefits set out above. A study by the Los Angeles Regional Transportation Commission showed that 85 cents of every dollar spent on petrol left the regional economy (and much leaving the USA as well). In contrast, an estimated 80 cents out of every dollar spent on public transport fares goes towards transport worker's wages. Those 80 cents circulate in the local economy and generate an extra $3.80 in goods and services in the region (CNTP, 1991).

This evidence clearly shows that planning and development policies for our built environment which encourage public transport while discouraging road transport will produce greater economic benefits and use land more efficiently, so reducing the surrounding pressure on greenfield sites. Indicative of this is an EU report (Transport Europe, 1992) declaring that a city without cars would be up to five times cheaper to run than a city with cars and furthermore would be a viable proposition. The research behind this statement demonstrated that the cost of a motor-free city chargeable to the public authorities could be up to five times less than in 'normal' cities where the cost is borne by the private sector. Above, we discussed the concept of demand side management and 'negawatts'.

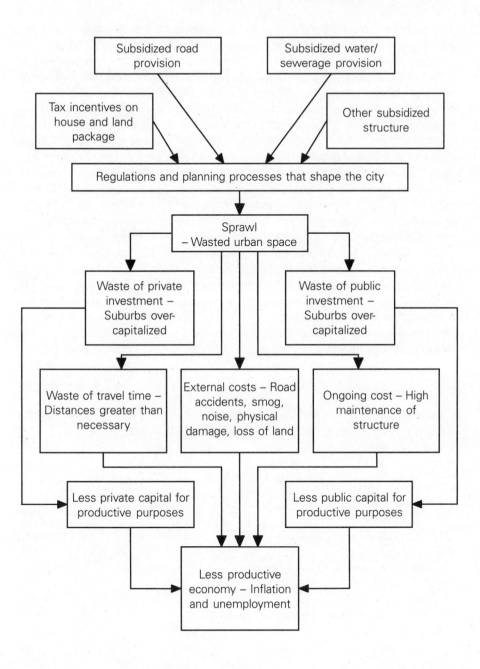

Source: Newman, 1995

Figure 9.1 *The Dynamic Mechanisms Linking Road Provision, Urban Sprawl and Economic Problems*

The evidence here suggests that using the concept of 'negahectares' would be just as constructive. Allowing expansion of the built environment only creates more pressure for more expansion, yet is of mixed benefit to the economy. Alternatively, seeking to control land use and gain maximum benefit from each hectare, we can maintain a dense built environment which is also a more pleasurable place to live and work in and which has a stronger economy. If we were to add the cost of loss of agricultural land to this calculation, the concept of 'negahectares' would become even more inviting. To demonstrate this, we need only look at North America where urban population growth has slowed to less than 1.3 per cent per year, but between 1982 and 1992 urban land area increased from 21 to 26 million hectares. In one decade, 2 million hectares of forestland, 1.5 million hectares of cropland, 1 million hectares of pastureland and 0.75 million hectares of rangeland were lost to urban spread. This pushes agriculture to new land, which is often inferior in quality (World Resources Institute, 1996).

Research has also quantified the hidden social and environmental costs of road transport. Teufel et al (1988) and Teufel (1989) have analysed the total costs imposed by cars and lorries and compared these with the totals of taxation of all kinds which they pay. Both pieces of research show that cars and lorries cost society more than the income gained by taxation. For lorries the deficit between taxation and overall costs is 85 per cent (see Table 9.2) and for cars between 71 and 74 per cent (see Table 9.3). Work by Maddison et al (1996)

Table 9.2 *Total Costs and Taxation Income for Lorries in West Germany, 1987 (middle estimates; all figures in million DM)*

Income (all taxes)	6724
Costs	
Road expenditure	8730
Accident costs	5030
Distress related to accidents	2600
Air pollution	6350
Noise costs (private dwellings)	9850
Other noise costs	2500
Congestion	2000
Water pollution (from dangerous goods)	3800
Water pollution (from road salting)	2800
Health damage to lorry drivers	1100
Other	1200
Total costs	45,960
Total costs not covered by tax income	39,236

Source: Teufel, 1989

Table 9.3   *Total Costs and Taxation Income for Cars in West Germany, 1987 (all figures in billion DM)*

	1960–1986 (cumulated)	1986 (one year)
Total income from taxes	441	31.4
Costs		
Expenditure on roads	551	29
Accident costs not covered	456–710	27–35
Air pollution	265	18
Noise	625	35
Total costs	1897–2151	109–117
Deficit	1456–1710	78–86

Source: Teufel et al, 1988

estimates that external costs for road transport in the UK amount to between £45.9 billion and £52.9 billion, yet road taxes generate only £16.4 billion; a difference of a factor of three. Given the relationship between road transport and land use, if these financial considerations were added to our notion of negahectares, the economic case for less road transport and more efficient land use would become even stronger.

Ecological tax reform would be an effective way in which to tackle the problems of inefficient road transport and land use. Rising fuel costs would discourage road transport and encourage the development of more environmentally responsible forms such as rail, light rail, cycling and walking. This change would then promote land use policies which reflected the new travel priorities of businesses and individuals within the built environment. Though there would be a change in use of different modes, overall it is likely that higher transport costs would mean lower levels of transport. This would promote more local forms of production and consumption and lead to more stable regionally centred economies. An example is the use of locally sourced construction materials. At present, slates used in the UK are as likely to come from Spain, Brazil or China as from local quarries, and traditional local materials might have been displaced because low transport costs encourage the use of many different materials from across a wide area. Under ETR, rather than source materials from across the planet, it would become cheaper to seek out the nearest sources and this would encourage a return to vernacular forms of construction.

IN CONCLUSION: AN ECONOMICS FOR OUR BUILT ENVIRONMENT

The fiscal measures set out above would produce an economy in which it was not 'cost effective' to move products great distances for the sake of so-called economies of scale, or to rely on distant superquarries supplying our mineral needs, or on a few sources of fossil fuels burnt in distant power stations and then delivered to our homes and workplaces via a vast network of pylons and cables.

Instead, our economies would become much more locally based, as it becomes cheaper to produce and buy products from the local area. Rather than acting at a national and increasingly at a global level, our economy would begin a partial return to one more rooted within the built environment and in the community. Commentators such as Sale (1980), Berry (1995), Bookchin (1980) and Daly and Cobb (1989) speak of promoting a community of communities, meaning that we would act much more as members of a community than as members of a country or members of a global trading block. As Daly and Cobb put it:

> 'The nation is a community very remote to most citizens. It is better to conceive it as a community of communities. The goal of an economics for community is to restore to communities at lower levels the power to determine their own affairs. That requires a regionalisation of economic power and activity that would attach capital to regions. A variety of industries would be needed in each locale, and these would identify their well-being with that of states and cities, working with them for the well-being of the community rather than playing states or cities off against each other to extract maximum concessions. This would be a deep reversal of current trends.'

Daly and Cobb, 1989, p 293

The phrase 'think globally act locally' still has significance because it recognizes that only at the local level can we effect a change. Furthermore, outside this area, we have little or no control over what happens. If, however, we are to move to such a community of communities, then it is important that our economy, which is one of the key elements of our society, supports rather than undermines these communities. In practice, this means making our built environment sustainable, for without sustainable surroundings our communities will remain trapped in unsustainable modes of behaviour. To do this, we need to change the nature of our economy so that it supports sustainable practices and nurtures our communities.

An economy which fosters the needs of the community is likely to be a vibrant one. In their study of Italian regional governments, Putnam et al (1993) found that those regions with a strong community and a high degree of 'social capital' were less marked by income inequalities, had better levels of health and stronger local economies. The supposition is that effective local economies both rely on and support effective local government, vibrant communities and a healthy population. The alternative is a culture of economic dependency at an individual and societal level. Individually, we have grown used to the market providing our needs. A prime example is our dependence upon others to provide for our housing needs. As Day notes:

> *'We have come to take for granted that buildings are provided ready-finished by others. The less we are able to do ourselves, the more dependent we become. Dependency is a step towards social malaise . . . Self-builders are estimated to build more houses than any firm in Britain, though very few start low on the ladder of privilege. My experience with volunteer building, however, demonstrates that even with no previous skill and low expense it is possible to break the links of individual-suppressing dependence, to afford and achieve surroundings that nurture the soul, to build self-confidence, community and, almost incidentally, learn employable skills by the back door.'*

Day, 1990, pp 136–137

At a larger scale, our built environment has been degraded by its dependency on the whims of market forces, something which is most apparent amongst our poorer communities; yet ultimately we have all been made dependent upon outside forces to provide our needs. There are many examples of regions scarred by such dependence, some of which have been raised in this book. This economic dependency is the outcome of our current economic model which assumes we all act selfishly and that overall this promotes general welfare in society. Acting in this way also leads to specialization, where we give up doing certain things for ourselves and pay others to do them for us. But in constructing this system, we have ignored the many external costs of our economic activities. These costs are social *and* environmental, and the consequences of these come back to roost within our built environment. New measures of economic growth and reform of the system using measures such as ecological tax reform are desperately needed if we are to reduce materials and energy intensities, improve employment opportunities and promote a sustainable economy to best meet the needs of our built environment, communities and society.

However, even without reforms such as ETR, looking at current problems from a fresh vantage point shows that actually our economy is already underperforming, and changes in construction practices and land use planning could bring major economic gains. Using demand side management techniques could help us use energy and land more efficiently and free up valuable capital to spend on rejuvenating our built environment. Policies which encourage public transport and discourage private motor vehicles could result in more effective land use and higher quality environments in which to live and work.

Our current economic system seems to downgrade all that is of importance to the long-term health of the built environment and, by implication of society.

Globally, the economy is responsible for the deterioration of the health of our planet. Within the local environment, problems such as poor health, unemployment, inequality, crime, the poor quality of our building fabric and pollution, are exacerbated by short-term economic policies which bring about so-called 'economic growth' but which ultimately put the greater wealth of society in jeopardy. An economy which ignores this problem and which is not responsible to the community in which it operates is not sustainable.

Alternatively, economic reforms and a better model of economic welfare would help us to promote the social capital and the environmental responsibility needed. Crucially, such reforms will strengthen our built environment and the economy itself by providing the foundation on which a strong, healthy economy can be supported. Of paramount importance is our adoption of sustainable development as the best model for our society and the built environment. Doing this will allow us to address economic, environmental and social concerns holistically and without conflict. Decision making which seeks to further sustainable development will begin to make our built environment sustainable. Changes like those detailed above will assist in steering the economy and hence the built environment along such a path.

10

THE WAY FORWARD

'. . . we can't have a sustainable economy unless we build a physical setting to house it. The physical setting we presently dwell in itself exhausts our capital. It is, in fact, the biggest part of the problem.'

Kunstler, 1994, p 246

On 27 October 1993, the 18-storey Dunes neon sign in Las Vegas was demolished. It was still functional and with careful maintenance could conceivably have continued to operate for some years (let us put on one side for the moment that it was consuming large quantities of electricity wastefully). In terms of the driving force of urban development in Las Vegas, however, it had to give way to more profitable structures. Steve Wynn, the proprietor of the Mirage and Treasure Island hotels, wished to create a super resort on the site, with lakes big enough for jet skiing. Las Vegas is continually being destroyed and recreated in order to increase the flow of tourists through the city. The most obvious physical manifestation of this is the themed hotel, one of the latest being 'New York New York'. It has over 2000 beds and is a mini replica of New York with one-third size skyscrapers, a Statue of Liberty and a Brooklyn Bridge over a mini East River. Some of the tourists who stay there will presumably be from New York, who could gamble at home and see the real thing. Other themed hotels include pyramids from Ancient Egypt, castles from Arthurian England and a galleon that sinks into the ocean several times a day. In conventional accounting terms, these developments are immensely profitable and Las Vegas is the most rapidly growing urban area in the United States.

The real costs of Las Vegas, however, far outweigh the benefits of this city in the desert. These costs have been highlighted by Mike Davis (1995) who describes the city as 'too many people in the wrong place, celebrating waste as a way of life'. The explosive urban growth in southern Nevada is having devastating environmental consequences, most notably in terms of water resources. Davis quotes the average water consumption per head in Las Vegas as 360 gallons per day, compared to 210 in Los Angeles and 110 in Oakland. This colossal rate is required to water the golf courses, fill the swimming pools and boating lakes, provide the oceans for galleons to sink in, and sustain the millions each year who go to Las Vegas to gamble. Unfortunately, Nevada's desert climate yields only four inches of rain per year, and the consumption of Las Vegas is equivalent to another 20–30 inches. The deficit is made up from groundwaters, which means the city is gradually desiccating the southwest United States, and from pumping from distant sources at the cost of fossil fuel consumption. The desert climate also demands air-conditioning to cope with the 100 degree heat; this raises the temperature outside the buildings to four or five degrees above the temperature in the open desert. Added to this is one of the highest levels of car dependency in the United States, which is destroying the clear desert air, one of the original attractions of the city. EPA data show that Las Vegas rivals New York City in terms of carbon monoxide pollution.

On top of these environmental problems, Las Vegas is experiencing heightened social stresses. Recent in-migrants include the affluent retired fleeing from Southern California, blue collar workers and, increasingly, Latinos seeking employment. The job creation rate is not matching the in-migration rate, however, and unemployment, especially among African Americans and Hispanics, is high. The gaming industry is noted for its low employment of minorities. The affluent are retreating to gated enclaves or to the suburbs, where the fragmented local government structure guarantees them low tax rates as well as physical separation from the negative side of Las Vegas. The city is unsustainable, demanding ever more consumption of non-renewable resources and expenditure on policing and welfare to keep it going. Davis maintains that Las Vegas demonstrates 'the fanatical persistence of an environmentally and socially bankrupt system of human settlement, and confirms . . . Edward Abbey's worst nightmares about the emergence of an apocalyptic urbanism in the Southwest'. Las Vegas is an extreme case, but elements of its unsustainability are to be found to varying degrees throughout the developed world.

The built environment is an expression in bricks and mortar, tarmac and concrete, of the society which has created it. It should not be a surprise that a materialistic society which takes a short-term view should create and live in a built environment that is being extended and continually recreated at the expense of the earth's capital resources. Las Vegas illustrates this perfectly, but so do more mundane examples such as every greenfield housing development and new out-of-town shopping centre. The requirements of individualized, short-term profit, justified by the unquestioning acceptance of the inevitability of globalization, the power of market forces and the imperative of technological change, together with privatized, personalized and internalized gratification of individual wants are the driving forces behind the shaping of our built environment. These forces have produced polluted, wasteful and socially divided cities, many of whose inhabitants are experiencing a steady decline in quality of life, and whose ecological footprint gets more extensive. The built environment we have and the lifestyles which have produced and maintain it, are not sustainable economically, socially or environmentally.

The root cause of the mess lies in an overwhelming emphasis on consumption as the route to human happiness and economic growth as the means of achieving it. As with all addictions, the underlying hollowness of the satisfaction yielded by consumption leads to the need for a bigger 'fix', more consumption, rather than a fundamental reassessment of the real foundations of human contentment. The spiral of consumption, environmental damage, and greater consumption is difficult to break once begun because of its own momentum and because the distribution of power in the developed world favours those who benefit from the processes of consumption, waste and circulation of financial capital, at least in the short term. The urban and ecological nightmare that is Las Vegas has made a small number of people immensely wealthy. It has also made a larger number of people comfortable in material terms and reduced the incomes of a growing minority below the poverty line. This is being maintained at an enormous cost, however, environmentally and socially. Environmental and social capital is being depleted at an increasing rate. In the long term, all will suffer from the breakdown of the ecosystem and the depletion of our capital resources, and the associated social dysfunction.

Tackling these problems – environmental, economic and social – in an effective way can only be done if their inter-connected nature is recognized and built into policy responses. The fatal flaw of existing management of the built environment is that it is compartmentalized within departmental areas of competence and jurisdiction, and set within a hierarchy of priorities headed by economic growth. All contemporary governments in the developed world assume that economic growth is not only the most important policy objective, but that all other objectives can be met only if economic growth is achieved. Hence, environmental protection is feasible only when we can afford it, and this will only be possible when we have an expanding economy which will produce the necessary financial resources. An expanding economy, however, will consume more resources. Similarly, the poor can be helped out of their poverty only with an expanding national cake of material goods and services. This usually means minimized transfer payments so that tax rates can be held down, perpetuating and in some cases exacerbating, social inequalities; rising tax rates would threaten the economic growth which is necessary to assist the poor.

The circularity in these processes indicates the problems with economic growth as a policy objective. The assumptions described above with regard to economic growth are false and dangerous, predicated on a further assumption that the Earth's resources are infinite. Economic growth in the conventional sense is the problem, not the solution; its pursuit damages the environment, leads to social injustice, and is detrimental to real economic development. As discussed in detail in Chapter 2, a more complete and integrated analysis of our problems is required which takes a more sophisticated view of what makes up quality of life. This would include non-material as well as material elements, and give the former as much priority as the latter. We must also consider the interests of generations to come and take a long-term view of quality of life. These factors can be encompassed within the concept of sustainability. Sustainability – how to achieve and maintain real quality of life for everyone – should be the central objective of policy across all areas, economic, social and environmental. This would ensure that policies do not pull in different directions, and would be the most effective way to achieve success across the range of problems to be addressed. Economic growth as an objective would be replaced by economic *development*, which would be only one of a set of related objectives including environmental protection, physical and mental health, and social cohesion. The achievement of sustainability would not only determine other policies, it would also guarantee their achievement.

Sustainability requires a fundamental shift in values and behaviour. In terms of values, a shift from materialism to a more holistic view of what constitutes quality of life is needed. Intangible, but real, elements of human contentment such as social cohesion, community and full self-development must be given greater priority. Health should be considered as something to be protected, not something to be regained with the assistance of medical technicians after its loss. Work should be considered as an activity of value in itself in addition to its function as an income earner. All of these are related and all can only be sustained within an environment which is itself sustained from one generation to the next. Care for the environment implies and demands a more cohesive and supportive society; we must care more for ourselves and each other. Such a transformation of social values would create the potential for profound changes to the built environment along the lines described in the previous chapters. Daly argues that if people's values do not change, then their behaviour will be changed either by a coercive social system, or by ecological collapse: 'If interior restraints on will and appetite diminish, then exterior constraints, coercive police powers, or Malthusian positive checks must increase' (Daly, 1993b, p 358).

There is a counter argument that material consumption can be maintained if we are more careful and less wasteful in the way we use resources, renewable and non-renewable (Weizsäcker et al, 1997) indicating that changes in behaviour are more important than changes in values. Whether we can maintain consumption or not in the long term, however, we are faced with problems in the built environment now that require urgent action and changes in lifestyle.

A SUSTAINABLE BUILT ENVIRONMENT

Achieving and maintaining a sustainable built environment will require significant changes in behaviour patterns. The profligacy with which materials, energy and space are used will have to be reduced so that our buildings, settlements and means of transport make fewer demands on resources and create less waste and pollution. The relationship between behaviour and the built environment is circular and reinforcing. The contemporary built environment reflects waste and carelessness, and in fact is so constructed that such behaviour is facilitated. Land uses are dispersed and segregated, increasing the need for travel. Transport infrastructure gives priority to the car and relegates public transport to second place. Public space is neglected and people retreat into poorly insulated, energy inefficient, private space. Income groups are physically segregated and social cohesion made more difficult. The requirement is a built environment that is not only a product of ecologically-minded and careful behaviour, but which also makes such behaviour easier. Our buildings and settlements should be of such a form and spatial arrangement that travel is minimized, energy consumption reduced, recycling more convenient and social opportunities maximized. This can be achieved by mixed land uses, priority being given to public transport, a prioritization of the creation of quality public space and careful use of resources from energy efficiency in buildings and the maximum degree of recycling. Instead of being centres of individualized consumption and profit generation, our towns, cities and villages should be communities of social interaction, human fulfilment and ambition which are as conscious of the next generation's needs as of their own.

The crucial question then becomes, what form of built environment will be both sustainable and facilitate sustainable lifestyles? It is tempting to start with an ideal form, such as Calthorpe's (1993) transit oriented developments of high density, mixed land use urban growth along major public transport routes, or the compact city as put forward by the Commission of the European Community (1990). These templates are useful in establishing general principles, but are not helpful as universal guides to future action since they do not necessarily apply in all circumstances and do not command unanimous acceptance (see Breheny, 1995 and Jenks et al, 1996, for arguments that the compact city is not necessarily environmentally benign). Furthermore, we have to deal with the built environment as it is. By the year 2000, more than half of the world's population will live in cities; in the developed world the proportion of the population living in urban areas is already over 70 per cent. The cities and towns that exist now, especially those of the developed world, are the source of the problem of non-sustainability and they must be the focus of any solution put forward. They are in any event the generators of human activity and innovation. Furthermore, it is not conceivable that the present urban population can be redistributed in a more dispersed pattern that would diminish its environmental impact.

Cities must be seen as not only the source of the problem, but also as the means of solving it. The general objective of achieving sustainability depends upon producing sustainable built environments from the cities and towns already in existence. In the short term, only limited changes can be made in a physical sense but more significant changes can be made in lifestyles. In the medium term, but starting immediately, the built environment can be changed in form to reflect and facilitate those lifestyles. The requirement is for steering rather than overnight radical change, whereby over a period of time gradual change to behaviour and action leads to substantial changes to the built environment. Sustainable development is itself a process and not an end-point; the objective is for sustainability to be the overarching guide to policy and behaviour permanently. Cities must be made more attractive places in which to live and their ecological footprint must be reduced. These two sets of processes are mutually reinforcing: greener cities will enhance quality of life, both for those who do and those who do not live within them. Furthermore, there are strong arguments to suggest that at current and projected levels of population, towns and cities are the most effective form of population distribution for lessening environmental impact, increasing the vitality of social interaction and reducing resource use. Infrastructure provision can be cheaper for a spatially concentrated population. Land is used more efficiently, preserving rural land for extensive, organic food production. Recycling and more efficient resource use, for example from waste exchange schemes, are facilitated when activities are located close together. A rich and diverse cultural life is easier to maintain in cities, historically the major sources of invention and innovation. A concentrated population has less need for travel and shorter distances to overcome, lessening energy consumption. For all these reasons, the built environment must be seen not only as the major source of environmental problems, but also as the locus of the solutions to those problems.

The details of the form a sustainable built environment could take have been discussed in earlier chapters. Here the practicalities of achieving this will be addressed. The most immediate of these is to cope with the non-sustainability of the existing built environment; we do not have a clean slate. A large part of the contemporary built environment consists of low density, car dependent suburbs and low energy efficiency buildings in older inner city areas. Development to cope with population increase and social change (in particular, the trend for household size to decrease and the demand for housing to increase commens-urately) makes up only a small part of the total built environment in any one year, but over the longer term could make significant contributions to overall urban sustainability. The British Government has estimated that between 1996 and 2016 the number of extra households in England will be 4.4 million (Department of the Environment, 1996), mainly due to the tendency for more and more people to live alone due to ageing, a rising divorce rate and delayed age of marriage. Such trends show how changes in patterns of work and living impact the built environment, and in particular how the loss of community and social concern can affect our towns and cities.

In the longer term a more cohesive society may find it acceptable to share space to a greater degree than we do now, through a greater willingness to live in flats or cooperative housing. In the short term, changes in society must be acknowledged. Action to meet housing need cannot be put off through reference to a desired future social state. In the past, extra housing demand would have been accommodated in a non-sustainable way on greenfield sites at low densities. This is the form of residential development marketed by the developers and preferred by them because it is easier and cheaper than building on 'brownfield' sites in existing urban areas. If a significant proportion of the extra households could be accommodated in existing settlements, several sustainability objectives could be addressed. Overall urban densities would be increased, making better use of existing urban infrastructure and decreasing the requirement for new infrastructure. The viability of public transport would be enhanced and the overall demand for travel diminished.

The degree of mixed land use in cities could be increased by using new residential schemes to regenerate older industrial areas where land is available. Unused sites could be developed and existing buildings used in some cases instead of new build. Where demolition is necessary, building materials could be recycled. Given that many of the extra households will be single persons, the demand for housing will not solely be in the form of low density family housing with gardens but will include demand for smaller dwellings, including flats, which can be built at higher densities and which are easier to obtain from the adaptation of existing buildings such as property above commercial premises. Not all of the extra households can be accommodated in existing built up areas – the British Government has set an optimistic target of 60 per cent – but those that can will be making an important contribution to sustainability, not only in that the new development itself is sustainable but also in the contribution it makes to reducing the environmental impact of existing urban areas. Where growth cannot take place on brownfield sites, care should be taken over the location and form of greenfield development (Breheny et al, 1993). The expansion of existing towns and villages would be preferable, all other things being equal, than totally new settlement. Where the latter is judged to be necessary, high density, mixed use development, including homes, employment and services, adjacent to public transport would be one possible form that would reduce its impact.

For individual buildings, domestic, commercial and industrial, higher standards of insulation and greater care in the choice of heating systems and building materials can make a significant contribution to reducing their environmental impact. Design features, such as placing windows to maximize solar gain and cooling and the use of passive stack ventilation, can reduce heating and air-conditioning needs. Retrofitting to existing buildings is more important in the long run than changing new build practices given the small percentage of the total building stock made up by new build, but is more difficult and less cost effective (although the differential could be reduced by fiscal arrangements which reflect real environmental and social costs). Incorporation of 'green' measures into standard maintenance and repair programmes is one way of reducing the financial costs of retrofitting and lengthening the useful lifespans of buildings. Building regulations can be used to great effect; in the UK, the regulations introduced in 1992 brought British standards of home insulation to the levels achieved in Denmark in 1954, indicating considerable potential for reducing environmental impacts.

There is general consensus on the validity of sustainability as a guide to the future across a wide area of policy issues, and national governments have agreed in principle that it should be the basis for policy formation. As the Rio Conference in 1992 and the New York Conference in 1997 illustrate, however, agreement in principle does not necessarily translate into action on the ground. Similarly, although there is not a detailed blueprint for the design and construction of a sustainable built environment, the principles involved are generally agreed and the sort of environments and buildings discussed in earlier chapters and summarized briefly above are accepted as being effective in moving towards sustainability. How quickly the existing built environment can take on these forms is another question and will depend upon the degree of resistance to the changes required, and whether decision-making processes in both the public and private sectors can move from short-term to long-term perspectives and from sectoral to more holistic criteria. This demands an integrated approach to problem solving, rather than current fragmented approaches which at best deal with one crisis and often create new problems or exacerbate existing problems in other areas.

Resistance to the changes required has come in the first instance from those who have vested interests in the status quo. The built environment is largely the product of the profit motive, rather than a consciously planned environment for the common good which gives particular attention to the weak, such as the poor, the handicapped, the elderly and children. The absence of real prices reflecting real costs in the markets concerned has resulted in lack of consideration for the environment and non-priced social issues. Those who have benefited in material terms from this, namely the rich and the powerful, have been resistant to the necessary changes. The interests connected with car dependence are the most significant in this respect and include the automobile manufacturers and the oil industry. In the 1940s, General Motors, Standard Oil and Firestone Tyres formed a company with the express intent of buying up tramcar systems to replace them with bus companies, thereby providing themselves with new markets for buses, fuel and tyres. This inadvertently promoted car use which proved to be of even greater commercial benefit. The hydrocarbon industry has funded research and organized the Climate Change Coalition as a pressure group to undermine confidence in the reality of anthropogenically induced climate change, while the car makers have opposed demand management responses to car dependence and encouraged faith in technological solutions to pollution problems such as the zero emission vehicle. Pollution is just one of the negative effects of car dependence, however, and the broader issues of urban structure, community and quality of life will not be addressed by a non-polluting vehicle.

The residential development industry has been reluctant to build on brownfield sites and has consistently opposed restraints on greenfield development. This is a rational response for commercial agencies operating in a market where the price signals do not reflect real resource use and where there are important environmental and social externalities. Until sustainability became a recognized issue in the land use planning process, intervention in these markets by the planners often had negative rather than positive effects in environmental terms. Decentralization and the lowering of residential densities, for example, was the mainstay of post-war planning philosophy until the 1990s; it is now accepted that sustainable development requires more centralization and an increase in residential densities. If the private sector agencies involved perceive that this sort of development will be less profitable, then they will be reluctant to engage in it.

These considerations apply to all sectors, residential, commercial, retail and industrial, but perhaps most tellingly to food retailing. The trend in the post-war period has been for the growth of large supermarkets on out-of-town sites at the expense of smaller, locally owned, centrally located traditional shops. These supermarkets consume large amounts of land, are dependent on car-borne customers and reduce employment in the retailing industry as whole. They are difficult to reach for the poorer households, who are faced with decreased choice and higher prices at the declining number of accessible traditional outlets. Their large buying power enables them to exert considerable control over suppliers, not only domestically but in the developing world as well. Until the 1990s, planning policy was to assist them in finding suitable decentralized sites on the grounds of consumer choice and preference. The large profits generated by the companies concerned are based on enormous environmental damage, hidden by conventional black ink accounting. Although in the UK policy on out-of-town retailing has been reversed and there is now a predisposition in favour of more central development, there are outstanding planning permissions not yet taken up to ensure that unsustainable retail developments will continue for several years to come. The car and the suburban supermarket are powerful symbols of the unsustainable nature of the built environment of the 1980s and 1990s.

Existing markets do not reflect real environmental costs and benefits and hence have failed to deliver sustainable development. It therefore falls upon government to intervene to ensure that sustainability policy objectives are met. This can be done either through regulation, or through pricing to ensure that all costs are reflected in the operation of the relevant market processes. Governments have accepted their responsibility in this respect, but translating responsibility in principle to effective action has proved difficult. In the broad sense, moving to a sustainable society is a long-term process with short-term costs; the latter may be politically difficult for a government to impose on sections of the electorate with four or five year electoral cycles, and difficult decisions may be ducked as a consequence.

In terms of decision making and the details of policy formulation and implementation in the public sector, particular difficulties are related to shifting from short-term to long-term perspectives, and from sectoral to integrated policies. It is very difficult for governments to follow policies which take a long-term view and whose benefits are not confined within narrow departmental definitions. For example, in the case of social housing for low income households this makes it difficult to shift to building practices which are more environmentally friendly and which provide better housing at lower long-term cost. Firstly, the higher initial capital cost may be constrained by short-term public expenditure limitations. Secondly, the reduction in lifetime costs will be enjoyed by the tenants in terms of reduced heating costs but will not be directly reflected in the budget of the housing provider; the latter however will still bear the burden of higher initial capital costs. There will be benefits to total public expenditure such as reduced medical care due to improved tenant health, reduced income support payments for tenants as a consequence of lower energy expenditure, and these will outweigh the initial additional capital expenditure. These changes to public expenditure patterns, however, fall on different government agencies (health services, social security, housing providers) who operate within their own budgetary constraints and are unlikely to spend more themselves for the benefit of other agencies' budgets. The obvious solution to such bureaucratic barriers is to make sustainability a central concern for all government departments. This would not only raise the profile of environmental issues but would also make it easier to integrate environmental and other policy issues, such as poverty and employment.

A possible mechanism for facilitating this is the European Union's Eco-Management and Audit Scheme, set up in 1993 to help industry address the complex issues involved in operating in a more environmentally friendly manner. It is designed to assist industry to institute environmental management systems that integrate environmental considerations with more general policy implementation. In 1995, the British Government extended this to local authorities to help them pursue Local Agenda 21 objectives (Department of the Environment, 1995), but it could usefully be adopted by all central government departments as well. The widespread application of international environmental management standards, in particular ISO14001, can also be helpful, but more important is the political will and commitment to achieve stated environmental objectives.

The integration of policies in terms of sustainability across departmental divides and vertically within government from local to central is vital. This can be usefully illustrated by the importance given to sustainability in Bedfordshire's Structure Plan, the targets for which are given in Table 10.1. The Structure Plan is prepared by the Planning Department, but the targets indicate that the plan has objectives much wider than land use; its successful implementation will require other departments within the authority (waste disposal, transport, environmental protection, leisure and recreation) to share the objectives set out in the plan and determine their actions accordingly. The local authority will also require the cooperation and assistance of central government. The imposition of a national landfill tax, for example, will assist the local authority in achieving its waste disposal target. National planning guidelines on greenfield development will reinforce land use policy. Grants for energy conservation measures will help in achieving local CO_2 emission targets. At present, departmentalism and horizontal divisions in government can hinder progress towards sustainability. A recent example of this in the UK was the cut in VAT on fuel in the June 1997 budget; this helped to reduce poverty in the short term, but damaged energy efficiency objectives.

A possible solution to the problem of short-term public expenditure constraints on investment for long-term sustainability is for government to transfer some of the cost to the private sector. The large size of public sector budgets can be used as an advantage in this context through purchasing power in the market. The United States Government has instigated this mechanism to upgrade the energy efficiency of 500,000 Federal buildings by 2005. Such a large amount of business places government in a strong position to bargain with the private sector. In the Energy Department FREE programme (Financing Renewable Energy and Efficiency), private companies will install energy efficient lamps, air-conditioning systems and heating equipment in Federal buildings at

Table 10.1 *Sustainability Targets in Bedfordshire's Structure Plan 1995*

Indicator	Target (by 2011)
New build in existing urban areas and transport corridors	80%
Loss of greenfield land	Reduce by 50% compared to 1986–91
Derelict land and vacant buildings	Reduce by 50%
Non-fossil fuel energy production	Increase by 100%
Waste disposed to landfill	Reduce by 25%
CO_2 emissions by buildings and transport	Reduce to 1991 level by 2001
Journey to work in urban areas	50% by public transport, cycle or walking
Area of woodland	Double by 2015

Source: Blowers, 1997

no cost to the Government. In return, the companies will receive part of the savings from the lower electricity bills for a designated number of years. Private sector companies are installing energy management systems (combined heat and power, for example) in British public sector institutions such as schools and hospitals, again providing the capital investment and earning income from the energy savings. The Royal Liverpool Hospital has entered into a contract with a private company who have invested £2 million to install a combined heat and power system. This provides all the steam, hot water and electricity requirements of the hospital with estimated annual energy cost savings of £500,000. The hospital has thus been enabled to invest more resources in medical care.

A combination of regulation and market-based mechanisms will be required to make the built environment more sustainable, implemented by local and central government in an integrated way with long-term policy objectives. Land use planning, economic development and transport departments at local level have a vital role to play in shaping the broad structure of settlements so that they conform to sustainability objectives. This will involve new regulatory practice, such as strict controls on greenfield developments and the abandonment of inflexible zoning, combined with the use of pricing to change behaviour. This could include road pricing to deter car use in urban areas as already in operation in Singapore and Oslo, and which is being actively considered for Edinburgh and Leicester. The revenues raised can be used in constructive ways, for example invested in public transport so that there is an attractive alternative to car use. If such hypothecation of tax revenues is not possible, or deemed undesirable, revenues can be used to reduce other taxes, for example business rates, and stimulate the local economy. It is important that land use and transport policies are integrated to ensure the success of both. There are car-free residential developments in Germany (Grünenstrasse, in Bremen for example) where residents agree not to own a car, but these are only successful if there are good alternative transport modes available; in most German cities, the public transport is high quality, affordable and reliable. Canmore Housing Association in Edinburgh is building a car-free housing scheme, a new departure for urban Britain, and the success of the project will depend upon the support for walking and cycling and the quality of the public transport available in the city. The road pricing plan mentioned above could play a crucial role in the success of the Canmore development.

Regulation and pricing can also be used at the level of individual buildings in a general set of sustainability policies. Building regulations can be drawn up to guarantee minimum levels of energy efficiency and can be extended to ensure that materials used are environmentally responsible. It is important that these are coordinated. In the UK at present, much double-glazing uses window frames made from UPVC, a substance being phased out in Austria and Germany; energy efficiency is enhanced but at the expense of using a toxic material. Building regulations could also be extended to cover water use, recycling and other environmental issues and applied to extensions and repairs as well as new build. A difficulty here is that construction costs may be increased as a consequence of the more demanding regulations, but these would be offset over the life cycle of the dwelling by lower energy use and maintenance costs. In America the Housing and Urban Development Department and the Department of Energy have provided finance so that mortgage lenders can offer more generous loans to buyers of energy efficient dwellings; the savings in heating and lighting costs offset the higher loan repayments. Over 7000 such mortgages were issued in 1997.

A carbon tax imposed by central government would help in this respect by making energy efficiency measures more cost effective. In the short term, there would be market resistance from both builders and customers to the higher price. A consumer survey in the United States found that though there was widespread support for environmentally responsible building practices, few were willing to pay extra to have them (Buchta, 1996). Only 7 per cent were unconcerned about their home's impact on the environment, but 25 per cent, though concerned, would not consider environmental impact in decisions about their homes. Half wanted an environmentally friendly home but wouldn't pay more for it; only 18 per cent were prepared to pay more. Other factors revealed as retarding market penetration of green building techniques were lack of interest in marketing environmentally friendly products and technologies by the building trades and manufacturers, causing problems of availability: many suppliers did not stock a variety of alternative building products. The higher price would be a reflection of better quality and a real increase in value, however; the dissemination of information on the long-term advantages of more environment-friendly building practices would be important in this respect, and an important part of local authorities' Agenda 21 responsibilities.

The Home Energy Conservation Act in the UK gives local authorities the responsibility for showing how domestic energy consumption could be reduced by 30 per cent over ten years, and given that most homes in the UK are privately owned, education of householders will be a vital part of their task. In the longer term, builders might compete on the basis of energy efficiency should energy prices rise to reflect the real costs of energy use. There are already instances in the United States where the extra costs of higher standards of energy efficiency have been guaranteed against reduced fuel consumption by the architect who designed the building. If energy performance does not live up to prediction, the buyer is recompensed commensurately. Regulation can improve the working of the market by, for example, a statutory requirement that all buildings offered for sale should have an official energy assessment similar to the National Home Energy Rating (NHER) scheme operated in the UK.

The initial costs of moving towards a sustainable built environment are immediate and easily identifiable, but the benefits are sometimes delayed (for example in reduced energy consumption) and sometimes not obviously linked to sustainability policies. They are nonetheless real and important. The environmental improvements are clear, but the economic benefits in terms of employment, and the social benefits in terms of reduced inequality, less so. This is why it is of paramount importance to recognize the interrelationships between the different issues covered in this book so that there is general recognition of how widely-felt the benefits of moving towards sustainability will be. If we fail to make these connections, then government, businesses and individuals will continue to assert that protecting the environment costs jobs, raises taxes and damages competitiveness, when in reality it safeguards the long-term stability of the economy while promoting health, equity and community within the built environment. The move towards a sustainable society would entail radical economic, social and political change. It has been argued in Chapter 7 that an important component of that change would be the lessening of social inequalities. There are two reasons for this. First, a society which protects its natural environment will inevitably have fewer and shallower inequalities in the long term simply because the measures intrinsic to that protection also create a more equal society. Material consumption will be less and hence differences in material standards of living will be compressed. People will place more value on non-material sources of satisfaction which will be more widely available and more dependent upon cooperation than competition. Different people will have different skills and different levels of skill, but they will derive satisfaction from the exercise of those skills as much as any monetary reward.

Second, any process of rapid social change imposes strains on social cohesion and has costs. Moves towards sustainability will mean significant shifts of resources according to environmental criteria and realistic and comprehensive pricing, and this could have a particularly adverse effect on the poor in the short term. To gain support for the necessary measures it will be vital to protect the weak from the costs of adjustment and persuade rich and poor alike that more consumption does not necessarily equate with a better standard of living. For example, it is widely accepted that one of the most effective ways to reduce CO_2 emissions is via the imposition of a carbon tax on fossil fuel consumption. This would increase fuel prices and, other things being equal, cause financial hardship to poor households. Particular environmental taxes could have a regressive effect when applied to basic necessities rather than luxuries and introduced singly rather than as an integrated package. As Turner et al (1994) have pointed out, however, this distributional unfairness can be overcome by constructive use of the extra revenues raised by the tax:

> 'The government can in turn compensate for the unwanted regressive aspects of taxes by giving money back to those worst affected. Such a redistribution to consumers could either be in the form of increased tax-free income allowances or through lowering taxes on other basic commodities (both of which will be of proportionately greater help to the poor than the rich)'

> Turner et al, 1994, p 177

As argued in Chapter 9, such ecological taxes could be used to reduce taxation on labour, thus reducing unemployment, and could also be offset by energy efficiency gains. A more direct way to use the extra revenues for both environmental and social purposes would be to allocate them to capital expenditure on energy efficiency measures for low income households, or even to subsidize such expenditure for all households. Ecological tax reform, which would include measures to protect the poor, would in fact have both environmental and equity advantages. It would in the long run prove more effective at redistributing quality of life – *real* income – than more conventional fiscal measures to redistribute income in favour of poorer groups which are transfer payments only rather than carefully designed measures with defined sustainability objectives. The general point to be made here is that radical change is more easily accomplished by a socially cohesive society which shares the same values and goals. A prerequisite for such a society is equity and justice, and these demand that the weak should not shoulder the burden of shifting to a sustainable society. The effect of policies based on sustainability is that different problems, for example climate change and long-term unemployment, can be tackled more successfully by identifying a common solution; this is the mark of true sustainability.

The most important single cause of poverty in the developed world is unemployment. Economic growth has failed to create the number of jobs required to make a dent in the unemployment statistics; indeed, technological change has destroyed jobs and society has not managed to replace them with alternatives. At the same time, there is so much that needs to be done in our towns and cities both for each other in terms of services and for the environment degraded by the economic growth that was supposed to solve our problems. Chapter 9 illustrated that the move towards a sustainable built environment will in fact create jobs, but without increasing total consumption. This will be an effective attack on poverty, reduce social inequalities and improve quality of life for everyone by enhancing the physical and social environments. Conventional economic growth – to which the mainstream political parties are committed – shifts resources according to imperatives of global competitiveness, creates inequalities, externalizes environmental and social costs and ignores local communities. Politicians have come to the conclusion that economic growth is the only way to solve a range of problems, economic and social, and do not, or will not, see that growth is the problem. It makes more sense to begin with an analysis of our major problems, which are environmental and poverty related, and work out what the most effective responses are likely to be. The transformation of our towns and cities so that they contribute to, rather than threaten, sustainability will simultaneously address both environmental and poverty issues. Effective responses require the integration of environmental and poverty policies. In the absence of that integration, both are liable to fail.

One of the major causes of the state of our built environment, social inequity and declining quality of life is an excessive centralization of power, especially commercial and governmental. Korten (1995) has illustrated the power that large corporations exercise in the interests of profit and their own growth, graphically shown in towns like Las Vegas. Globalization, the expansion of international trade, the increasing flexibility of labour and the mobility of capital have taken more and more control away from people over their lives and lifestyles. In the field of government there has also been a centralization of control, with local authorities losing power over time to central government, and hence becoming less able to influence the development of their own areas. This has been particularly evident in the UK in the 1980s and 1990s, where local government has had its powers to act and raise finance reduced; in some policy areas this has been accompanied by the imposition of increased responsibilities, such as energy conservation. The combination of responsibility without power is a guarantee of failure. Centralization of power has led to feelings of impotence and hopelessness within individuals and local communities. Our contemporary political institutions and governmental processes are remote from the public, who are given little real power to influence them apart from voting at election time. This has led to disillusionment with the political process and the resort to direct action such as protests against road building and airport extensions in the UK. It is regrettable that when people do participate in the political process, for example by deploying rational argument at public inquiries, they feel that the situation is rigged against them. Non-violent direct action can delay developments, but its impact on halting work is limited; it is also damaging to the long-term health of democracy if there is a widespread rejection of normal political processes. These must be made more responsive to real democratic control, exercised at the local level in the first instance.

It is at the local, community level that the impacts of the decline in the environment, social and physical, are felt most acutely and the deterioration in quality of life directly experienced. Decision makers in government, commerce and industry are to a large extent divorced from the negative consequences of their actions and operate within a context where criteria such as profit are paramount rather than quality of life and environmental protection. The immediate adverse impacts of an out-of-town supermarket fall on those who suffer the pollution from the increased car traffic and those who bear the loss of their local, within walking distance shop. They have little control over, or even input into, the decision making processes which lead to the construction of such developments. This decision making is theoretically politically accountable through planning procedures, but in the past local councils have been influenced more by non-valid arguments about jobs and central government guidelines than concern for the totality of the built environment. This has been shaped more by McDonalds and Tesco than by local communities, and in the interests of profit and the narrow, advertising industry-determined definition of consumer preferences than a holistic view of what constitutes quality of life, a healthy community and a sustainable environment.

A strengthening of local control and greater community involvement in local government would lead to wiser and more environment-friendly decision making and to a healthier, more democratic and participatory political system. This is why it was thought that the commitments to sustainable development made by national governments at the 1992 Rio Conference would be most effectively fulfilled through local action. Sustainable development as a process must begin at the local level, involving all sections of the community: individuals, businesses, local government and voluntary organizations (stakeholders in the contemporary jargon). All these groups must share a commitment to the principles of sustainable development and the objectives of Agenda 21, and act together to achieve them. This can occur only with consent and through democratic processes. Any other way forward will be non-sustainable. They must also have the power to resist the ambitions of larger, non-local agencies whose interests are not consistent with local sustainability.

Chapter 28 of Agenda 21 placed a large responsibility on local governments to fulfil the objectives of sustainable development, and part of their task was to be the inclusion of as many stakeholders as possible in a process of defining what was required. The consultation processes involved as implemented by local authorities have had a tendency to be complex and bureaucratic, as illustrated by the prefecture of Kanagawa in Japan and Lancashire County Council in England.

> '*Agenda 21 Kanagawa was formulated by an Interdepartmental Liaison and Co-ordination Committee, made up of the heads of every department within the Prefecture and chaired by the Vice Governor. A working level committee made up of section chiefs from each department was established to review detailed proposals. A secretariat within the Environment Department managed the public consultation and internal review processes. Public input was provided through three sectoral "conferences" or committees: one for citizens and non-governmental organizations, one for private enterprise, and one for local municipalities in Kanagawa. In addition, neighbourhood consultative meetings were organized and a direct mail package and questionnaire was sent to thousands of residents. The final Agenda 21 Kanagawa is a detailed and comprehensive document.*'

ICLEI, 1995

'. . . the development of a multi-stakeholder Environmental Forum for the purpose of discussing environmental issues and identifying co-operative solutions. The Forum has over 200 members representing over 80 organiz- ations, including national government departments and agencies, industries and utilities, local governments, health agencies, public interest groups and academic institutions. The Forum is co-ordinated by a smaller Steering Group. The Steering Group reports to an Environmental Policy Unit within the County Council, which in turn reports directly to the Council's Planning Committee. The Forum, focused through an Environment Unit, developed a "Green Audit" which identified the assets and quality of both natural and man-made resources, and considers how human activities and natural processes are influencing them. This information was widely circulated by distributing the Green Audit report to libraries, schools, colleges, Council offices, etc, by hosting a travelling information display at each community in the County, and by circulating 40,000 information leaflets throughout the County. Through this circulation process, citizens and Forum members were canvassed to identify priority issues. The Forum then developed four Specialty Working Groups which evaluated these priority issues and prepared proposals for action. These proposals were critiqued (sic) internally within the Forum, and were also released for public review, prior to being integrated into Lancashire's Environmental Action Programme (LEAP). LEAP includes over 200 proposals for action. Each proposal identifies an authority or agency responsible for implementation, and includes targets to be achieved and time-lines for implementation. LEAP also identifies mechanisms for monitoring and reporting progress. Annual progress reports will be released to the community. The Green Audit will be updated every 3 years, and LEAP itself will be updated every 5 years to address changes and to incorporate new approaches.'

ICLEI, 1995

Unfortunately, this has often resulted in a top-down process in which local authorities control rather than facilitate the formation of Local Agenda 21 strategies. The end-product is documentation setting out sustainability objectives and action plans, but nothing which engages the public intellectually, emotionally or practically, and which would lead to significant changes in individual, agency and institutional behaviour. Consultation does not guarantee effective involve- ment which is essential if Agenda 21 objectives are to be met at the local and global levels. The key to the success of Local Agenda 21 strategies is the empowerment of local communities so that they are given the means to control their own environments. The role of local government should be to facilitate this, not for local government itself to develop those strategies. In the latter case, the policy development process becomes professionalized, centralized and non- democratic, thereby guaranteeing failure.

The local government response to Agenda 21 has tended to be most active in countries where sustainability has in the past received a low priority in management of the built environment. There have been more Local Agenda 21 strategies developed by British than German local authorities for example, although the latter have been aware for a much longer period of the importance of environmental issues and have had in place appropriate management responses predating the Rio Conference. Unfortunately, the Local Agenda 21 strategies developed by British local authorities and elsewhere have tended to be of the bureaucratic, top-down type discussed above. There are examples, however, of initiatives coming from local communities which are more promising, and which have been supported, rather than controlled, by local government. Chapter 8 stressed the importance of community to sustainability and gave examples of how people, by coming together to address their quality of life, had begun to live in more sustainable ways and to take control over the local environment. The example of Greenpoint-Williamsburg in New York shows how a deprived community, with the assistance of local government, managed to reduce pollution and at the same time enhance self-confidence and community cohesion.

There are also examples in the UK of local government helping communities to live in more sustainable ways by responding to their initiative rather than paying lip-service to community involvement through an elaborate public consultation exercise. The Urban Oasis project in Salford is one such example in which the tenants of a public sector tower block, Apple Tree Court, have attempted to create a sense of community within the block through the mechanism of a project to improve the local environment. This has taken the form of using derelict land around the block for a garden and the production of organically grown fruit and vegetables. A safe area has been created where residents can meet, community cohesion has been enhanced through cooperation in building and maintaining the garden and the involvement of local schools, and productive activity and training have been provided for unemployed residents. The produce grown has also improved people's diets with direct benefits to health, and surpluses sold to reinvest in the project. Crucial elements for the success of the scheme have been the enthusiasm of the tenants, who initiated it and the transfer of responsibility for management of the flats and the surrounding land from the local authority to the tenants themselves. The contribution of the local authority derived from its shedding of power, not exercising it. Agenda 21 is about how people live, not about how local authorities interpret and administer national commitments to international agreements.

Local authorities do have a role to play in the success of Local Agenda 21, however, beyond passing power downwards. They can be instrumental in helping people to live more sustainably. In Kanagawa, for example, the Prefecture has been involved in the construction of 100 'eco-housing' units which make use of rainwater and recycled materials and are highly energy efficient. A Prefecture-wide system has been established to recover and destroy ozone depleting CFCs, and subsidies provided for the purchase of non-CFC equipment. More generally, local authorities can provide infrastructure and services, such as recycling and waste management, and efficient public transport, which contribute towards sustainable lifestyles. These measures will only be effective if they have widespread public support, and perhaps local authorities' most valuable contribution may lie in the field of education in disseminating the importance of sustainable living and offering guidance on how to achieve it. The City of Göteborg in Sweden has produced an Eco Handbook providing information on how to live in more environmentally friendly ways, and in April 1992 more than 400,000 copies of the second edition were distributed concurrently with telephone directories to all households and businesses in the city. In Olympia, Washington State, the local authorities have targeted the business sector by organizing Operation Waterworks. This provides small businesses with education, technical assistance and community recognition opportunities to increase their practice of environmental stewardship, concentrating in the first instance on waste management and water quality issues.

THE COST OF INACTION

The changes suggested in this book to the built environment and the behaviour within it are radical and to some they may appear unnecessary given the cost and the disruption in lifestyle required. Those who doubt the need for change and question the usefulness of the concept of sustainability as a guide to the future development of the built environment, should consider what the likely costs are of not changing. These can be considered at the global and local scales. The use of energy for buildings accounts for half of the UK's emissions of greenhouse gases, two-thirds of this coming from housing (Shorrock and Henderson, 1990). A further one-third of the total is derived from transport, mostly from car exhausts. Similar figures apply to the rest of the developed world. The changes suggested in this book to our towns and cities and the way we move between and within them, have the potential for making significant reductions in the rate of climate change; indeed, significant reductions are dependent on these changes. Those who take the threat of anthropogenically induced climate change seriously must accept the need for change to the built environment. At the local level, the social, economic and environmental problems of our major metropolitan areas, and quality of life for those living within them, will continue to get worse, and affect a growing proportion of the population, unless the interconnected nature of these problems is recognized. If they are not tackled together, then none will be effectively addressed. Most immediately, those concerned with poverty, inequality and social cohesion must recognize the vital role of the environment and the pointer that environmental issues have given to the ineffectiveness of policies dependent upon economic growth as conventionally understood. A more sophisticated and holistic view of quality of life will lead to more effective protection of the environment and more potent attacks on poverty and inequality.

Those who accept the need for change but who doubt whether the necessary transformation in the built environment is feasible, should look to cities in Europe, especially in the Netherlands, Germany and Scandinavia for examples of good practice where the environmental impacts of urban living have been reduced and where towns and cities are attractive places to live. There can be no greater contrast than between Las Vegas and Vienna, for example. Vienna has low levels of car use as a consequence of an integrated, high quality and affordable public transport system. The density of population is high, and land uses mixed, but the quality of life is also high. The city is a concentration of culture and activity, providing varied opportunities for work and leisure. Vienna has quality public space, both recreational, commercial and functional. In summer, squares are used for eating and conversing. Public transport stops are also used for retailing and meeting. Most public space in Las Vegas is devoted to the car and it has one of the lowest acreages of public parks of all American cities. Although a tourist attraction, Vienna is also a satisfying place to live; Las Vegas is the former, but not the latter. Vienna's ecological footprint is admittedly large in terms of comparison with cities in the developing world, but proportionately smaller than that of Las Vegas. Many towns and cities in Europe (though few in the UK) are like Vienna: Amsterdam, Stockholm, Copenhagen and others. The survival of towns and cities into the next century depends upon following and building upon their example, not that of Las Vegas.

There are encouraging signs that in some areas of the United States the necessity for change in the built environment is being recognized. As long ago as the 1970s, Portland in Oregon limited urban expansion outwards, dismantled a major freeway and placed restrictions on downtown parking. This was accompanied by the construction of a light railway and improvements to bus services in the metropolitan area. Although there are now signs that the original limits may have been too tight, revealed by rising house prices and increasing congestion, expansion beyond them will be strictly controlled and linked to light rail links. In 1996 Seattle adopted similar measures including a $4 billion rail and bus system, rejected by voters 30 years earlier. San Jose, the capital of California's Silicon Valley, has established a permanent green line around the city outside which no new development will be allowed and no services provided. More radically, at Civano in Arizona work has just begun on the construction of a 2500 home development designed to be self-sufficient and energy saving. Unlike most residential developments in recent years, Civano will have jobs, schools, churches and shops, all within walking distance, and recycling and composting facilities will be available in all homes. The City of Tucson has sponsored the project and will share some of the risk with the developers. The city hopes to recover some costs through savings on road maintenance, waste disposal, pollution abatement and water treatment. Projects like Civano may not be immediately successful, but they point the way to a sustainable built environment. More importantly, the challenge in the future will be to make our existing cities sustainable.

REFERENCES

Adalberth, K (1994) *Energi för att bygga Bruka Riva småhus*, Department of Building Physics, Lund University

Adams, J (1991) *Determined to Dig: The Role of Aggregates Demand Forecasting in National Materials Planning Guidance*, Council for the Protection of Rural England, London

Advertising Association (1994) *Retail Marketing Pocket Book 1994*, Advertising Association, Henley on Thames

Alexander, C (1965) 'A city is not a tree', *Architectural Forum*, 122, April also pp 118–131 in Le Gates, R T and Stout, F (eds) *The City Reader*, Routledge, London

Alexander, C (1985) *The Production of Houses*, Oxford University Press, New York

Ambrose, P and Colenutt, R (1975) *The Property Machine*, Penguin, London

Ambrose, P et al (1996) *The Real Cost of Poor Homes*, Royal Institute of Chartered Surveyors, London

Anink, D, Boonstra, C and Mak, J (1996) *Handbook of Sustainable Building*, James and James, London

Antonovsky, A (1984) 'The sense of coherence as a determinant of health', *Advances,* 1, pp 37–50

Appleyard, D (1981) *Livable Streets,* University of California Press, Berkele

Architectural Review (1995) 'Comment', *Architectural Review*, 1179, May, p 4

Armstrong, H, Darrall, J and Grove-White, R (1994) *Building Lancaster's Future: Economic and Environmental Implications of Lancaster University's Expansion to 2001*, Department of Economics and Centre for the Study of Environmental Change, Lancaster University

Arrington, G B (1993) 'Transportation and Land Use – A Shared Vision', *Passenger Transport* 2 (3), pp 4–14

Ashton, J and Seymour, H (1988) *The New Public Health,* Open University Press, Milton Keynes

Atkinson, C, Collins, R and West, J (1994) 'Use of Waste Materials in Building Products', *First International Conference on Buildings and the Environment*, CIB and BRE, Watford

Atkinson, M (1997) 'Fewer hubs – aye, there's the rub', *The Observer*, 23 February, Business section, p 4

Baird, R (1996) 'Stormy weather will cost us more', *The Guardian*, Society, 3 July, pp 4–5

Bank of America (1995) *Beyond Sprawl: New Patterns of Growth to Fit the New California*, Bank of America, San Francisco

Barclay, P (1995) *Inquiry into Income and Wealth,* Joseph Rowntree Foundation, York

Barker, T (1997) 'Taxing Pollution Instead of Jobs', in O'Riordan, T (ed) *Eco-taxation*, Earthscan, London

Barrie, C (1996) 'Grid teetered as viewers switched on 10pm cuppa', *The Guardian*, 2 May, p 17

Berglund, B (1993) *Community Noise*, Environmental Health Criteria Document, External Review Draft, World Health Organization, Copenhagen

Berman, F (1996) *Trash to Cash: How Businesses Can Save Money and Increase Profits*, St Lucie Press, Delray Beach, Florida

Berry, W (1995) 'Conserving Communities', *Resurgence*, 170, May/June, pp 6–11

Berz, G (1996) quoted in Smith, P *Options for a Flexible Planet*, Sustainable Building Network, School of Architectural Studies, Sheffield

Blowers, A (1993) *Planning for a Sustainable Environment*, Earthscan, London

Blowers, A (1997) 'Environmental planning for sustainable development' pp 33–53 in Blowers, A and Evans, B (eds) *Town Planning into the 21st Century*, Routledge, London

Boardman, B (1991) *Fuel Poverty: From Cold Homes to Affordable Warmth*, Belhaven/Wiley, London

Boardman, B (1994) 'Energy Efficiency Measures and Social Inequality' pp 107–127 in Bhatti, M, Brooke, J and Gibson, M (eds) *Housing and the Environment: a New Agenda*, Chartered Institute of Housing, Coventry

Böge, S (1994) 'The well travelled yoghurt pot: lessons for new freight transport policies and regional production, *World Transport Policy and Practice*, 1, pp 7–11

Bookchin, M (1980) *Toward an Ecological Society*, Black Rose Books, Montreal

Bookchin, M (1992) *The Ecology of Freedom*, Cheshire Books, Palo Alto

Bovin, K and Magnusson, S (1997) *49 Local Initiatives for Sustainable Development*, Swedish Society for Nature Conservation, Stockholm

Bradford Hill, A (1965) 'The environment and disease: association or causation' *Proceedings of the Royal Society of Medicine*, 58, pp 295–300

Breheny, MJ (1995) 'Compact cities and transport energy consumption', *Transactions, Institute of British Geographers*, 20, pp 81–101

Breheny, M and Rookwood, R (1993) 'Planning the sustainable city region' in Blowers, A (ed) *Planning for a Sustainable Environment*, Town and Country Planning Association and Earthscan, London

Breheny, MJ, Gent, T and Lock, D (1993) *Alternative Development Patterns: New Settlements*, HMSO, London

Brickner, R et al (1994) private communication 23 August 1994, quoted in Roodman and Lenssen, 1995

British Medical Association (1997) *Road Transport and Health*, British Medical Association, London

British Road Federation (1993) *Basic Road Statistics*, British Road Federation, London

Brolin, BC (1976) *The Failure of Modern Architecture*, Van Nostrand Reinhold, New York

Brown, L et al (1996) *State of the World 1996*, Earthscan, London

Browning, R, Helou, M and Larocque, PA (1998) 'The impact of transportation on household energy consumption', *World Transport Policy and Practice*, 4, 1

Buchta, J (1996) *Minneapolis Star Tribune*, 16 November

Burkhardt, R (1994) 'Straw Bale Construction', in Schaeffer, J (ed) *Solar Living Sourcebook*, 8, pp 43–46, White River Junction, Vermont

Burrows, R (1997) *Contemporary Patterns of Residential Mobility in Relation to Social Housing*, Centre for Housing Policy, University of York

Calthorpe, P (1993) *The Next American Metropolis,* Princeton Architectural Press, New York

Cappon, D (1990) 'Indicators for a healthy city', *Environmental Management and Health*, 1, pp 9–18

Charter, M (1996) 'Industrial ecology: interview with Dr Braden R Allenby', *Eco-Design*, IV, 1, p 8

CIRIA (1997) 'Standardisation and pre-assembly provide better value for money', *CIRIA News*, 3, p 3

City of Calgary (1995) *Sustainable Suburbs Study*, Calgary, Canada

CNTP (1991) 'Urban Transportation: Programs and Policies for More Liveable Cities: Washington D.C. Campaign for New Transportation Policies', in Lowe, MD (1994) *Back on Track: The Global Rail Revival*, Worldwatch Institute, Washington, DC

Cockersole, M (1994) *Local Transport Today,* 14 April 1994, pp12–14

Cole, I et al (1997) *Creating Communities or Welfare Housing?* Chartered Institute of Housing, Coventry

Commission of the European Communities (1990) *Green Paper on the Urban Environment* Commission of the European Communities, Luxembourg

Commission of the European Communities (1993) *Trans European Networks: Towards a Master Plan for the Road Network and Road Traffic*, Directorate General for Transport, Brussels

Commission of the European Communities (1995) *Europe's Environment – The Dobřiš Assessment*, Commission of the European Communities, Luxembourg

Conaty, P (1995) 'From illth to wealth', *Resurgence*, 171, July/August, pp 18–19

Connaughton, JN (1993) 'Real low-energy buildings: the energy costs of materials', pp 87–100 in Roaf, S (ed) *Energy Efficiency*, Oxford University Press, Oxford

CPRE (1993a) *Driven to Dig,* CPRE, London

CPRE (1993b) *Planning for the Future,* CPRE, London

CPRE (1997) *Planning More to Travel Less,* CPRE, London

Currivan, T (1996) 'Buildings with a future', *Building for a Future*, 6, 1, pp 2–6

Daly, HE (1993a) 'Introduction to Essays toward a Steady-State Economy', pp 11–47 in Daly, HE and Townsend, KN (eds) *Valuing the Earth*, MIT Press, Cambridge, MA

Daly, HE (1993b) 'The Steady State Economy' pp 325–364 in Daly, HE and Townsend, KN (eds) *Valuing the Earth,* MIT Press, Cambridge, MA

Daly, H and Cobb, JB (1989) *For the Common Good: Redirecting the Economy Towards Community, Environment and a Sustainable Future*, Green Print, London

Darley, G (1993) 'Local Distinctiveness: An Architectural Conundrum', in Common Ground, *Local Distinctiveness: Place, Particularity and Identity*, Common Ground, London

Davies, JK and Kelly, MP (1993) *Healthy Cities*, Routledge, London

Davis, M (1995) 'House of cards', *Sierra Magazine*, 80, pp 36–42

Day, C (1990) *Places of the Soul*, Aquarian Press, London

Department of Energy (1994) *Energy Digest 1994*, HMSO, London, in Friends of the Earth (1995) *Working Future: Jobs and the Environment*, Friends of the Earth, London

Department of the Environment (1993) *Merry Hill Impact Study*, HMSO, London

Department of the Environment (1994a) *Sustainable Development: the UK Strategy*, Cm 2426, HMSO, London

Department of the Environment (1994b) *Planning Policy Guidance 13:Transport*, HMSO, London

Department of the Environment (1995) *EC Eco-management and Audit Scheme for UK Local Government*, HMSO, London

Department of the Environment (1996) *Household Growth:Where Shall We Live?* Cmnd 3471, HMSO, London

Department of Health (1991) *The Health of the Nation*, Cm 1523, HMSO, London

Department of Trade and Industry (1995) *Digest of United Kingdom Energy Statistics*, HMSO, London

Department of Transport (1990) *Trunk Roads, England into the 1990s*, HMSO, London

Department of Transport and Midland Expressway (1994) *Birmingham North Relief Road Environmental Statement: Non Technical Summary*, Department of Transport and Midland Expressway

dk-TEKNIK (1995) *Thermal Insulation Products: Impact Assessment and the Criteria for Eco-labelling*, Draft Report, dk-TEKNIK, Søborg, Denmark

Dobson, A (1990) *Green Political Thought*, Andre Deutsch, London

Dockery, DW (1996) 'Acute Respiratory Effects of Particulate Air Pollution' pp 49–52 in Curtis, CJ, Reed, JM, Battarbee, RW and Harrison, RM (eds) *Urban Air Pollution and Public Health*, Ensis Publishing, London

Douthwaite, R (1996) *Short Circuit*, Resurgence Books, Totnes

Doyal, L (1979) *The Political Economy of Health*, Pluto Press, London

Durning, AT (1992) *How Much is Enough?* Earthscan, London

ECMT/OECD (1993) *Transport Policy and Global Warming*, OECD, Paris

Eco-Logica (1995) *Transport's Total Land Take*, Report for CPRE, Eco-Logica, Lancaster

Ecological Design Group (1996) *Specify Benign, Environmentally Benign Building Materials Audit: A Bioregions Approach for Scotland*, Robert Gordon University, Aberdeen

Elliott, L (1996) 'Return of the feudal barons', *The Guardian*, 24 January, p 15

Ellis, W (1947) 'Cottage Building in Cob, Pise, Chalk and Clay', *Country Life*, London

Elsom, D (1996) *Smog Alert*, Earthscan, London

ENDS (1991) '£10–£30 billion and still rising – UK contaminated land clean up', *ENDS Bulletin*, 201, October/January

Energy Efficiency Office (1994) *Benefits to the Landlord of Energy Efficient Housing*, BRECSU, Watford

ETSU (1996a) *Hatherleigh: A Community Renewable Energy Planning Study*, ETSU, Harwell

ETSU (1996b) *Renewable Energy Scoping Study for Broughton Village*, ETSU, Harwell

Etzioni, A (1993) *The Spirit of Community: the Reinvention of American Society*, Touchstone, New York

European Centre for Environment and Health (1996) *Environment and Health 1: Overview and Main European Issues*, European Environment Agency and World Health Organisation, Copenhagen

European Union (1993) 'Economic Growth, Employment and Environmental Sustainability: A Strategic View for the Community', *Working Paper of the Informal Environmental Council*, European Commission, Luxembourg

Evans, B (1993), 'Integrating fabric and function', *Architects' Journal*, 2 June, pp 44–48

Expert Group on the Urban Environment (1996) *European Sustainable Cities*, Commission of the European Communities, Luxembourg

Fairlie, S (1996) *Low Impact Development: Planning and People in a Sustainable Countryside*, Simon Carpenter Publishing, Charlbury

Fisk, W and Rosenfeld, A (1997) 'Improved productivity and health from better indoor environments', *Center for Building Science News*, Summer, p 5

Flavin, C and Lenssen, N (1995) *Power Surge: A Guide to the Coming Energy Revolution*, Earthscan, London

Flood, M (1993) *Power to Change – Case Studies in Energy Efficiency and Renewable Energy*, Greenpeace International, Amsterdam

Friends of the Earth (1995) *Prescription for Change: Health and the Environment*, Friends of the Earth, London

Friends of the Earth Europe (1995) *Towards Sustainable Europe*, Friends of the Earth Europe, Brussels

Freund, P and Martin, G (1993) *The Ecology of the Automobile*, Black Rose Books, Montreal

Galbraith, JK (1958) *The Affluent Society*, Hamish Hamilton, London

Galbraith, JK (1973) *Economics and the Public Purpose*, Houghton Mifflin, Boston

Gee, D (1997) 'Economic Tax Reform in Europe: Opportunities and Obstacles', in O'Riordan, T (ed) *Ecotaxation*, Earthscan, London

Ghosh, D (1996) *Sustaining Calcutta*, Present Status Report of the Urban People's Environment, Calcutta Metropolitan Water and Sanitation Authority, Calcutta

Gilbert, R et al (1996) *Making Cities Work: the Role of Local Authorities in the Urban Environment*, Earthscan, London

Gill, J (1996) Speech at 'A Future for Our Cities' conference, Manchester Town Hall, 29 May

Giradet, H (1996) *The Gaia Atlas of Cities*, Gaia Books, London

Glotz-Richter, M (1994) 'Living without a car: the Bremen-Hollerland experiment', *World Transport Policy and Practice*, 1, pp 45–47

Göldner, A (1994a) 'Eco-property development', *Eco-Design*, III, 2, pp 36–40

Göldner, A (1994b) 'Eco-property development', *Eco-Design*, III, 3, pp 40–42

Golton, B (1991) 'Obsolescence – a holistic view for professionals', in Barrett, P and Moles, R *Practice Management, New Perspectives for the Construction Professional*, E & F Spon, London

Golton, B (1994) 'Affluence and the Ecological Footprint of Dwelling in Time – a Cyprus Perspective', *First World Conference on Sustainable Construction*, CIB TG16 Group, Tampa, Florida, 7–9 November

Golton, B, Atkinson, S, Fletcher, S, McCurry, K, Rowland, J and Vincent, C (1995) *Demolition in Manchester – A Case of Long Distance UK Recycling*, mimeo

Golton, C and Golton, B (1995) *The Perception of Obsolescence – A Conceptual Model*, mimeo

Goodacre, C (1998) *An Evaluation of Household Activities and their Effect on End-user Energy Consumption at a Local Scale*, PhD thesis, Geography Department, Lancaster University

Goodmans Group (1992) *Energy Efficiency: Opportunities for Employment*, prepared for Greenpeace UK/International by Krier, B and Goodman, I, Goodmans Group Limited, Boston

Gorz, A (1983) *Ecology as Politics*, Pluto Press, London

Greenpeace (1996) *Solar Electric: Building Homes with Solar Power*, Greenpeace, London

Gryzywinski, R (1996), quoted in Douthwaite (1996) *Short Circuit*, Resurgence Books, Totnes, p 153

Guardian (1996) 'Belgian drought', *The Guardian*, 6 August, p 7

Hamilton, K (1995) 'Village Homes, In Context, Late Spring', in Roodman and Lenssen (1995) *A Building Revolution: How Ecology and Health Concerns Are Transforming Construction*, Worldwatch Institute, Washington, DC, p 43

Hancock, T (1993) 'The Healthy City from Concept to Application', pp 15–24 in Davies, JK and Kelly, MP *Healthy Cities*, Routledge, London

Hancock, T and Duhl, L (1986) 'Healthy Cities: Promoting Health in the Urban Context', *WHO Healthy Cities Paper 1*, FADL, Copenhagen

Hansen, J et al (1996) '*Table of Global-Mean Monthly, Annual and Seasonal Land-Ocean Temperature Index, 1950–Present*', Goddard Institute of Space Studies, Internet document http://www.giss.nasa.gov/Data/GISTEMP

Haq, G (1997) *Towards Sustainable Transport Planning: A Comparison Between Britain and the Netherlands*, Avebury, Aldershot

Hapland, E (1993) *Eco-renovation*, Green Books, Dartington

Hayward, T (1995) *Ecological Thought*, Polity Press, Cambridge

Headicar, P and Bixby, B (1992) *Concrete and Tyres: Local Development Effects of Major Roads, M40 Case Study*, CPRE, London

Helliwell, B and McNamara, N (1978) 'Hand-Built Houses of Hornby Island', *Architectural Design*, July, p 478

Hewett, J (1995) *European Environmental Almanac*, Earthscan, London

Hillman, M, Adams, J and Whitelegg, J (1990) *One False Move: a Study of Children's Independent Mobility*, Policy Studies Institute, London

Holdsworth, B and Sealey, A (1992) *Healthy Buildings*, Longman, Harlow

Houben, H (1994) 'Ecological and Energy Saving Advantages and Benefits of Building with Earth', *First International Conference on Buildings and the Environment*, CIB and BRE, Watford

Hudson, RC, and Shoarin-Gatterni, K (1993) 'Car parking in Central London', *Traffic Engineering and Control*, January, pp 15–19

Hutton, S and Harmon, G (1993) *Assessing the Impact of VAT on Fuel on Low Income Households*, Social Policy Research Unit, University of York

Hutton, W (1997) 'Sun, wind and loneliness down under' *The Observer*, 2 November, p 26

ICLEI (1995) *Case Studies on the Local Agenda 21 Process*, Internet site, http://www.iclei.org/csdcases/la21int.htm

Illich, I (1975) *Medical Nemesis*, Calder and Boyars, London

Illich, I (1977) *Disabling Professions*, Marion Boyars, London

Ineichen, B (1993) *Homes and Health*, E & FN Spon, London

Ingersoll, R (1992) 'The Ecological Question', p 46 in Papanek, V (1995) *The Green Imperative*, Thames and Hudson, London

Intergovernmental Panel on Climate Change (1996) *Climate Change 1995: Second Assessment Report* (3 volumes), Cambridge University Press, Cambridge

Jackson, JB (1984) 'Concluding with Landscapes', p 140 in Least Heat-Moon, W (1991) *Prairyerth*, Picador, London

Jackson, T and Marks, N (1994) *Measuring Sustainable Economic Welfare – A Pilot Index 1950–1990*, Stockholm Environment Institute, Stockholm

Jacobs, J (1961) *The Death and Life of Great American Cities*, Random House, New York

Jacobs, M (1996) *The Politics of the Real World*, Earthscan, London

Jenks, M et al (1996) *The Compact City: a Sustainable Urban Form?* E & FN Spon, London

Kåberger, T (1996) *Environmental Power in Competitive Electricity Markets*, Institute of Physical Resource Theory, Göteborg

Katz, P (1994) *The New Urbanism: Toward an Architecture of Community*, McGraw-Hill, New York

Keynes, JM (1951) *Essays in Persuasion*, Macmillan, London

Knight, B and Stokes, P (1996) *The Deficit in Civil Society*, Foundation for Civil Society, Birmingham

König, H (1989) *Wege zum Gesunden Bauen*, Ökobuch, Freiburg

Korten, D (1995) *When Corporations Rule the World*, Earthscan, London

Kunstler, JH (1994) *The Geography of Nowhere,* Simon and Schuster, New York

Kunstler, JH (1996) *Homes from Nowhere,* Simon and Schuster, New York

Lalonde, M (1974) *A New Perspective on the Health of Canadians,* Ministry of Supply and Services, Canadian Federal Government, Ottawa

Lancashire County Council (1997) *Lancashire's Green Audit 2,* Lancashire County Council, Preston

Langdon, P (1994) *A Better Place to Live,* University of Massachusetts Press, Amherst

Lansley, S (1994) *After the Gold Rush,* Century, London

Lawson, WR (1994) 'Design for Deconstruction', *First International Conference on Buildings and the Environment,* CIB and BRE, Watford

Liddell, H, Stevenson, F and Kay, T (1994) 'New From Old: The Potential for Re-Use and Recycling in Housing', *Innovation Study No. 1,* Scottish Homes, Edinburgh

Litman, T (1996) 'The External Costs of Road Transport in North America', pp 178–217 in Maddison, D, *Blueprint 5: The True Costs of Road Transport,* Earthscan, London

Lothian Regional Council (1992) *Comparative Parking Statistics for Central Areas of Selected Larger Towns in Great Britain,* Highways Department, Edinburgh

Lovins, AB (1991) 'Energy, People and Industrialization', pp 117–149 in Trudeau, PE (ed), *Energy for a Habitable World,* Crane Russak, New York

Lowry, S (1991) 'Housing and health' *British Medical Journal,* 301, XXXI

Link Quarry Group (1996) *The Case Against the Harris Superquarry,* Link Quarry Group, Perth

MacGillivray, A (1997) 'Why don't economists measure happiness?' *New Economics Magazine,* 42, pp 4–7

MacGregor, A, Fitzpatrick, I, McConnachie, M and Thom, G (1995) *Building Futures: Can Local Employment be Created from Housing Expenditure?,* SAUS Publications Bristol

Maddison, D et al (1996) *Blueprint 5: The True Costs of Road Transport,* Earthscan, London

Martell, L (1994) *Ecology and Society,* Polity Press, Cambridge

Martin, N (unpublished) *Hockerton Housing Project: A New Way of Living for the 21st Century,* design notes and plans, Hockerton Housing Project, 2 Mystery Hill, Gables Drive, Hockerton, Southwell, Notts NG25 0QU, Tel: 01636 816902

McAllister, D (1997) *Multilateral Agreement on Investment and its Negative Impact on Democracy and the Environment,* Ocean Voice International, Ottawa, Internet document http://www.ovi.ca

McKeown, T (1976) *The Role of Medicine – Dream, Mirage or Nemesis,* Nuffield Provincial Hospitals Trust, London

McMichael, AJ (1993) *Planetary Overload,* Cambridge University Press, Cambridge

Meadows, DH et al (1972) *The Limits to Growth,* Universe Books, New York

Meadows, DH, Meadows, DL and Randers, J (1992) *Beyond the Limits*, Earthscan, London

Meeker-Lowry, S (1995) *Invested in the Common Good*, New Society Publishers, Philadelphia

Meikle, J (1996) 'Foster's vision: a tower to trump the rest of the city', *The Guardian*, 10 September, pp 1–2

Metron (1989) *Verkehrsflachen der Schweiz*, Justiz und Polizeidepartement, Bundesamt fur raumplanung, Bern

Miljø and Energi Ministeriet (1996) *Energy 21: The Danish Government's Action Plan for Energy 1996*, Danish Ministry of Environment and Energy, Copenhagen

Mintel (1995) *Survival of the High Street*, Mintel, London

Mohan, J (1985) *Transport to Derriford Hospital, Plymouth*, Department of Geography, Plymouth Polytechnic, Plymouth

Morgan, R (1996) *Digitations*, Michael O'Mara Books, London

Myhrman, M (1993) 'A brief history of hay and straw as a building material', *The Last Straw*, 2, 1, pp 12–13

National Resources Defense Council (1996) *Flying Off Course: Environmental Impacts of America's Airports*, Washington, DC

NSDC (1995a) *Sustainability: Towards an Autonomous Building Strategy*, Housing and Environmental Health Committee Minutes, 2 February, Newark and Sherwood District Council

NSDC (1995b) *Newark and Sherwood's Housing Energy Strategy*, Housing and Environmental Health Committee Report, 6 July, Newark and Sherwood District Council

New Economics Foundation (1996) 'CHP for jobs', *New Economics Magazine*, 37, p 4

New Economics Foundation (1997) 'New economics snapshot', *New Economics Magazine*, 41, p 1

New Economics Foundation and Friends of the Earth (1997) *More Isn't Always Better: a Special Briefing on Growth and Quality of Life in the UK*, FoE and NEF, London

Newman, P (1995) 'The end of the urban freeway', *World Transport Policy and Practice*, 1, pp 12–19

Newman, P and Kenworthy, J (1989) *Cities and Automobile Dependence: an International Sourcebook*, Gower, Aldershot

Newnham, D (1996) 'Vorsprung durch shopping', *Guardian Weekend*, 23 November

Nordhaus, WD (1994) 'Do real output and real wage measures capture reality? The history of lighting suggests not', *NBER Working Paper and Cowles Foundation for Research into Economics at Yale, Discussion Paper 1078*, in Wilkinson, R (1996) *Unhealthy Societies*, Routledge, London

OECD (1991) *Fighting Noise in the 1990s*, OECD, Paris

OECD (1993) *OECD Health Systems: Facts and Trends 1960–91*, OECD, Paris

O'Neill, B (1996) 'Tall storeys and eco trips', *The Guardian,* On-Line, 22 September, pp 1–2

OPCS (1984) *Key Statistics for Urban Areas,* HMSO, London

OPCS (1993) *Housing and Availability of Cars,* 1991 Census, HMSO, London

O'Riordan, T (1993) 'The Politics of Sustainability' in Turner, RK (ed) *Sustainable Environmental Economics and Management,* Belhaven, London

O'Riordan, T (1997) 'Ecotaxation and the Sustainability Transition', in O'Riordan, T (ed) *Ecotaxation,* Earthscan, London

Orr, DW (1979) 'Modernisation and the Ecological Perspective' p 80 in Orr, DW and Soroos, MS (eds) *The Global Predicament,* University of North Carolina Press, Chapel Hill

Owens, M (1994) 'Building Small...Thinking Big', *New York Times,* 21 July

Papanek, V (1995) *The Green Imperative,* Thames and Hudson, London

Pauen-Höppner, U (1987) 'Was weiss man uber Flachenverbrauch und Verkehr?', pp 14–23 in *Flachenverbrauch und Verkehr,* ILS, Dortmund

Pearce, J (1996) 'The village that refused to die', *New Economics Magazine,* 40, pp 8–9

Pearson, D (1989) *The Natural House Book,* Conran Octopus, London

Pearson, D (1995) *Earth to Spirit: In Search of Natural Architecture,* Gaia Books, London

Piano, R (1992) *Renzo Piano Building Workshop: buildings and projects, 1971–1989,* Process Architecture Series, Murotani Bunji, Japan in Lawson, W (1994) 'Design for Deconstruction', *First International Conference on Buildings and the Environment,* CIB and BRE, Watford

Poloniecki, JD, Atkinson, RW, de Leon, AP and Anderson, HR (1997) 'Daily time series for cardiovascular hospital admissions and previous day's air pollution in London, UK', *Occupational and Environmental Medicine,* 54, pp 535–540

Potter, S (1997) *Vital Travel Statistics: a Compendium of Data and Analysis about Transport Activity in Britain,* Open University, Milton Keynes

Pout, C (1994) 'Relating CO_2 Emissions to End-Uses of Energy in the UK', *First International Conference on Buildings and the Environment,* CIB and BRE, Watford

Power, A (1996) Area-based poverty and resident empowerment, *Urban Studies,* 33, pp 1535–1564

Power, A and Tunstall, R (1995) *Swimming against the Tide: Progress and Polarisation in Twenty Unpopular Council Estates,* Joseph Rowntree Foundation, York

Putnam, RD (1995) 'Tuning in, tuning out: the strange disappearance of social capital in America', *Political Science and Politics,* December, pp 664–683

Putnam, RD, Leonardi, R and Nanetti, RY (1993) *Making Democracy Work: Civic Traditions in Modern Italy,* Princeton University Press, Princeton

Radford, T (1997) 'A drop in the Oder', *The Guardian,* Online, 31 July, p 4

Rajan, V (1993) *Rebuilding Communities,* Green Books, Totnes

Rapaport, EN and Sheets, RB (1995) 'A Meteorological Analysis of Hurricane Andrew', and 'Lessons of Hurricane Andrew', Special Publication of the Annual National Hurricane Conference, 13–16 April, in Brown, L et al (1996) *State of the World*, Earthscan, London

Redclift, M (1996) *Wasted: Counting the Costs of Global Consumption*, Earthscan, London

Renner, M (1991) *Jobs in a Sustainable Economy*, Worldwatch Institute, Washington, DC

Rifkin, J (1995) *The End of Work*, G.P. Putnam's Sons, New York

Roberts, J (1991) *Changed Travel . . . Better World? A Study of Travel Patterns in Milton Keynes and Almere*, Transport 2000, London

Roberts, J (1992) *Trip Degeneration: a Literature Review*, TEST, London

Rocky Mountain Institute (1995) '"The Economic Renewal Project" of the Rocky Mountain Institute', quoted in Meeker-Lowry, S *Invested in the Common Good*, New Society Publishers, Philadelphia, pp 127–132

Roodman, DM and Lenssen, N (1995) *A Building Revolution: How Ecology and Health Concerns Are Transforming Construction*, Worldwatch Institute, Washington, DC

Rostron, J (1996) *Sick Building Syndrome*, E & FN Spon, London

Royal Commission on Environmental Pollution (1994) *Transport and the Environment: Eighteenth Report*, HMSO, London

Ruch, M, Schultmann, F and Rentz, O (1994) 'A Case Study of Integrated Dismantling and Recycling for Residential Buildings', *First International Conference on Buildings and the Environment*, CIB and BRE, Watford

Rudlin, D and Falk, N (1995) *Building to Last*, URBED and Joseph Rowntree Foundation, York

Ryle, M (1988) *Ecology and Socialism*, Century Hutchinson, London

Sale, K (1980) *Human Scale*, Secker and Warburg, London

Schor, J (1995) 'Can the North Stop Consumption Growth? Escaping the Cycle of Work and Spend' in Bhaskar, V and Glyn, A (eds) *The North, the South and the Environment*, Earthscan, London

Schult, R and Holzwarth, J (1988) 'Der Flächenbedarf repräsentativer' *Latzug- und Sattelzugkombinationen in Straßenverkehrstechnik*, 1, pp 8–16

Scott-Samuel, A (1997) 'Sweeping changes' *The Guardian*, 16 July, p 9

Seabrook, J (1996) 'You ain't seen nothing yet', *The Observer*, Review, 12 May, p 4

Shorrock, LD and Henderson, G (1990) *Energy Use in Buildings and Carbon Dioxide Emissions*, Building Research Establishment Report BR170, Garston

Simon, M (1997) 'The Politics of Ecodesign', *Eco Design*, 5, pp 12–13

Smith, M, Whitelegg, J and Williams, N J (1995) *Life Cycle Analysis of Housing*, Scottish Homes Technical Research Report, Edinburgh

Smith, M, Whitelegg, J and Williams, NJ (1997) 'Life cycle analysis of housing', *Housing Studies*, 12, pp 215–229

Smith, P (1996) *Options For a Flexible Planet*, Sustainable Building Network, School of Architectural Studies, Sheffield

Smith, S (1989) 'Housing and Health: a Review and Research Agenda', *Discussion Paper 27*, Centre for Housing Research, University of Glasgow

Soros, G (1997) 'Capital crimes', *The Guardian*, The Week, 8 January, pp 1–3, originally printed in the *Atlantic Monthly*

Spreiregen, PD (1965) 'Urban Design: the Architecture of Towns and Cities', p12 in Sale, K *Human Scale*, Secker and Warburg, London

Steen, A, Steen, B and Bainbridge, D (1995) *The Straw Bale House*, Chelsea Green, White River Junction, Vermont

Steinhart, JS and Steinhart CE (1974) 'Energy use in the US food system', *Science*, 184, p 307

Stephenson, N (1993) *Snow Crash*, Roc, London

Sustainable London Trust (1996) *Sustainable London*, Sustainable London Trust, London

Taylor, L (1992) 'Employment aspects of energy efficiency', p 51 in FoE (1995) *Working Future? Jobs and the Environment*, FoE, London

TEST (1984) *The Company Car Factor: a Report for the London Amenity and Transport Association*, TEST, London

TEST (1989) *Trouble in Store: Retail Locational Policy in Britain and Germany*, Transport 2000, London

TEST (1991) *Wrong Side of the Tracks: Impacts of Road and Rail Transport on the Environment*, TEST, London

Teufel, D (1989) *Gesellschaftsliche Kosten des Strassen-Güterverkehrs: Kosten Deckungsgrad in Jahr 1987 und Vorschläge zur Realisierung des Versacherprinzips*, Bericht Nr 14, Umwelt und Prognose Institut, Heidelberg

Teufel, D (1991) *Ökologische und soziale Kosten der Umweltbelastung in der BRD 1989*, UPI-Bericht 20, January

Teufel, D et al (1988) *Ökosteuern als marktwirtschaftsliches Instrument im Umweltschutz – Vorschläge fur eine ökologisches Steurreform*, Umwelt und Prognose Institut, Heidelberg

Thatcher, M (1988) speech to the Royal Society, 22 September

Thomas, R (1996) *Environmental Design*, E & FN Spon, London

Tickell, O (1997) 'Sparks might fly', *Green Futures*, 4, April/May, pp 6–7

Tindale, S and Holtham, G (1996) *Green Tax Reform: Pollution Payments and Labour Tax Cuts*, Institute for Public Policy Research, London

Town and Country Planning Association and Manchester Metropolitan University (1996) *Manchester 2020: Sustainable Development in the City Region, Overview* Manchester

Townsend, P and Davidson, N (1982) *Inequalities in Health; the Black Report*, Penguin, Harmondsworth

Tranæs, F (1996), quoted in Douthwaite, R *Short Circuit – Strengthening Local Economies for Security in an Unstable World*, Green Books, Totnes, p 204

Transport Europe (1992) *The Community Framework: Infrastructure, Transeuropean Network: Implementation of Maastricht Treaty*, 19, May, European Information Service, Brussels

Tsouros, A (1990) *World Health Organisation Healthy Cities Project: A Project Becomes a Movement,* WHO/FADL, Copenhagen

Tucker, G (1989) *Air Pollutants from Surface Materials: Factors Influencing Emissions,* Environmental Protection Agency, Washington

Tucker, SN and Treloar, GJ (1994) 'Energy Embodied in Construction and Refurbishment of Buildings', *First International Conference on Buildings and the Environment,* CIB and BRE, Watford

Turner, RK, Pearce, D and Bateman, I (1994) *Environmental Economics,* Harvester Wheatsheaf, Hemel Hempstead

Tutt, P and Adler, D (eds) (1979) *New Metric Handbook,* Architectural Press, London

UNCED (1993) *Agenda 21: Program of Action for Sustainable Development,* United Nations, New York

UPI (1993a) *Oeko-Bilanzen von Fahrzeugen,* Umwelt und Prognose Institut, Heidelberg

UPI (1993b) *Scheinlösungen im Verkehrsbereich. Kontraproduktive und ineffiziente Konzepte der Verkehrsplanung und Verkehrspolitik,* Umwelt-und Prognose Institut, Bericht 23, Heidelberg

Vale, B and Vale, R (1975) *The Autonomous House,* Thames and Hudson, London

Vale, B and Vale, R (1991) *Green Architecture,* Thames and Hudson, London

Vale, B and Vale, R (1993) 'Green housing: can we afford it?', *EcoDesign,* II, pp 16–17

Wackernagel, M and Rees, W (1996) *Our Ecological Footprint,* New Society Publishers, British Columbia

Ward, D (1995) '"Sick" offices sent to early grave', *The Guardian,* 1 April, p 2

Webber, M (1964) *Explorations into Urban Structure,* University of Pennsylvania Press, Philadelphia

Wedge, P and Prosser, H (1973) *Born to Fail?* Arrow, London

Weizsäcker, EU (1994) *Earth Politics,* Zed Books, London

Weizsäcker, EU and Jedinghaus, J (1992) *Ecological Tax Reform: A Policy Proposal for Sustainable Development,* Zed Books, London

Weizsäcker, EU, Lovins, AB and Lovins, LH (1997) *Factor Four: Doubling Wealth, Halving Resource Use,* Earthscan, London

Welford, R and Starkey, S (1996) *Business and the Environment,* Earthscan, London

Whitelegg, J (1993) *Transport for a Sustainable Future: The Case for Europe,* Belhaven, London

Whitelegg, J (1995) *Freight Transport, Logistics and Sustainable Development,* Eco-Logica, Lancaster

Whitelegg, J (1996) 'Evidence on Sustainable Development', LAH/2031 Local Authorities Against Terminal 5, Surrey County Council

Whitelegg, J (1997a) 'Traffic Plan versus Traffic Jam', *NHS Magazine,* 8, Spring, p 7

Whitelegg, J (1997b) *Critical Mass,* Pluto Press, London

Whitelegg, J (1998) *A Guide to Achieving Traffic Reduction Targets in England and Wales*, Friends of the Earth, London

Wilkinson, RG (1996) *Unhealthy Societies*, Routledge, London

World Bank (1995) *Monitoring Environmental Progress: A Report on Work in Progress*, The World Bank, Washington, DC

World Commission on Environment and Development (1987) *Our Common Future*, Oxford University Press, Oxford

World Health Organization (1986) *The Ottawa Charter for Health Promotion*, WHO, Copenhagen

World Health Organization (1992) *Our Planet, Our Health*, WHO, Geneva

World Resources Institute (1996) *World Resources: A Guide to the Global Environment 1996–97*, Oxford University Press, New York

WWF International/CECET (1995) *Saving the Climate – That's My Job – Potential Employment Effects of Achieving the Toronto Target, Case Study: The Netherlands*, WWF International, Amsterdam

Wyeth, A (1987) 'The Helga Pictures', p 141 in Least Heat-Moon, W (1991) *Prairyerth*, Picador, London

Young, J (1990) *Post Environmentalism*, Belhaven Press, London

Young, M and Willmott, P (1957) *Family and Kinship in East London*, Routledge and Kegan Paul, London

INDEX